THE
NINE
LIVES
OF
MICHAEL
TODD

BOOKS BY ART COHN

The Joker Is Wild:
THE STORY OF JOE E. LEWIS

The Nine Lives of Michael Todd

THE
NINE
LIVES
* of *
MICHAEL
TODD

ART COHN

RANDOM HOUSE · NEW YORK

This true fable * is for my sons,
Ted and Ian

* *fable:*   a short tale to teach a moral, often with animals or inanimate objects
as characters . . .

The American College Dictionary

PUBLISHER'S NOTE

At the time of the tragic airplane accident
on March 22, 1958, in which Art Cohn and
Michael Todd were killed, the foreword
and the first thirty-six chapters of this book
had been completed in final draft. Chapters 37 and 38 were not finished, but the
author's wife, Marta Cohn, was readily able
to construct them from the copious notes
he had taken. Her invaluable help in the
final preparation of the manuscript is
gratefully acknowledged.

✳ CONTENTS ✳

ILLUSTRATIONS

Between pages 238 and 239

Michael Todd at the age of five, with his brother and sister, Frank and Edith, and his mother, Sophia Goldbogen.

Chaim Goldbogen, Michael Todd's father.

Michael Todd (age twelve) and friend.

Michael Todd at seventeen.

Michael Todd and Michael Todd, Jr. (Los Angeles, 1931).

At Gay New Orleans (World's Fair, 1940).

World's Fair, 1940.

Mayor Fiorello H. La Guardia and Michael Todd at World's Fair Grounds, 1939.

Michael Todd with Michael Todd, Jr., 1942.

Michael Todd looks over the line of legs of the swimming chorus of *A Night in Venice.*

Michael Todd with Cantinflas and David Niven.

Michael Todd and Shirley MacLaine on location.

Director Michael Anderson, Michael Todd and Frank Sinatra.

Michael Todd, Elizabeth Taylor and Fernandel.

Michael and Elizabeth Todd and daughter Elizabeth Frances.

* Conception *

I have one test for biography: Would the subject, regardless of name, fame or infame, make a good novel? Mike Todd, yes. He could have been conceived by Shakespeare, Cervantes or Dumas.

Seeking the truth of Todd, often in spite of the facts, I have sought the truth of our time that created him.

Before me are my typewritten pages: Mike Todd's laughter and tears, triumphs and catastrophes, loves and hates, dreams and denouements. In assaying them, a reflection by Isaac Newton comes to mind:

"I do not know what I may appear to the world, but to myself I seem to have been only like a boy playing on the seashore, and diverting himself now and then finding a smoother pebble or a prettier shell than ordinary, whilst the great ocean of truth lay all undiscovered before me."

Mike Todd, a bold adventurer fighting middle age as if he

were going to beat it, is a twentieth-century Renaissance man. His universe is a dream, his life a search for something outside of himself. He is a citizen of the world no less than was Erasmus; he has been all his life, unconsciously until the past year, a votary of Don Quixote and that "happy Age . . . because those two fatal Words, Mine and Thine, were Distinctions unknown to the People of those fortunate times."

Todd has, unintentionally, frustrated every would-be biographer. He never looks back. He is reborn each day without knowledge of the past. He has no yesterdays, no reminiscences or regrets. The man he was the day before or twenty years before is a stranger to him and he has no interest in knowing him. What is gone is done for; he must start clear at each moment.

At eighteen he was president of a $2,000,000-a-year construction company. A year later he had a credit balance of $820,000. At twenty he was broke, unable to pay his rent, existing on his wife's dole of a dollar a day.

He produced sixteen shows that grossed $18,000,000, among them *The Hot Mikado, Something for the Boys, Mexican Hayride, Up in Central Park,* a Molière satire and the longest-running *Hamlet* in Broadway history. When he was thirty-seven he had four plays running simultaneously, netting him $20,000 a week. The following year he went into bankruptcy for $1,105,616.78, and, while in hock, lived on a thirty-acre estate at Irvington-on-the Hudson, supped on caviar and champagne at "21" *and* raised more than half a million dollars to produce two shows.

Currently, in *Around the World in Eighty Days,* he has the first motion picture likely to gross a hundred million dollars, and befittingly, in a single week of June, 1957, he bought half a million dollars' worth of jewelry and paintings.

"Dad," his son, Michael, Jr., observed, "you're going now like you did when you *didn't* have it."

As his shadow for more than a year, I have seen him in rage and ecstasy countless times.

I was with him when he did not have money enough to finish *Around the World in Eighty Days,* and on the night he won the Academy Award for it, and in London when the *Daily Mirror* urged in a front-page article that Queen Elizabeth knight him.

I watched him, when the going was rough, stutter so badly he was unintelligible, and I heard him hold an overflowing assemblage of students at Harvard University spellbound for almost two hours.

I was with him the day he met Elizabeth Taylor aboard a yacht off the California coast and, a few weeks later, the day he introduced her to his grandson in his son's farmhouse at Croton, New York.

I was with him when he stood before the Massachusetts Legislature in session and stated brashly, "All you guys are actors too." I was with him the day a doctor peered into his throat and said, "You can't smoke again as long as you live."

I was with him in Chicago the night the Governor of Illinois and the Mayor of Chicago vied for his arm. And I was with him in London when a newspaperman, Alan Dick, told him, "Mike, you talk constantly to prevent yourself from saying anything."

Mike Todd's mask is *comoedia.* Even when his worlds toppled—when he was rousted out of Chicago by gangsters, when his first wife died tragically and mysteriously, when Joan Blondell, his second wife, left him, and when he was buried under an avalanche of debts—he was not a tragic figure. He never lost his resilience, his urchin's sense of fun and his genuine affection for the human race.

"He has a great natural instinct for dealing with the young," Wolcott Gibbs wrote me, "a rarer quality than you might suppose." Not rare for one reborn each day.

There is mischief but not malice in him. His humor is antic and bears out John Dryden's contention that *great wits are sure to madness near alli'd, and thin partitions do their bounds divide;* or, in the words of Don Quixote, "For a Knight Errant to run mad upon any just Occasion is neither strange nor meritorious; no, the rarity is to run mad without a Cause, without the least constraint or Necessity: There's a refin'd and exquisite Passion for you!"

Todd is a primitive who has successfully resisted all attempts to civilize him. "Educate me," he told an associate who tried, "and we'll both be out of work."

His thoughts soar far beyond the proscenium arch.

I was with him when he shook a remonstrative finger under the nose of the U.S.S.R.'s Vice-Minister of Culture, Vladimir Surin. "You Russians have the wrong attitude," he lectured. "Be a man, Vladimir, but also treat others like men. Learn to say *Can I?* not *I want.*"

Mike went to Russia, and a fellow American, Morris L. Ernst, the noted lawyer, who was visiting Moscow, reported:

"One sign of great hope—Mike Todd took over by seduction the government of Russia, special food, planes, *et alii.* He was fabulous and improbable. He, unlike a government official, having no enduring responsibility, knew that only the fantastic and improbable could find an excited response in the dictators of Russia. I'm not suggesting that he be employed in our foreign service, but when he can get pronto a girl friend a special visa and a plane out of Paris to Moscow, in a matter of hours, because he's lonely, the Todd psychology is worth studying. The willingness to give him whatever he wants for a motion picture—7,000 horses, 40,000 soldiers, the use of Leningrad—deserves a study by our State Department not as to merits of co-operation but as to the psychology that brings the response. That he telephoned to bring in by special plane cases of special liquor for a party he gave is only a symbol, not an evidence as to *means of seduction.* This episode in which I lived is one of the odd hopeful signs I saw on how to find weaknesses in the armor of the hierarchy."

Behind the obvious purpose of showing off was a quixotic

desire to bring two hostile nations a bit closer to understanding.

The pitchman who gave Broadway its lustiest burlesque in *Star and Garter* and *Peep Show* is equally devoted to all the senses. "Trust a man with your money, your wife, your reputation, everything—except your liberty," he says seriously. "Never trust leaders, only the people. When people are permitted to meet people—*all people*, freely—there will be understanding and peace, not before."

Of all the accolades he received for *Around the World in Eighty Days*, the one he treasures most, and quotes on all advertising matter in larger type than any other comment, is that of Mark Barron of the Associated Press: "Mike Todd's show makes this a better world."

Of him it can be said, as of few others, that he is a man who has no price.

He was directing a large company for the Indian massacre episode of *Around the World* on location at Durango, Colorado, when he ran out of money. He had to meet a payroll of $329,000 that Black Saturday before Thanksgiving Day, 1955, and he did not have $3.29. The long Western sequence had cleaned him out. There was nothing left to soak, no one left to bite. He stopped shooting and went East. If he didn't raise half a million dollars in two days he could not finish the picture.

Two days later he was driving Roy Little, the financier, along the Hudson. Little wasted no words.

"I'll buy you out, Mike, your company, the film, your Todd-AO commitments, the works: ten million."

Not a muscle in Todd's face flexed. The needle of the speedometer did not quiver. The man Damon Runyon had called "the greatest natural gambler I've ever known" drove on impassively as if deaf.

"I said ten million," Little repeated.

"Thanks, I'm flattered," said Mike.

Little was astonished. "Is that all you can say?"

"It's interesting," Mike said, "but I don't think I'll take it."

It was final.

"The word was out that I had pulled up lame," Mike explained to me. "The boys who had jobbed me out of the Todd-AO Company were hammering my brains out, waiting for me to quit so they could grab the film from me. Yet I turned down more money than a guy can make in five lifetimes. Anybody who does that, the world figures, must have an angle. 'What's Mike's angle?' they asked. 'What's his hole card?' That's the trick: knowing your opponent's hole card, or knowing one more fact than he does. I didn't have a hole card but they thought I did, which is just as good as having one. I knew someone would stake a guy who had turned down ten million bucks. Someone did. And I didn't have to sell myself out."

He is a man of many talents, not the least as a chef. "I *know* this," he said as he barbecued a beef roast superbly. "Everything else I'm just guessing. Dames always wind up sighing, after one of my dinners, 'Mike, if you could only make love . . .' "

A few weeks ago, as we gazed over the Côte d'Azur from a promontory on Saint Jean Cap Ferrat, Mike mused, "I had no philosophy until ten years ago. All I thought about was survival. As you grow older you realize that *your* survival is comparatively unimportant. I'm a hustler and an opportunist. Anyone who isn't shouldn't be in show business. You romanticize what you don't know fully. Knowing it, no magic remains. This may be life." The mask with the mischievous smile came on. "I have a strong suspicion I haven't said or done anything that should be carved on Mount Rushmore. But I think I'm more good than bad."

There are contradictions in this book and variances of opinion. Some are in Todd's favor and some are not. The appraisal of friends can be trusted as much, or as little, as the judgment of enemies. Where lies the truth? First, what *is* truth and how can you recognize it?

"The *truth*, Mike: How old are you?"

"I was born June 19, 1911, according to my new birth certificate."

"You were born June 22, 1907, according to your Selective Service record, U.S. Army files, your passport, the International Motion Picture Directory and Who's Who in the Theater . . ."

"That was the Old Todd, before Liz began courting me."

"I didn't finish. You were born June 20, 1908, according to your brother David—and in 1909 or 1910, according to your brother Frank. When *were* you born?"

"You went to research, you tell me."

"For the last time, Mike, how old are you?"

"I don't know. As a kid I lied about my age, always putting on two or three years so I could get jobs. It caught up with me. If I had to take a guess, I'd say I'm a year *older* than it says in my new birth certificate. I *think* I was born in 1910, but you put down any year you want."

"You don't care?"

"Why should I? It's *your* book and, anyway, it can't change my true age, whatever it may be."

Michael Todd, born Avrom Hirsch Goldbogen, entered this world June 22, 1909.

This book is not an indictment or an apologia. I have no desire to condemn or justify, only to portray a phenomenon. I did not use a tape recorder or a lie detector. A man can prevaricate as easily into a machine as he can to your face. Until Univac writes a biography comparable to the works of Plutarch and Boswell, I will rely on human judgment, inaccurate as it is.

It is not a commissioned biography. This is wholly my work in conception and execution, and I insist on taking full responsibility for it. I have not been intimidated by skeptics who, without knowing a word I have written, have prophesied I would "whitewash" Mike. I like Mike Todd. If I didn't I would not write a book about him.

Why do I like Mike Todd?

One day during the shooting of *Around the World*, he stood on the bridge of the *Henrietta*, the three-masted, paddle-wheeled vessel that was bringing Mr. Phileas Fogg back to England, and noticed hundreds of sea gulls following the ship.

"What are they doing?" Todd, a landlubber, asked.

"Following us for food—the garbage," the first mate answered.

"Garbage!" Todd was horrified. "No sea gulls following *my* boat are going to eat garbage. Toss them some decent food. We go first class."

To repeat, I like Mike Todd, but, paraphrasing his words, I would not trade my liberty for his friendship. I would compromise for an enemy before I would for a friend. I have striven to please one man, myself.

Step inside, folks, the show is about to begin!

ART COHN

Rome-New York-Beverly Hills
1956–58

THE
FIRST
LIFE

"I was a Boy Wonder.

That was before

I was a Boy Failure."

☀ 1 ☀

Avrumele

The sun was sinking behind the bagnios of Hennepin Avenue.

"Shoeshine! Get your shoes shined!"

The boy walked fast, his shoeshine box swinging jauntily from a shoulder strap, his darting eyes searching for a customer. He caught one at Washington Avenue, a *Bashik* he surmised. He could spot a Swede from Duluth a block away, at least a block away from the Great Northern Depot.

"Lookin' for a little fun?" he asked as he blacked the man's massive shoes.

The Swede was astonished at the boy's prescience. "Everybody look for little fun, sonny," he laughed, somewhat defensively.

The boy fished a card out of his back pocket and handed it to him. The man read it, nodded, and stuck it in his pocket with feigned casualness. The boy suppressed a smile. This *Bashik* was a cinch four bits. Plus a nickel for the shine.

He looked up at a clock in front of a jewelry store. It meant nothing to him. He couldn't tell time. But he *knew* the time: the saloons' free-lunch signs were coming out. He scurried up the street to Moler Barber College.

"This way, kid!" a young barber called out.

The boy passed him. No freshmen for him, even though haircuts by them were free. He paid a nickel for the advanced students, at least they didn't remove hair by handfuls. He was proud of his thick black hair.

Groomed, his day's work done, he was ready to eat. This called for a decision, whether to dine out or go home. He deliberated a moment and strolled into the Baltimore Dairy Lunch.

His hungry eyes raced down the counter. Pork chop sandwich, eight cents. T-bone sandwich, eleven cents. Banana short cake with a blob of cream on top, four cents. He licked his lips.

The counterman glared at him. Avrom was a familiar customer and an unwelcome one. No one—no *two*—consumed the quantities of extras he did. Immense pitchers of cream and platters of pickles disappeared into his seemingly bottomless stomach every time he came in. He had to climb on tiptoe to reach the ketchup, but, on an average night, emptied three bottles.

"That ain't for kids," the counterman would growl.

Avrom would not dignify the admonition with a retort. He could not if he had deigned: his mouth was full. He looked at his critic with disdain, his money was as good as anyone else's.

A forbidding figure appeared from the kitchen. Avrom tightened. The manager was his enemy. He could not stop Avrom from filling up on relishes but he could spoil his enjoyment of them. The manager was a hard man.

The boy sighed. He was not in a mood for an argument tonight and, to the manager's relief, he turned around and walked out.

"Avrumele!" his mother called with affection and frustration from behind the pot-bellied stove as he ran into the kitchen and up the stairs. He couldn't stop now, he had to get his mail.

It was a good haul: two dozen boxes of bluing, six automatic pants pressers and a carton of ointment guaranteed to cure acne.

"I'm going to tell!" a girl's voice shrilled behind him. He did not bother to turn. He wasn't afraid of his sister Edith. He wasn't afraid of anyone.

"You'll go to jail!" she reinforced her threat from the doorway, and left.

He continued unpacking the merchandise, unperturbed. This was his business. He searched every newspaper and magazine he could lay his hands on for advertisements that began BOYS WANTED! or WIN VALUABLE PRIZES! He filled them out and mailed them, at a considerable investment of time and stamps.

He remembered, a long time ago, when he'd received his first shipment, two dozen boxes of starch. He sold them in three days, mailed the full amount to a post-office box number in Chicago, as instructed, and anxiously awaited his prize, "a beautiful, handmade Hawaiian ukulele."

The ukulele arrived at last. He twanged the strings. Three of them snapped. Disgusted, he tried to sell it, and discovered, to his disenchantment, that it was not worth as much as the sum he had collected from the starch. Thereafter he eschewed the prizes and kept the money from the sales. After a few letters demanding an accounting, he would write, "Sorry, I lost the stuff." Did they think they were playing with children?

He was answering his voluminous correspondence when Edith's clarion voice announced that dinner was on. He raced to the outhouse, almost a block away, and got back just as the family was sitting down.

Edith and Shirley were helping their mother serve. Carl was proudly inspecting his new printer's card in the Typographical Union. Aunt Zisse was tying a napkin around little David's neck. And Uncle Elya was talking to his father.

Avrom waited until his mother kissed him and then ran to kiss his father on the cheek: this was his equation of love for his parents.

"Avrumele!" Uncle Elya was patting him on the head. "Have you been behaving yourself?"

"What goes on behind those *gnaivishe eigen* [cunning eyes]?" his father nodded with a smile. Avrom self-consciously went to the other side of the table, his father's gaze following him. "That boy is going to amount to something," he went on. "He takes after my father, *olav hasholem* [rest in peace]. His mind is ahead of everybody. He knows what you are thinking before you open your mouth."

"He is beautiful like an angel, my Avrumele." His mother beamed.

"Aw, Ma, cut it out," he said, trying to hide his deceptively cherubic face.

Whenever Aunt Zisse and Uncle Elya came to dinner, Avrom only half listened. First they would discuss the war. The Kaiser had been winning until America got in, a few months ago, but it would be over next year, 1918. Frank said so and Frank ought to know, he was in the Navy. He had enlisted when he was fourteen by swearing he was eighteen. Nobody could keep Frank out of the war, not even his father. Frank was tough.

About the time the meat plates were cleared, his mother would ask Uncle Elya how business was, and he would answer, "Just so and so," which was one of his jokes—because he was a tailor and, as he explained every time, he meant, "Just sew and sew." Then Aunt Zisse would ask his father how business was and he would change the subject. Invariably they wound up reminiscing about "the old country."

The conversation never changed, except on rare occasions, and he could tell by listening every ten or fifteen minutes—for key words like Drubnin, Malava, *Tate* Hellerman and Monte Carlo—how far they had progressed on the agenda. He always waited for the part about Monte Carlo, then listened attentively although he knew every word by heart.

He was lost in thought when Carl's startled voice broke through his reverie. "We're moving to Bloomington?"

"Bloomington, Indiana?" Shirley asked hopefully. She had passed geography the year before.

"Why are we going to Bloomington?" Edith asked. Surprise had already given way to trepidation.

Uncle Elya held up his hands for silence and, assuming the role of spokesman, announced, "Your papa has found a wonderful business opportunity, only twelve miles from here."

"*That* Bloomington!" Shirley groaned.

"I don't want to go to Bloomington," Edith announced.

Chaim Goldbogen surveyed his gaggling flock. "We are not moving tomorrow," he said softly. "Like your Uncle Elya said, there is a fine business opportunity in Bloomington, a vacant general store. I'm going in with my friend Suntig."

It was an old story to the children, only the names were different. Once it was a bottling business with his friend, Fred Nixon. Another time it was peddling fruit for his friend, Meyer Weinstock. Or selling dry goods for another friend who ran a department store. Or peddling junk for another friend, shouting in the streets, "Any rags, any bones, any bottles today?" twelve hours a day, a tragic desecration of a magnificent voice that had been trained to sing psalms in the synagogue. But it paid eight dollars a week. Now it was to be a general store with his friend Suntig in Bloomington.

Their father never ran out of friends, only jobs.

He read the expressions on their faces and he was sad, for them. He had not forgotten the dreams of his youth. As a boy in Poland he had wanted, more than anything in the world, to become a scholar and dedicate his life to the Talmud, studying it and teaching it. Falling in love with Sophia Hellerman, and marrying her, had enabled him to follow his star. Her family had provided *kest,* the ancient Jewish practice whereby the bride's parents supported, in their own home, their daughter and son-in-law for a specified time after their marriage. Until the *kest* was guaranteed, the groom would discuss no other particulars of the prospective union.

The specified time expired, alas, and Chaim reluctantly entered the world of commerce. He started out selling leather supplies to shoemakers, and failed; he brewed mead in the basement of his own saloon, and failed; he opened a soap factory, and failed; he managed an estate, and failed; he immigrated to Minneapolis, peddled everything from dry goods to junk—and failed every time.

His only steady income came from being a kosher slaughterer of cattle and poultry. Two cents a pigeon; three cents a chicken; and four cents a turkey, they were tough and struggled. He was a good craftsman, the birds bled well. His lifetime ambition was to become a learned rabbi like his father, Moishe Mordecai, but he had never had enough money to join the Rabbinical Society.

Chaim Goldbogen accepted his destiny as the Lord's will. He was not ashamed or remorseful, this gentle, kind man. He had done his best. He had sired nine children, eight living; he had brought his family from the tyranny of Poland to the freedom of America. They had received educations, as much as they wanted, and two were already married with children of their own. He had always provided sufficient food, clothing and a roof over their heads, but he understood their fears. He wished with all his heart he could give them more.

"It's your own fault, Chaim," Uncle Elya chided, half in jest. "If you had only been a better farmer . . ."

Avrom stopped listening and returned to his own thoughts. For the next ten minutes his mother, Uncle Elya and the older children would relive their days in Bugsa, when they had been rich. But not his father. He didn't listen either.

"That was an estate you had!" Uncle Elya exclaimed, as if it were the first time and not the thousandth or more he had assayed it. "*Hundreds* of acres: fruit trees, apples, pears! Lumber!

Your own water mill, your own stream! Thirty people working for you!"

"Thirty-five," Mama corrected; she looked at her sons one by one, and shook her head sadly. "A Hellerman's grandson reduced to this . . ."

Uncle Elya nodded and sighed. "Worth half a million rubles if it was worth a cent. By today's standards and exchange, half a million *dollars!*" He paused for dramatic effect, and all the children except Avrom sat in awe, as they always did. "And what happened to it?"

"What happened to *your* share, Elya?" Mama loyally intercepted, with fire.

Avrom automatically tuned in on the conversation.

"What really happened at Monte Carlo, Uncle Elya?" Carl asked.

Uncle Elya grimaced. "You know what happened!"

"Uncle Elya lost a hundred and *fifty* thousand rubles!" Mama interjected. "His whole share of the estate. He tried to double it and left *all* of it there. Monte Carlo!"

"Easy come, easy go," Uncle Elya said with a pathetic chuckle, and the children laughed dutifully at his sad and time-honored joke, but not too hard. They knew how badly he felt.

Avrom's eyes glistened. What if Uncle Elya *had* doubled his money? He would have had *three* hundred thousand rubles! His father had lost his share without going to Monte Carlo, without having a *chance* to double it. Uncle Elya had lost his money in a few weeks, enjoyably he admitted, while drinking champagne and eating caviar. It had taken his father years of hard work, disappointments and betrayals by trusted friends to lose everything he had inherited. Since life seemed to be largely a matter of luck, regardless of how you played it, Uncle Elya's method made more sense. And Monte Carlo sounded more exciting than Bugsa.

"It's better you lost the money," Chaim said.

Avrom looked up.

"If it had not been for you, Elya," Chaim continued emotionally, "none of us would be here. Who knows how many of us would even be alive?"

Elya's honor was restored. Elya Eisenberg did not think of himself as a pioneer, and yet he was. He had been the first member of the family to leave Drubnin, a village north of Warsaw, and settle in America. He had helped to found the Society of Drubnin in Minneapolis, a link between the place of his birth and the home of his choice. He loved Minneapolis—the Sunday picnics on the banks of the Mississippi, swimming and boating at Lake Calhoun or Lake Harriet, the great flour mills and their towering elevators, the opportunity and, most of all, the liberty and freedom. Here a man could say what he wanted to, no matter how foolish. When he had gone back to Poland in 1903 for his short-lived inheritance, he entreated Chaim to bring his family to America and he promised to help.

The seed Elya had planted, the alluring pictures he had drawn, took root in the imaginations of the older children. They beseeched and harassed their father to emigrate, and three years later, having run the Hellerman estate into the ground, he agreed. The government did not: the borders were closed and no citizens were allowed to leave. This had not discouraged Chaim. Against tremendous odds, the man who had failed in everything he had ever attempted took his wife and six children, ranging in ages from two years to fifteen, smuggled them across the German border, transported them to Rotterdam and got them aboard a ship bound for America.

They had few possessions and little baggage, but one trunk was filled with food Sophia Goldbogen had prepared. Her husband was a pious Jew, and even aboard ship he would not eat food forbidden by dietary laws.

The years passed swiftly for Chaim and Sophia. In June, 1909, they were blessed with Avrumele, a black-haired, blue-eyed boy who took after Grandfather Hellerman, for whom he was named. He was their first child born in America. Then came

David, born in St. Paul. He was the only glowing memory of their short stay there, as Chaim had been unable to secure work.

They had moved back to Minneapolis and into the fine five-room house on 718 Girard Avenue North, where the rent was twelve dollars a month, next door to the home of Floyd Olsen, the former Governor of Minnesota, no less. God willing, it would be even better in Bloomington.

"The house is back of the store," Chaim told his family, then added cheerfully, "I forgot, a gas pump goes with it."

"I'll run the pump," Avrom said instantly.

"I want to run the pump," Edith demurred. "Toat gets to do everything." Toat had been Avrom's nickname since, as a baby, he had mispronounced the word "coat" as "toat."

There was a low whistle outside. Avrom edged off his chair.

"Make him help with the dishes!" Edith insisted.

"I gotta go," Avrom said and ran.

"Be home by eight o'clock, not one minute after!" his mother charged. "And put on your sweater."

"Be careful, Avrumele," his father said gently as the boy sped past.

His best friend, Carl Feller, was waiting. They walked downtown, sharing their day's happenings, discussing the good guys and the bad guys of the world. The good guys were General Pershing, William S. Hart and the great Australian fighter, Stingaree. The bad guys were the Kaiser, the truant officer and the cops on Hennepin Avenue.

"Toat, look! Sally's!" Carl exclaimed suddenly and pointed. A police van was pulling up in front of a cigar store half a block away. They raced to the scene and, with other curious onlookers, watched until the last offender was escorted into the paddy wagon.

After the crowd dispersed, Avrom and Carl ducked into an alley, walked around the back and, finding a door unlocked, entered. There was only a handful of cigars in the blind boxes on display. The cash drawer had been emptied save for the pennies. Avrom took the cigars and the coins and, in the parlor behind the store, he picked up a handful of calling cards. They would be good for four bits apiece when Sally reopened. He hoped she wouldn't be closed for long.

They scuffed toward the river, the pennies jingling in their knickers.

"Step in closer, folks, I won't bite you!"

They joined the gathering crowd that huddled obediently in a semicircle.

The speaker, a handsome gray-haired man, elegantly dressed, with an elk's tooth suspended from a thick gold chain spanning his checkered vest, nodded gratefully and cleared his throat. "Ladies and gentlemen!" There was a note of esteem in his resonant voice and his eyes roved perspicaciously from face to face. "Instead of spending the money on advertising in the *Saturday Evening Post* and other periodicals too numerous to mention, the manufacturers of these products"—he grabbed two handfuls of merchandise from an oversized case spread open on a folding table —"wish to place them in the hands of responsible citizens."

Avrom listened, enrapt. Carl was restive.

"You want to know what the catch is. There always is one!" The pitchman smiled disarmingly. "In this case, we want you— *if* you like the product—to tell your friends. If any of you think this is too much to ask for the placing of our merchandise, please be honest enough *not* to accept these products—*absolutely free!*"

He made a sweeping gesture with one hand and, in an instant, there was a wild scramble for the shower of samples. Avrom leaped but his reach was too short.

"Ladies and gentlemen — *please!*" The pitchman lifted his voice in entreaty. "There is a city ordinance against creating a public disturbance. But there must be *some* way of giving away merchandise without causing a riot." He mulled the problem a moment, then broke into a triumphant smile. "Of course! How many of you have a dime?"

Several hands went up, each clutching a coin. The pitchman walked among them, took the dime or two nickels from each upraised hand and replaced them with a sample. The customers eagerly unwrapped them and, to their consternation, discovered styptic pencils that could be purchased anywhere for a nickel.

The pitchman returned to his soapbox podium, looked down at the increasingly hostile crowd and chortled, "I told you there's always a catch!"

They were shocked by his effrontery and an ominous undertone could be heard. Avrom's face was expressionless.

Again the pitchman held up his hands. "Will those who had ten cents' worth of faith in me and my products, please raise their hands—and show their merchandise?"

The same hands went up again, suspiciously. He walked among them and this time, to their astonishment, handed each one back a dime. A moment later they watched with new belief as he displayed the next item.

"If I were to sell you an automatic razor hone for twenty-five cents, you would . . ." He stopped suddenly, his eyes shooting to a fictional critic at one side, and then back. "I heard what that man over there said. He said it's just a piece of stone." There was an expression of hurt on his seamed face. "All right, I'll tell you what I'm going to do . . ."

He looked down at his case and, after a judicious search, picked up a small black box with a curved periscope. "Do you know what this is?" he asked, holding it aloft. "It is a Magic Eye. Do you know how much it is worth? Decide for yourselves. How much is an eye worth?"

Avrom had a gift for recognizing talent. He had heard every peddler, spieler and con man on the street. This one had a fresh come-on. It was the third time he had heard his pitch, and his respect for the man's virtuosity increased with each performance.

"I know a man who looked in a keyhole. Do you know what happened?" The pitchman's face clouded. "He has only one eye now. Somebody stuck a hatpin through the keyhole. Do *you* want to go through the rest of your life with only one eye?" He put the contraption to his right eye. "You're always safe with a Magic Eye." He picked up the hone in his other hand. "Be honest with me, neighbors, do you believe the automatic razor hone *and* the automatic keyhole-looker are worth twenty-five cents?" He paused. "How many of you have two bits' worth of faith in what you see with your own eyes and hear with your own ears?"

A wave of hands went up, each clasping a quarter or the equivalent in change.

The pitchman collected the coins, distributed the hones and periscopes, then after the customers had examined them with varied degrees of satisfaction, he asked, "Will all those who just paid twenty-five cents, please raise their hands and show their merchandise?"

The same hands went up joyfully; it was a game now, and again he reimbursed them. He repeated the process until he had worked them up to a dollar for a set of bone-handled cutlery, a pair of pearl cuff links and an unbreakable fountain pen. Again he went through the mummery of collecting the money and, moments later, returning it.

"Is everyone satisfied?" he asked as he closed his case.

Satisfied? Their arms were loaded with merchandise, there had been nothing to sign, no strings, everything absolutely free, as he had promised.

He read their looks of incredulity. "I told you," he said, tightening a stout strap around his case, "the only reason I'm here is because the manufacturers of these products want to put them in the hands of responsible people."

He started to leave, stopped suddenly and turned to the crowd that was reluctant to disperse. "Are there any *really* responsible people here?"

Heads nodded automatically. Shouts of "Yes!" answered him.

He unfolded, with seeming reluctance, his tripod and placed the case back upon it. "I have here," he said, removing the strap and spreading the case, "something extra special: a *perpetual* watch."

"How many times can you watch him?" Carl nagged. "Let's go home, Toat."

Avrom did not hear him. The one passage of the pitch he had not yet committed to memory was coming up. Tonight he would have it.

"I got to go home," Carl said.

Avrom nodded absently, his eyes never leaving the man in the checkered vest.

"This fine gold-plated watch is guaranteed to last *one hundred years!*" The pitchman held up a pocket watch in a simulated gold case. "Now some of you may not expect to live one hundred years, but you can always pass it on to your children or your grandchildren." He stopped, a self-conscious smile of guilt on his face. "There I go exaggerating already! And the manufacturers cautioned me not to exaggerate. The truth, folks, is that this watch will last you only a lifetime, a *long* lifetime."

After a silent plea for forgiveness, he brought out a handsomely embossed certificate and studied it. "This guarantee comes from Geneva, *Switzerland,*" he said, impressed by its contents. "Read the engraving—" He pointed and looked up. "We don't ask you to buy this wonderful watch. Our problem is how to introduce it in the United States. The manufacturers asked the question: 'How do you get them in the hands of the people?' And the answer was: '*Put* them in their hands!'"

He fondled the timepiece. "Is this worth five dollars? Some of you will say it isn't. But, then, I couldn't sell five-dollar gold pieces for a dollar. You're too smart for me." He chuckled. "Would any person here give me five dollars for this watch?"

A shill who had led every previous response impatiently pressed through the crowd.

"No, son"—the pitchman shook his head—"you're too young. This is for *responsible* people. Is there a responsible person here with five dollars' worth of faith in this fine watch?"

Hands flew up, the most yet, this time with fistfuls of bills.

"There's one condition," he warned. "Only *one* watch to a customer!" He walked among them as before, collecting the money and passing out the watches.

"Sir, I *cannot* be bribed!" He raised his voice to a shill in feigned rage. "If you want a watch for your uncle, *bring* your uncle!"

Moments later he stopped in front of another prospective customer. "Your face is vaguely familiar, neighbor," he said suspiciously; then after a reflective pause, he added forbearingly, "But I'm going to give you the benefit of the doubt. If you have taken advantage of me by acquiring *two* watches, that shall remain between you and your conscience."

The pitchman returned to his table. "Will everyone who purchased a watch, please raise his hand," he requested by rote, "and show his merchandise?"

The same hands shot up.

"Is everyone satisfied?"

Of course, their faces told him, let's get on with the show.

"Would you be satisfied," he asked with practiced guilelessness, "if the watch was not worth a penny?"

Why not? In a moment he would give them back their money. "Yes . . . ! Yes . . . !" they chorused with good-natured shouts even before the shills. They did not mind playing straight men for him.

Avrom's eyes glistened. He had the pitch, letter-perfect.

"Good." The pitchman beamed. "Please keep your hands raised."

He walked among them once more, and into each hand that was confidently expecting a five-dollar bill he placed a watch fob worth all of four cents.

"Thank you very much, ladies and gentlemen," he said and,

to their chagrin, locked his case for good. If he detected any
resentment his face did not betray it. He felt no sense of guilt.
He had put out about ten bucks' worth of slum to this crowd
before he had brought out the watches. He had not been compelled to return their money for the slum: they had not demanded or even requested it, neither had he promised to do
so. He had chosen to convert the "sales" into gifts. They could
have gone home with their loot free if they hadn't been greedy
and wanted a watch *too.* As for the watches, he had been scrupulous not to misrepresent the transaction. At no time had he
promised, even by inference, to return their money, and this
time he had exercised his prerogative of *not* doing so. Moreover, he had asked them if they would be satisfied if the turnips
were not worth a penny, and they had assured him they would
be.

The sheared lambs left quietly, their newly gained wisdom to
last as long as their "perpetual" watches. One person remained.
The pitchman had noticed him throughout this spiel and on two
previous occasions.

"Young man"—he eyed the boy solemnly—"do you trust me?"

Avrom grinned knowingly.

"How old are you, son?"

"Ten." He always added two years to his age, it gave people
more confidence in him.

"What's your name?"

"Avrom H. Goldbogen," he said proudly.

"Glad to know you, Av. My name is Doc. How would you
like to work for me?"

"Sure. Doin' what?"

The pitchman reached into a pocket and pulled out an oddly
shaped break-away blade. "I demonstrate this potato peeler,"
he said, brandishing it close to Avrom's right ear, "by passing it
through a person's neck. Like this . . ." He made a menacing
sound and, with a dexterous sleight of hand, performed the illu-

sion of decapitating the boy. "Without spilling a drop of blood
—very often." He chuckled.

Avrom remained impassive during the demonstration.

"You didn't bat an eye!" the pitchman exclaimed in genuine
surprise.

"How much a day?" Avrom asked impatiently. Poking a tip
(a free act to attract a crowd) was an old story to him.

"Two bits," said the pitchman.

"Four bits," said Avrom.

"We'll see how you work out. One P.M. tomorrow."

"I'll be here."

He did not walk, he bounced. He was late as usual, but no
one checked him in.

They would be moving to Bloomington soon, he reflected as
he stretched out in the bed he shared with his brother Carl.
That was all right with him. He didn't feel he *belonged* in
Minneapolis. He didn't belong to any place or anybody, even
his family. He knew they loved him but he felt apart.

Most people wanted to stay in the same place, talk about the
same things and do the same things day after day. He didn't
want to do anything twice, not the same way. He didn't get
any fun out of repeating things, because it was a waste of time
and there was never enough time.

Why, he wondered, did people want to be *like* everyone else?
Why were they afraid of change? Why were they afraid of anything new and unusual? People were scared of being different,
he figured: they were scared to do things alone, they wanted to
be part of a crowd. Suppose Columbus had believed everybody
who said the world was flat? He said everyone was crazy and
then went out and proved it. That's how you became famous:
by not taking *anyone's* word for *anything*, but finding out for
yourself, following no one but *discovering* things, then going
out and proving you were right and everybody else was wrong.

The family never stopped talking about what they had done

or not done or should have done. He got bored listening to them. It was past and done with, so why keep talking about it, good or bad? Like Minneapolis. He liked living in Minneapolis, it had been a good life, but he wouldn't miss it. . . .

He trusted his senses, sharpened them and lived by them. They were faithful to him and showed him how to enjoy life to its fullest. Most people didn't have fun, as far as he could see. They said they wanted adventure, and were always talking about people who lived exciting lives, but they were afraid of going out and *having* adventures. Like his poor father. Why did he have so much trouble making money? *He* had no trouble and he was only eight. Not that he blamed his father, for anything. He loved him more than anyone else in the whole world. His father never raised his voice to him or scolded. He was good and kind. He even brought a pot of tea to his mother in bed every morning.

They talked behind his father's back, Uncle Elya and Aunt Zisse, sometimes his mother, too, when she was sore. They called him an "easy mark" and a *schlimazl* (luckless man)— books he knew but business he didn't. But Avrom knew how brave he was. How about the night the mattress caught fire? Avrom had been only two years old then but he remembered his father running into his room, through the smoke and flames, picking him up from his crib and carrying him out in his arms. Papa had saved his life.

He loved his father and he had failed him. His father had been so proud of him when he'd learned the Hebrew alphabet in two lessons, faster than any of the others, and so disappointed when he lost interest in the language almost immediately.

"What's the use, Papa?" he asked. "It goes in one ear and out the other."

"No, my son, you learn quickly and you have your *zeida's* memory.

"But what good is saying words if you don't know what they mean?"

There was a hurt look in his father's eyes. "It is our language," the man who read and spoke six languages said. "You may not know each word but you can feel what it means."

His father felt the meaning and the beauty of the symbols, but he did not. It could have been Greek. He stopped going to Hebrew school.

Avrom's eyes moved around the cluttered room and stopped at a cornet on the table. He wouldn't be playing in the Minneapolis Boys Band any more; guess he'd hock the cornet. He wondered how much he would get for it.

What would he miss? The Zone Theater, yes. He had spent some of his best days in the little movie house at Sixth Avenue and Girard. He would never forget Charlie Chaplin's films or the serial every Thursday. Admission was five cents until war was declared, an excuse to double the tariff. Getting a nickel was not too difficult but promoting a dime was often impossible, not for him but for his friends. Avrom balked at the extra nickel on general principles. More and more youngsters were sneaking in via the fire exit. Not Avrom. To him anything that had already been done was suspect; there had to be a better way. He went to the manager of the Zone Theater.

"I'll guard the fire exit," he told the manager. "No one will get by me."

And for the next three months, no one did unless he was a relative or friend. Avrom collected a nickel from those he knew to have the price, and he was clairvoyant in assaying a person's worth; to those who protested, he suggested they enter the front way for ten cents.

Soon Minneapolis would be behind him. He had no regrets. He had done everything in Minneapolis he had wanted to do.

Carl came in and started undressing.

"How do you feel about moving to Bloomington?" Avrom asked.

"I'm joining the Navy," his brother said.

Avrom bolted up in surprise. "The Navy? Papa said you couldn't."

"I'm twenty-one," Carl said. "I can do what I want."

"But Papa said . . ."

"Papa said I couldn't go on the stage, remember?" Carl pointed out with resentment. "How many get a chance with Gus Edwards' Revue? I have to have a father who says no son of his will ever go in show business."

"The Navy's different."

Avrom was impressed with Carl's theatrical career, but it was over, so why talk about it?

"You'll be Papa's right-hand man," said Carl, "with Joe, Frank and me away."

Avrom thought about his new responsibilities, but not for long. He kept thinking about Doc and the expressions on the faces of the people listening to him. Everyone had wanted something for nothing, but that wasn't new to him. Everyone was positive he was going to get a gold watch for nothing, *that* was remarkable.

He had a feeling that even those who didn't believe what Doc said listened because he was telling them what they *wanted* to believe. He gave them a styptic pencil and a Magic Eye keyhole-looker, and they thought he was the greatest man in the world. They would have bought the Hennepin Avenue Bridge if he had asked them to. They had faith in him even though he was a stranger. And they followed a leader, any leader, like kids who blindly followed the leader during recess games at school. If one man bought from Doc, the others did too. They believed in the judgment of a leader. People just wanted to believe, he concluded. He must remember that, he told himself, envisioning himself not as a sucker but as Doc.

It had been a wonderful day and, for a man of eight who had played hooky from Anderson School, he had learned a great deal.

Tomorrow, he knew, would be more wonderful because it would be different. He closed his eyes reluctantly. He begrudged every minute that he would be unconscious.

* 2 *

The Commuter

The conductor took the commuter's ticket, a little red pasteboard, old and frayed.

"How were things in Minneapolis today?" he asked.

The commuter looked up from his newspaper. "No complaints," he said and stuck the ticket in his pocket. The conductor, a true friend, had given it to him gratis, punching it each time in lieu of taking the twenty-two-cent fare, for appearance's sake and in case an inspector was checking up on him.

The commuter wiped the sweat from his forehead. It was the last train and he had had to run to make it. If he had missed it, not an infrequent occurrence because of the press of business, he would have had to walk six miles. That was a long hike after a full day spent operating his various enterprises.

He gazed out the window. A narrow stream wound through the countryside. One day he would have to conquer Nine Mile Creek. Thus far it had defied him. He could not tolerate that. To him everything was a contest, and he had to win.

He recalled his last challenge and winced at the memory. He had launched a tin-bordered wooden bathtub he had promoted from a forgotten benefactor. For ballast he put aboard several

large rocks from the banks of the creek; a sturdy tree branch
was converted into an oar and he rowed for the middle of the
stream, his destination the broad Mississippi into which it
emptied.

He had relived Huckleberry Finn, for a few seconds. The
swift current was his undoing. The rocks shifted, the tub cap-
sized and Avrom was almost drowned. He took off his clothes to
dry but it was to no avail. His mother greeted him with a sharp
pinch, then worked up to giving him the worst hiding (or the
best, according to his brothers and sisters) of his life.

Had she suspected how close he had come to a watery grave
she would have smothered him on her bosom. The licking was
for the devastating report she had been given that afternoon by
the truant officer.

Poor Mama, she didn't understand him any better than she
did Papa.

The lights of Bloomington twinkled in the distance. It wasn't
a bad town in which to bring up kids, but he wasn't a kid and
never had been. He was a man, age nine.

The months had passed swiftly. Carl had come home from the
war and had settled in Minneapolis to work as a printer. Frank
had finished his hitch with the Navy, but he had become so
accustomed to life aboard the U.S.S. *Huron,* he re-enlisted for
another five years and was now with the Asiatic Fleet. Joe had
found and lost a diamond mine, married and divorced an heir-
ess, and was drifting around South Africa.

Avrom attended Consolidated Grade School occasionally but,
with the exception of history, he had little interest in studies
and no time for homework. He was too busy playing in the
Working Boys Band and commuting to Minneapolis. The only
thing to which he gave anything at school more than passing
attention was the annual play, *The Mikado*. He did not rest
until he had promoted the job of stage manager. He and his
friends made up parodies to "Three Little Maids From School
Are We" and "Let the Punishment Fit the Crime" but pru-

dently did not sing them within earshot of any members of the faculty.

"Another day, another dollar," sighed the conductor as he stopped at Avrom's seat.

"This is my last trip," the boy said and held out his hand.

The conductor's face clouded. "Lost your job or something?" He grasped the boy's hand affectionately.

Avrom shook his head. "The family is moving to Chicago," he said. "My father has a big opportunity there. So have I!"

No use telling the conductor that the general store, in less than two years, had gone the way of all Goldbogen enterprises. No use telling him that his father was going to Beth Ahren Congregation, a small synagogue in the Wicker Park section of Chicago's North Side. He might not think it was a big opportunity.

"You'll do all right in the Windy City, son," the conductor said.

Avrom was ready for Chicago. Keep moving, keep changing, keep hustling: that was the only way to keep from dying, at least from stagnating. He had not read much but he had opened *Alice in Wonderland* once and he hadn't forgotten what some character called the Red Queen said:

It takes all the running you can do to keep in the same place. If you want to get somewhere else you must run at least twice as fast as that.

Where would you go, he wondered, if you ran *three* times as fast?

"Bloomington, all out!" shouted the conductor.

It was another end of the line for him. He took the worn commuter's ticket from his pocket and tossed it away. He saved nothing that was used.

* 3 *

No Cement

Every bell in Chicago pealed joyfully the day the Goldbogens arrived. It was November 11, 1918, the end of World War I. Avrom ran out in the street and was lost for two days.

"Win a live duck!" the barker in the small carnival on Division Street shouted. "Not an ordinary duck but a big fat Jewish duck, a *katchke,* the finest you ever ate, for ten cents, a thin dime, one tenth of a dollar! All you have to do is toss three little balls in the big basket and . . ." He stopped. No one was listening to him except a thin, dark-haired boy.

The barker looked around. No one was in sight, it was early in the evening. "You look like a smart kid," he addressed the boy, sotto voce. "Can you keep your mouth shut?"

"About what?" Avrom asked.

"Follow me." The barker led him to the rear of the booth. "See that basket?" He pointed. "See the spring in the bottom? Look closer. If it's pulled tight the balls will hit it and bounce *out.*" He winked at Avrom. "You're small enough so you can crawl under the platform. When you hear me holler, 'Don't miss it!' you pull the spring. Remember, when you hear me holler, *'Don't miss it!'* you pull the spring. Two bits a night, okay?"

"Okay."

"You're hired. Call me Duke."

His back muscles ached, hunched under the platform for hours, his conscience hurt too, and the second night he asked for fifty cents.

"Are you trying to ruin me?" Duke shouted. "Our deal is for two bits and that's all you're getting."

The next night Avrom was under the platform, pulling the spring every time Duke called out, "Don't miss it!" Then a young boy, Lester Kaplin, known as Legs, stepped up to the booth. He put a dime on the counter and Duke handed him three balls.

"Throw 'em in the basket, son, and you win a live duck. Come one, come all, watch the boy win a *katchke!*"

Legs took aim.

"Don't miss it!" Duke raised his voice for Avrom's cue.

"I won't," said Legs and let go. The ball hit the basket and did not bounce out.

Duke's face clouded a little. "All right, son, try the second one. And *don't miss it!*"

"I won't," said Legs and fired. The ball landed in the basket and, like its predecessor, remained there.

Duke stiffened. Something was wrong but he did not know what it was. Everything had gone along perfectly until now. Had his kid fallen asleep?

"Get this one and the duck is yours," he said hollowly, and added, in a booming voice, *"DON'T MISS IT!"*

Legs Kaplin didn't. The crowd shouted as Duke, with a sickly smile, took a live duck out of a cage and handed it to him. "The little gentleman wins a fine fat duck," Duke said grudgingly. "Now, who's next?"

"Hold it," Legs said, "I feel lucky. I'll try for another one."

Three times Legs pulled back his right arm. Three times Duke called out, "Don't miss it!" with mounting anguish. Three times Legs assured him, "I won't." Three times the balls landed and remained in the basket.

Legs did not stop. A large crowd was clustered around him, cheering his unprecedented feat, and Duke was helpless. His supplications of "Don't miss it!" descended in volume in direct ratio to his ducks' departure, until, at last, Legs mercifully put him out of business.

"One for you and one for me." Legs divided the spoils equally later that night with Avrom, his best friend and next-door neighbor, who had conceived the conspiracy and made it possible by neglecting to pull the spring each time he heard Legs give the prearranged signal, "I won't."

"That'll teach him," said Avrom, "not to run a gyp game."

His education was consummated at Wicker Park Grammar School. Here he learned how to gamble: how to weigh odds, how to judge character by the way a person bet and, most important, how to parlay. From then on, life to him was a parlay.

They wore seventeen-button vests and bell-bottom trousers. They called themselves the Sleeve Tossers, derived from an ancient wheeze, "We'll give you the sleeves out of our vests." They shot craps every day; Avrom ran the game. He decided who could play, when and where, usually in the back of the school playground. For his services he took a cut of every pot, customarily ten cents from each winning roll. His only expenses were a modest pay-off to the school janitor and a nickel an hour to a lookout, Fat Libitsky, a classmate with the belly of a whale and the eyes of an eagle.

One day Fat fell asleep at his post, and the Sleeve Tossers were arrested. After a trip to the station, they were let off with a warning. The game was resumed immediately after Avrom paid Libitsky the two months salary he owed him. Fat did not fall asleep again, nor was there a second pinch.

Avrom's virtuosity as a hustler increased. Within an hour after his tonsils were removed he was back in the schoolyard, inviting one and all to examine his raw throat, at five cents a look.

He never stopped promoting. He promoted a man named Moore, who ran a boiler factory on the North Side, to put up a clubhouse with a pool table and buy baseball uniforms for the Ranger A.C., Avrom's private club. Moore was proud of the uniforms but not of their wearers, and, at the close of the season, called the team to his factory.

"You have won only one game all year," Moore said sadly. "Why?"

"It was by default," the catcher, Fat Libitsky, said. "The other team didn't show up because they couldn't steal enough bicycles to bring the whole team."

Avrom glared at his catcher. "You ought to be a comedian," he said. He was prophetic. Fat Libitsky became Jack E. Leonard, a comedian.

To implement his income, Avrom got a job as soda jerk at a pharmacy on Division Street. The first day, as he swept out, he found a ten-dollar bill under the cash register. He wrestled with his conscience for almost an hour and then turned it in, surmising it was a plant. Once past his trial, he figured, he would be safe.

One day a desperate cry for help from the back of the store brought him on the run. The druggist, a stout clumsy man, was wedged in the doorway of the narrow stockroom, incapable of getting in or out. Avrom liberated him and learned this was a daily occurrence, and a critical one; the carboys of grain alcohol that he was bootlegging at twenty dollars a gallon were stashed behind the pharmaceutical bottles.

The druggist looked at Avrom's lean, lithe figure and instantly promoted him from soda jerk to stock clerk in charge of alky. He learned quickly. A customer had only to mention that his horse had kidney trouble and Avrom was on the run for ample quantities of spirits of niter. It was an effective nostrum for indisposed plugs, and, by a coincidence, if boiled until the water evaporated, produced an odd-tasting potion not unlike gin, at least in its effect. The boy's efficiency and ingenuity were rewarded with lavish gratuities by appreciative distillers of bathtub gin, brewmasters of needled beer and red-ink vintners.

Soon he was filling prescriptions. It was illegal but so were many of the prescriptions. The label, "For Medicinal Purposes," covered a multitude of ninety-proof bottles. Despite the hanky-panky produced by the Eighteenth Amendment, he decided to learn pharmacy; and after eight weeks of exhaustive study, he passed a two-day examination. He was not interested in pharmacy but in the ten-dollar-a-week minimum paid to apprentices.

The drug store went out of business during a wave of reform, and a coincidental spate of liquor robberies, and Avrom utilized his vast knowledge of medicine and Yiddish to promote a job at Michael Reese Hospital. His first assignment was to frisk Jewish visitors. They were killing the charity patients with *gefüllte* fish, *kreplach* and stuffed derma.

"In bedpans there's no future," a paying patient told him. "I make thirty thousand a year on the road for Florsheim Shoes, just Texas and Oklahoma. I'll start you out as a trunk boy."

Avrom quit Tulle High School; it was his first year and he had had enough. He became an apprentice in the Florsheim factory, and, to augment his income, he worked Saturday afternoons at Cutler's Shoe Store. Veteran salesmen watched him with awe and envy.

As he was preparing the trunks for his first trip to Texas, his sponsor died. He remained with the company but not for long; his ambition was his undoing. Florsheim's had hopefully invited employees to make suggestions for improving the business. Avrom submitted so many that his superiors, no doubt reckoning it was a case of them or him, let him go.

He next promoted a job as a window-display assistant for a magnesia patent medicine company. His boss was a lush and Avrom soon moved into his job, trimming one drug-store window free, featuring his company's products, and receiving three to five dollars for doing a second window. He had imagination. Once he built an immense toothpaste tube that covered an entire window of the Logan Drug Store; it won the fifty-dollar first prize in a contest. He quit after a few months because of the monotony, but he learned one thing from his prize window: *people are impressed by bigness, regardless of content.*

By natural progression, he went into high-pressure merchandising. Having mastered the art of window display, he added a dimension and, with a capital of eighty dollars, launched a Get-Rich-Quick-Wallingford-type promotion in the cut-price-shop field of small storekeepers.

He shot his entire bankroll on the opening production, a shop on Milwaukee Avenue. "BUILDING COMING DOWN—SELLING OUT TO THE BARE WALLS!" read one sign. "FORCED TO VACATE— ENTIRE STOCK AT A SACRIFICE! OUR LOSS IS YOUR PROFIT—HURRY!" read another. Actually, the owner of the building had just offered the tenant a five-year lease, but the shop owner needed cash and agreed to give Avrom thirty percent of the take for running the sale.

It was a tremendous success, more than six thousand dollars' worth of merchandise was sold. Early on the Monday morning following the end of the sale, Avrom gaily went to the store for his money. He had spent the week end contemplating how he would parlay the two thousand dollars he had coming.

The store was *really* vacated. The sale had been so successful that the owner vanished.

Avrom was shattered. It was the first great betrayal of his life. "No one will ever do that to me again," he swore to his current "best friend," Wally Hoffman, who drove a beer truck for one of the bootleg syndicates.

"You can always come to work for my outfit," Wally told him.

Avrom had no interest in muscle jobs; he worked above the neck. An omnivorous reader of newspaper classified advertisements since his BOY WANTED! days, he conceived his first major project on reading, "MEN WANTED! MAKE $15 A DAY AS A BRICK-LAYER." Fifteen dollars a *day*! And they had to advertise for them! How, he thought, does one become a bricklayer?

"YOU TOO CAN BE A BRICKLAYER!" read his first advertisement in the classified sections. "BE A CAPITALIST, EARN TWO DOL-

LARS AN HOUR!" announced a sign over the store on Robey Street
he had rented and converted into a hall of learning.

The faculty of the College of Bricklaying of America consisted
of Professor Stevens, an Assyrian. His laboratory was a load of
one thousand bricks and a pile of sand, purchased on credit.
Cement was not permitted in the mortar lest it harden and be
unusable the following day. The students, mostly Poles, were
compelled to clean their own bricks after each class, an essential
part of the course.

Classes were slowed down by Avrom's insistence on inter-
rupting Professor Stevens' lectures to expound his own theories,
but Graduation Day came at last and, at an impressive ceremony, approximately one hundred seniors received their di-
plomas. Unfortunately, the Bricklayers Union refused to recognize the College of Bricklaying of America as an accredited
institution and its alumni were *persona non grata.*

President Goldbogen took his profit, about three thousand
dollars, returned the thousand bricks and the pile of sand for a
refund, and philosophically closed his university.

Failure did not discourage him. The greatest ball player of
all time, Ty Cobb, failed to get to first base six times out of ten.
Play percentage, take the odds and keep rolling: that was the
combination. He hadn't learned it, it was instinctive.

He would cut a corner here and there but he was not a thief.
He had roamed the streets of Chicago at night since he was a
little boy, out of curiosity and for adventure, but his curiosity
ended at the border of larceny.

"Come on, Av!" the leader of a gang would plead. "It's nothing." Breaking into a house or a store and lifting anything that
could be carried *was* nothing in a city where murder was a mis-
demeanor.

"If you don't go, you're *chicken!*" The most dreaded epithet
in the lexicon of adolescence, the one word responsible for more
crime than any other, had been hurled at him countless times.

It was easy to say, "No, I'm *not* chicken!" and the best way to prove it was to go along, but, to his way of thinking, it took more courage to be chicken than not.

"Aren't you *one of us?*" a companion tried to shame him.

He could not be shamed, lured or intimidated. *He* knew he was not chicken. They *had* to break into houses and stores to prove they had moxie. He didn't. He, who did not even feel the need of belonging to his own family that loved him, had no necessity to belong to *them.* He didn't have to belong to anyone. He was not *one of the boys* and never would be.

He was the grandson of a rabbi and the son of a *tzaddik* (Hasidic rabbi) who was the president of the Northwest Synagogue. He was proud of his name and would not dishonor it. There was a selfish reason too. He had noticed that almost everyone on the take whispered. He had a loud voice and he enjoyed using it, shouting for what he liked and against what he did not like. He was a resourceful promoter, hard and sharp: he lived by his wits but, within the flexible limits of the law, they were honest wits. The worst that could be said of him was that he had *chutzbah,* and he did not deny it. What was *chutzbah* but audacity and courage?

He had an insatiable curiosity and he tried everything his fertile imagination conceived. He wasn't afraid of making mistakes. That was the secret: to have no fear of consequences, no repressions and no regrets. The important thing was doing what you wanted to do. The result was unimportant and boring, whether it was a success or a failure. It was only the doing that mattered.

This was the greatest truth he had learned in his sixteen years.

* 4 *

Enter Bertha

The long, sleek gondola glided through the labyrinthian canal. On the shore, festooned with lights, harlequins and dominoes in masks and spangles, effervescent with the spirit of *carnevale*, laughed, danced, blew horns and clanged other noisemakers. The gondolier, in the traditional white costume topped by a brown straw hat with red ribbons, softly sang *"Torna a Surriento"* as the young man and the young girl, arms entwined, gazed at the stars.

"I could go on like this forever," she sighed.

"At seventy-five cents an hour?" he asked.

"Don't make jokes, Av. This is the most wonderful night of my life."

"It ain't bad," he admitted, drawing her closer.

There wasn't a sound except the lapping of the water against the black sides of the gondola.

"Av . . ." she sighed. "Avrom. It's a nice name."

"Not as good as Sam. Sam Zayel."

"I told you we're not going steady. I just went out with him a few times." Bertha Freshman was a virgin and self-conscious about it.

"His family owns a furniture store. You could do worse."

She bristled and squirmed in his arms. "How about you and Leah Comroe? You're practically married!"

"Leah and I had a fight."

"But you didn't break off."

"I'm here, ain't I?"

"On a switch date."

"Listen to the music. It cost six bits."

The gondolier, an adenoidal tenor, had gone into *"Luna Rossa."*

"How old are you now?" she asked.

"Nineteen." He was seventeen. He had assumed the two extra years to get a work permit in Bloomington; by now, he *believed* he was nineteen.

"How old are you?" he asked.

"Eighteen," she answered truthfully, but quickly turned the questioning back to him. "What are you going to be, Av?"

He was going to be Somebody with a capital S and not be lost in the faceless millions. He was going to play life by ear, do the strange and the unusual, have fun and make a buck. He was going to do everything once and nothing twice. He wasn't going to be bored, least of all by *himself.*

He knew she was just making conversation, waiting for him to kiss her. Other gondolas with romantic couples, many in costume, passed. The gondolier stood on the *poppa,* softly chanting *"Vieni, Vieni."* Avrom had brass when it came to promoting deals, but now, in this ideal setting, he was diffident. He had been so preoccupied with learning how to become a hustler that he had not found out how to handle girls. He was shy and ill at ease. It took his last ounce of courage to touch her lips.

She responded to his embrace and he was grateful. He wanted and needed love, more than he realized or would admit to himself.

"Have you had many girls, Avrom?" she asked.

"A few . . ."

He had fallen in love when he was fourteen, with the most beautiful girl he had ever seen. And he had not even made a play for her. He had been afraid of failure and had felt inadequate because he was poor. So he worked hard and gambled hard, and a year and a half later, was ready to court her. He had a hopped-up Chevrolet coupé, new clothes, and money in his pocket. Now he would impress her.

Their first date was their last. She was not the breath-takingly lovely girl he had enshrined in his memory. She was plain, even unattractive. He was incredulous. Had she, or his eyes, changed so much in the year and a half? He looked at her and then at his highly polished car and his sharply pressed suit. Was this why he had schemed and saved—for an illusion? Was this life?

He wanted love and did not know where to find it. He went with his friends to honky-tonks on the Levee; he would go upstairs with a girl and pay her fee, but only to talk to her. He would boast of his conquests to his friends, in the belief this made him one of them, but he was only compounding his self-deception. He was never a member of any group. He was alone.

"Finito, Signore e Signorina," said the gondolier as he paddled to a landing.

Avrom helped the tiny, dark-haired girl out of the gondola and, arms locked, they walked into the Villa Venice and became a part of the revelry. It was not Mardi Gras but Halloween, 1926. It was not the Grand Canal or even Venice, Italy. This Villa Venice was a roadhouse, a bootleg joint on the outskirts of Chicago, past Evanston. The canal in the back was a canal.

In a moment they were drinking hooch and pretending to like it. In a few moments they were dancing the Black Bottom. Three and a half months later, on St. Valentine's Day, 1927, they were married by a justice of the peace at Crown Point, Indiana. Two friends, hers, were present. Later they were married by a rabbi in Chicago with their families present.

His father had no objections. When he was Avrom's age he was already a father. Bertha was a Jewess, beautiful, sensible;

she came from a good family, who were in wholesale groceries. Chaim's only prayer was that she would make a good home for his restless son.

* 5 *

The First Million

Philip Mass was five feet two. He drank every night until he was six feet two. Then he played his opera records. He spoke Italian and understood the lyrics, no matter how sodden he became. Philip Mass was a successful builder; he owned one building with a hundred apartments, but he was unhappy. He shouldn't have left Poland. He had been an important man in politics there, so important he had shared a prison cell with the President, Ignace Paderewski. He shouldn't have married Shirley Goldbogen. And he shouldn't have been five feet two.

Avrom was his chauffeur by day and his opera companion at night. He was good to Philip and Philip was good for him, he stimulated the boy's desire for culture.

Aïda . . . La Traviata . . . Cavalleria Rusticana . . . La Bohème . . . Pagliacci . . . Carmen. Night after night, over and over again, Avrom wound the victrola and spun the records while Philip, between drinks, translated and commented upon them. *The Barber of Seville . . . Faust . . . Rigoletto . . . Il Trovatore . . . Boris Godunoff.* Avrom came to know them by heart and to appreciate them.

Their nights were filled with majestic music and yeasty philosophy. "'Since it is impossible to have the truth about life anyway,'" Philip would sigh in distilled reverie, "'let us have only the pleasant hallucinations, for they are quite as likely to be true as the others.' Walpole."

Avrom respected Philip more than any other man except his father. Philip was a poet and a promoter, in his eyes the ultimate in achievement. He wanted to be like Philip, except for the drinking. He had no taste for the stuff.

The idea to follow Philip into the construction business was crystallized when the family decided to buy a home at 2034 LeMoyne Avenue on the northwest side, a half block west of Wicker Park. Before that they had lived in a half basement. Avrom made the down payment of fifteen hundred dollars; he was surprised, when it came to alterations, that he had to deal with a dozen contractors. "Why not just one?" he asked Philip.

Philip shrugged. He had more important things on his mind and on his victrola. Turiddu had just discovered that Santuzza had been spying on him and Lola.

Avrom learned that the cost of alterations on a house preceded the first mortgage on a builder's lien, a law that was subsequently changed because of abuses. Unless or until legislation was passed to protect mortgagers, however, Avrom was certain that the scheme now taking form in his brain could not miss.

He needed a partner—and, as if produced by a personal genie, his brother Frank suddenly returned home, his seven-year Navy career at an end. Avrom had his man. Frank was over twenty-one years old and could sign contracts. Equally important, Frank was a thrifty man who had saved his entire compensation in the Navy as well as a considerable amount, at half a cent profit a paper, he had earned as a newsboy before he enlisted.

Avrom and Frank formed the Atlantic and Pacific Ready Cut Houses, Inc., opened a lavish office in the Builders Building at 221 North La Salle Street and inserted advertisements in the foreign-language newspapers attacking Chicago's architecture. "MODERNIZE YOUR HOME WITH THE HAPPY HOME BUILDERS!" the ads advised. "SEE THE ATLANTIC AND PACIFIC CONSTRUCTION COMPANY AND IT WILL MAKE YOU HAPPY TOO!"

People will buy anything, Avrom contended, if you dramatize it well. He even used the partially completed houses of competitive contractors as billboards and, during the night, tacked signs on them: "ANOTHER ONE MADE HAPPY BY THE ATLANTIC AND PACIFIC CONSTRUCTION COMPANY."

He called himself "Estimator, Supervisor and Salesman," but he had special cards printed "Avrom H. Goldbogen, President." He subcontracted the carpentering, painting, plumbing, electrical work, *et alii,* and concentrated on baiting his psychological hooks.

Modern residential tracts, he contended, were a libel on architecture and a disgrace to the creative, nonconformist spirit that had made Chicago great.

"Every house is identical!" he charged. "If you have three drinks you can't find your own." He vowed to liberate his adopted city from the shackles of uniformity.

You had to be a genius, if you were in the construction business in Chicago in 1927, *not* to become a millionaire. It was common practice to borrow more money on a blueprint than the cost of the building. Even the most respected companies, which were supposed to borrow sixty percent legally on estimates, were getting ninety percent.

At eighteen, Avrom was operating a two-million-dollar-a-year business.

"He's only a kid, he doesn't know what he's doing," competitors warned prospective customers, but they forgot his age when he went into a hard sell. The head of the Federal narcotics division, who prided himself on his acumen, gave him the bid to build a sixteen-flat house. Goldbogen homes rose in Evanston, Park Ridge and Gary.

He built an elegant studio apartment for himself and Bertha

on Goethe Avenue between the Ambassador East and the Lake. She wanted position in Gold Coast society and for a few months they mixed with the elite, but Avrom couldn't take it. Her friends bored him unbearably.

Avrom was wealthy on paper. He did not have the heart to dispossess bankrupt tenants; instead, he insisted they remain indefinitely. For several months he brought groceries and loaned money to several show girls living in one of his apartment hotels. He had no ulterior motive; he just could not take advantage, let alone be ruthless with people in trouble.

He enjoyed building and rebuilding but, most of all, he liked to talk about each transaction, on one of half a dozen phones always within his reach.

In 1928 he had a credit balance of $820,000 at the bond house that was backing him. The bond house failed. So did the Atlantic and Pacific Ready Cut Houses, Inc. It owed "only" $100,000, and the first mortgage on one of its buildings alone was more than three million dollars, but Avrom was out of business.

Overnight the Boy Wonder became the Boy Failure. The genius who had built thousands of homes for others now faced eviction from his own apartment. It was time to move on.

THE
SECOND
LIFE

"It's better to pull up lame

in the Handicap than to

win a claiming race."

* 6 *

Pears Fall from Apple Trees

The idea came to him as he sat up in the coach car of the California-bound train, as he was reading a news item that *The Jazz Singer,* a semi-talking picture, had revolutionized the film industry.

The tumblers of his brain rotated: Sound movies . . . They will need soundproof stages . . . Celotex is a sound deadener . . . I know more about Celotex than Metro, Goldwyn *and* Mayer.

"I'm a soundproof expert," he announced to Bertha, seated beside him, and before the train pulled into Glendale he was. During his first week in Hollywood he contracted to soundproof two silent stages at Columbia Pictures and one at Universal Studio.

He had no interest in movies beyond the soundproofing. He was a builder and he went back into the construction business. His mentor, Philip Mass, who had gone broke, eagerly accepted his invitation to come west, with his opera records, to become Avrom's foreman.

The company grew. Impressive office buildings rose on Seventh Street facing Westlake Park and at Beverly Boulevard and Lake. Roads were widened. A subdivision in the Sawtelle district was opened. At twenty Avrom was one of the most successful builders in Los Angeles, well on his way to his second fortune.

He took up golf and made friends in the movie business. One of them, Murray Piver, showed him how Spanish versions of Hollywood films were made at Chadwick Studios, a subsidiary of Columbia Pictures on Sunset Boulevard. Avrom was fascinated by the technical skills of the industry and amused by the so-called producers who employed them. He rarely found one who was original or even bright. Most of them were opportunists who took themselves with deadly seriousness. How, he wondered, could anyone without a sense of humor succeed in the business of mass entertainment?

It looked like it could be fun, he thought as he watched the cameras grind. One day, he mused, he would like to learn how to make pictures.

Bertha gave birth to a son, Michael, at Hollywood Hospital, October 8, 1929, seventeen days before the Black Friday that ushered in the Depression.

Avrom's second empire collapsed. He lost everything, including his apartment. He had to promote a home. He found a lot that had been condemned, wangled a vacated house and moved it onto the lot.

They lived simply. Avrom was completely devoted to little Michael, more than he was to Bertha. His greatest relaxation was playing with his son and, after putting him to bed, visiting his brother Carl, who had married and moved to California in 1924. Carl and his wife Esther lived in a modest bungalow on Dillon Street in downtown Los Angeles. They existed from pay check to pay check, a printer's minimum at the Los Angeles *Herald,* but there was a warmth in their home Avrom could not find in his own.

Tragedy made its first strike on September 30, 1931. Avrom's father, age fifty-five, died of stomach ulcers in Chicago. He had been rushed to the hospital after a severe attack but it was too late for surgery.

It was a numbing blow. This was his first encounter with Death. His father dead? It could not be, he had not said goodbye to him. He had not said so many things he had wanted to say, so many things he should have said. How much he loved him. How much he respected him.

His father had been a great man. No conspiracy of circumstances could strip him of his pride. He had commanded respect solely by his presence. He had spoken broken English but he was the best American Avrom had ever known. His proudest possession had been his United States citizenship certificate, framed and hung in the living room of every home he had. It had been as sacred to him as his prayer book.

His little congregation on Crystal Street had been so poor he had to act as his own *shammis* (sexton), but even when performing the most menial duty, he was a rabbi.

In his sorrow, Avrom envied his father's dignity and grace. Pears fall from apple trees, he sighed to himself.

He was no longer a child. Avrumele was gone forever.

He picked up little Michael, now one week from being two years old. What a pity his father had never seen his grandson. What a pity his son would never know his grandfather, never feel the touch of his gentle hand or hear the sound of his soft voice.

"You will be a good man, like your *zeida,*" he said, clasping his son to his bosom.

It was a moment of consecration, father to son. He felt a compelling desire to give a sign of his devotion. He looked into his child's face. "Michael . . ." he murmured. A smile fought through his grief. "I know what . . . I'll be Michael too!" He hugged his son tightly and kissed his cheek to seal the covenant.

Michael Goldbogen. No, it didn't fit. Michael . . . Avrom's nickname was Toat. Michael . . .

Thus on the day Chaim Goldbogen went to his Maker, Avrom Goldbogen died, too, and Michael Todd was born.

It was his first flight, on a chartered two-passenger ship, and he was arrested as he stepped off the plane in Chicago.

"What is this?" he demanded of the two officers who took him into custody.

His bank account in Los Angeles had been attached by a creditor, and when another creditor presented a $150 check for encashment and was refused, he went looking for Goldbogen. Learning he had suddenly flown out of town, he went to the police.

"His father died," Mass explained. "He went to the funeral."

"A likely story," the creditor sneered, and swore out a warrant for Avrom Goldbogen's arrest.

It took a few hours for his brother Frank and his sister Sadie's husband to raise bail and spring him.

He stood at graveside with his mother, Sadie, Shirley, Edith, Frank and David as the coffin bearing Chaim Goldbogen's remains was opened. He watched in transfixed horror as his father's frail corpse was lifted out of the box and put in a shroud, to be buried face down touching the earth, in accordance with Jewish Orthodox rites.

"Dust thou art and to dust thou returneth," a rabbi intoned, and David, as the youngest child, tossed the first spade of earth upon his father. Ironically, David was the only one of the five sons who could say the *Kaddish* (Hebrew mourning service).

"*Yisgadal, v'yiskadash, sh'mai rabau . . .*"

David finished the prayer and there was a silence.

"Stop!"

Avrom's angry voice halted two assistant undertakers in their tracks as they started to take away the empty coffin.

Frank and David went to their brother's side.

"We paid for that coffin," Avrom said in a low, warning voice. "It is ours."

The undertakers started to protest, but thought better of it and left. They did not know what they would tell the boss. They had never returned from an Orthodox Jewish funeral without the coffin, the same one that had been used for years, charged for each time but never buried or lost—until now.

Avrom had recognized the larceny and, even in the moment of his greatest grief, he could not allow it to pass.

Without another word, he lit a match and handed the matchbox to Frank. He struck a match and David did the same.

In a moment the coffin was a pyre.

He gazed into the flames and saw his father walking through fire to snatch two-year-old little Avrom from the blazing mattress in his crib.

After a moment he thought of another little boy the same age in his crib. His beloved Michael.

∗ 7 ∗

The Flame and the Flesh

He was a builder with nothing to build, a promoter with no one to promote: he was merely a cipher in the 14,000,000 unemployed. He did not have the fare to Los Angeles, and there was nothing to return to even if he had.

Bertha doled out a dollar a day to him.

What had been Depression was now panic. The Bonus Army marched and retreated, under fire. The Little Bull Market proved one word too long. Families hoveled in wretched shacks on vacant lots called Hoovervilles, and proud men sold apples on street corners, those fortunate enough to have apples. A queue outside a building denoted a bread line or a bank run. Al Capone was in Alcatraz and his Chicago was insolvent.

When all other gods fail, when all the accepted principles of conduct are annulled by want, a solitary hope remains for the hopeless: Chance. The greater the desperation, the greater the need to gamble.

There had to be a resurgence of gambling that terrible fall of 1931. Benjamin Franklin was a liar. A penny saved was not a penny earned. A penny saved was a penny lost. No four-letter word was as obscene as *bank*. It was short for bankrupt. The promised rewards for diligence were fraudulent. It was impossible to work hard: there was no work. There was only one deity left: Luck. The have-nots must have an opiate. Gambling was, as it always had been, the bridge between them and the haves.

Todd, opportunist and salesman, at last had something he could sell. The only question was what form of chance he would peddle. He cased the town. People who could not afford a pair of shoes or a square meal were putting their rent money on *any* form of gambling, the longer the odds the better, in the frantic hope of *getting even*. Lotteries flourish only on the parched soil of the poverty-stricken, where there is no middle class, only the rich and the poor: in Mexico, Spain, Italy, China and, during the Depression, in the United States.

Mike conceived a legal lottery and called it the *Play Sheet*.

"This sheet is sold solely for the *information* included herein," he advertised in the newspaper classified sections, "and not as an inducement to gamble. Any prize given is absolutely free. It is *not* a game of chance."

Actually, it was a variation of a scratch sheet, a kind of punchboard, horse selections punched *at random,* the winners determined by races run at standard tracks. A player who could pick seven winners in a day might win a million dollars, a possibility even more remote than Mike's capability of paying off such a parlay.

A Philadelphia newspaper circulation man named Annenberg would build an empire on a questionably superior scratch sheet. Todd could not stick to his *Play Sheet.* He went farther afield.

Horse racing was insufficient for the public's needs, so the racing of whippets was cultivated. Dog racing was easier to control than thoroughbred racing. Now and then a jockey had compunctions about pulling a mount or riding the needle. Whippets could not talk.

The time was ripe, Todd concluded, to race indoors on a smaller scale, at the countless speakeasies on the West Side. It would give people something to do while drinking. With Joe Bigelow, a boyhood friend, he rented a loft on State Street and Lake and began experimenting with white mice imported from South America. The idea was to race them on a platform fashioned like a miniature track.

The tails of the mice were clipped and they became known as clippets. Daily, painstakingly, Todd and Bigelow trained them, but they never went to the post. The experiment cost Mike a thousand dollars.

He opened a bookie joint with Tom Walsh, a boxing manager whose stable included Jock Malone, a middleweight contender. The enterprise was as legal as bootlegging but not as profitable, and Mike lost his entire investment, $1,500, borrowed *in extenso.*

He was not cured because he was certain the public was not cured. He opened another horse parlor with Ray Florine, a friend as desperate as himself. While one was taking a bet, the other hid behind a partition and, through a loud speaker, simulated a radio broadcast of the race being run. The customer's choice always ran out of the money. They took bets on losing mounts after the returns were in. Even in an unethical business they were, in a word, unethical.

The Depression was throwing millions of Mike Todds. Some took to the jug. Some tap danced on air. Some sought refuge in the Communist Party. Mike pawned his soul in a crooked bookie joint. He was going down the drain, six to five to end in the sewer of Chicago gangsterdom along with many of his boyhood companions from Randolph Street and Division Street. And he knew it.

That saved him.

Call it conscience or cowardice, morality or pride, instinct or delusion, or the simple realization that he had lost *himself*—whatever, he refused to surrender and be smashed by life. He remembered his father's heroic struggle against humiliation and degradation of the spirit, in the direst poverty, and it gave him strength. If he was to remain faithful to Chaim Goldbogen's memory, he must fight for survival.

It was not easy to go back to Bertha's dole, but he did.

He walked the streets, looking for jobs that did not exist. He had to create work, so, before Christmas, he went back to his old business of window displays. He talked a Cicero manufacturer into making up, without a cash deposit, a felt Santa Claus with a beard thirty inches long and a magnetic clip, concealed behind the fingers, that could pull up articles of merchandise. It was crude, but Mike knew his neighborhood stores: they could not afford decorators, so they would go for it as a window centerpiece.

He rented a desk for five dollars in an office that had thirty-some names on the directory outside, inserted come-ons as of old in the newspaper want-ad sections, and went peddling. It was an awful comedown for a Boy Genius who had operated a two-million-dollar business at the age of eighteen, but he was oblivious of it: he was born with an inability to look backward.

It was Christmas money. He had to find a more seasonal business.

He listened to the radio for hours. It was the only entertainment he could afford. An idea came to him one night during Eddie Cantor's weekly program in which the comedian was not at his best. *I can write funnier than that,* Mike said to himself, but unlike millions of others who probably had the same feeling, he wrote Cantor and asked for a job as a gag writer. The comedian replied in a few days that he had all the writers he needed.

He tried other comedians. Ken Murray came to the Palace Theater to head the stage show, and Mike begged Will J. Harris, the director of production, for an introduction. He met Murray, applied for a job as a gag writer and was turned down.

A few weeks later Hitler appeared on the screen in a newsreel, gave the Nazi salute to a tumultuous throng in Berlin's Sportspalast and, in a dubbed Yiddish accent, said, *"Oi vei,* I'm dying from leffing at Olsen and Johnson."

The audience roared with laughter. Mike was glum. He had written the gag for an Olsen and Johnson show. He also sold special material to a comedian called "Senator Murphy." Gag writing, as an occupation, was neither gratifying nor steady but it was a temporary relief. For a few days, at least, he would not have to ask Bertha for his daily dollar.

He drifted almost two years without direction or meaning. When he got out of this, *and he would,* he vowed to himself, he would never be without money again. He would get it, inside the law, but he would get it. Money was a defense against contempt.

Bertha was hounding him to go to work. Her family had obtained, through a friend, a job that would pay him thirty-five dollars a week. Mike refused to take it; from that day, every hour at home was a hell of recrimination. Bertha's shrill, indicting voice drove him to despair. There was no communication between them: she could not understand him and, though he understood her, he was helpless to change the situation. He could not pay the rent; friends and relatives visited them via the fire escape. And he would not go to work for thirty-five dollars a week.

"If I take that job," he said, "it'll be the *end* . . . the end of everything." He ignored Bertha's entreaties and threats. He continued to write gags and skits that no one would read. He thought they were funny.

Mike stood impatiently in front of a slender, dark-haired young man typing at a small desk in the cubbyhole that passed for *Variety's* office.

"I hear *Variety* has a copyright service for original vaudeville material," Mike said at last.

"Put it in an envelope, seal it and leave fifty cents," the young man responded perfunctorily without looking up.

"Want me to tell you the skit?" Mike asked eagerly.

"Put it in an envelope, seal it and leave fifty cents," the young man repeated with total apathy.

"It's a 'hide-under-the-bed, that's-my-husband' blackout with a new switch," Mike went on, unabashed.

Danny Goldberg looked up wearily.

"Have dinner with me," Mike half begged, half insisted.

Hours later, at the Greek Café on Dearborn Street, Mike was still reciting his repertoire to his captive listener. Danny finally interrupted him; he was two hours late for an appointment with Dick Hood and John MacMahon at the Fair, formally known as the Century of Progress Exposition. Mike went along.

Hood and MacMahon, operators of the *Streets of Paris*, were disconsolate, and with good cause. Sally Rand, the greatest attraction on the Midway, had just given them notice she was leaving to star at the Italian Village.

"Danny," Hood implored, "if you hear of a big name who can follow Sally . . ."

In the stillness of early morning, Mike and Danny sat on

the end of a pier jutting out into Lake Michigan, talking and dreaming.

"They're taking in a hundred million bucks a year at the Fair," Mike sighed, "and I can't get a buck of it."

"All you need," Danny said, "is another Sally Rand."

Mike shook his head. "There's no money in imitations, you got to come up with an original."

He discovered a dancer named Shannon Dean, pretty and personable, but he was at a loss how to display her. There must be a way to undress a dancer artistically, he thought, like Salome. He was pondering, outside Shannon's dressing room, when Danny tapped him on the shoulder. "Don't play with fire, Mike," he cautioned. "I hear your wife is a jealous woman."

Mike was perplexed for a moment, then he broke into a grateful smile. "Thanks, Danny!" he exclaimed, not for the advice but for reminding him of the maxim, "Play with fire and you'll get burned."

He was impatient to tell Shannon. "You know the story of the flame and the moth . . ." he began.

Weeks later, in the vacant Swift Pavilion, the allegory of the moth and the flame came to life. Shannon, in the diaphanous costume of a moth, fluttered about the stage, drawing closer and closer to a huge candle, the flame of which Mike controlled by manipulating a machine beneath the floor. He had experimented with sixteen different chemicals, and had worked with an engineer for five weeks, but the problem had been solved by the gas company. Use plain gas, he was told.

At the climactic moment of the dance, as Shannon brushed the flame, Mike turned on the gas full blast. Her gauzy wings caught fire, the appendages fell and, seemingly nude, she scampered off stage. He had found a way of stripping a girl without doing it physically.

Shannon rehearsed the dance for a few weeks, but Mike was not satisfied and, badly as he needed money, he refused to open the act. Necessity could not stampede him into a premature decision. He continued searching . . .

He found her in Fred Evans' chorus line at the Chicago Theater. She was seventeen years old, five feet five, one hundred twelve pounds, and had long brunette hair—an exquisite bon-bon of French descent. Her name was Eva Gardiner and she had been trained in the Pavlui Ukrainsky Ballet.

Eva was an accomplished ballerina, a professional since she was twelve. Though Mike was instantly captivated by her, he could not visualize yokels on the Midway paying two bits or even a dime to see her execute an *entrechat*. Highbrow culture was a drug on the market; people had stopped reading H. L. Mencken and were writing chain letters. Graceful Eva could not compete with Sally Rand and her fluttering fans.

Could he persuade her to do his Flame Dance? What a question! He was the greatest salesman in the world.

"We have to change your personality," he told Eva the day after he met her. "From now on you're a society girl from Philadelphia. Your new name is . . . Page. Muriel Page. You know the story of the flame and the moth . . ."

Eva rehearsed the dance tirelessly.

"Be careful," he jested. "I've already burned up three girls."

There was a risk and his name was Gatty, the prop man. He regulated the gas machine, a chore that required a deft, steady hand. Now and then, after a nip or two, Gatty's hand was not as deft and steady as it should have been. Once he turned the jet to full flame an instant too soon, and Eva's leg was singed. She winced in momentary pain.

Mike, ashen, ran to her.

She read the alarm in his face. "Don't worry, Mike, we'll get it."

He was concerned. "Maybe it's a mistake, Eva," he said. "Maybe you ought to go back to the ballet. This could be hazardous."

"What girl wouldn't go through fire for you, Mike?" she

asked, pretending it was a joke, but she meant it. In a moment she was pirouetting toward the flame.

Persuading tough showmen like Hood and MacMahon to accept an unknown ballet dancer as a replacement for Sally Rand was easy for Mike. To him it was just another pitch, another sale.

The act opened over the protests of Eva's mother, who had been visiting friends in Canada and was unaware that her daughter had given up her career as a ballerina to become an incendiary carnival peeler. The Gardiner family, her uncles, aunts and cousins who lived in Chicago, were shocked by her "nude" dance, unaware she wore a flesh-colored leotard under her wings, and disowned her. It was an ordeal, but she refused to quit the act or Mike.

Mike, infuriated by her family's intolerance, determined to do something about it. Shortly thereafter, a prominent pastor delivered a sermon in which he stated, "The Moth and Flame is the most moral dance I have ever seen and teaches a great lesson." His opinion touched off a controversy that raged in the newspapers for weeks and made Muriel Page one of the leading attractions at the Exposition. Somehow he had convinced Chicagoans that the Flame Dance best symbolized their city's first hundred years of onward and upward progress.

It was a revelation to Mike—his first experience in public relations and the art of getting space in the newspapers, front-page space. The infallible sign of a salesman is his ability to make people fight for the article he is trying to sell. His was, from the beginning, an instinctive talent for converting publicity into news, at least what the press and the public *considered* news, which, for practical purposes, amounts to the same thing.

In the midst of the nation-wide debate he received an offer to take his Flame Girl to the Casino de Paris in New York for $750 a week. Show business was all right, he decided. He had signed Eva at $65 a week.

Her mother went along to keep an eye on the wardrobe mistress. To save time, if no one was watching, wardrobe mistresses would glue on the chemically treated wings instead of sewing them. Wet glue was inflammable.

Mrs. Gardiner also went along to keep an eye on Mike.

The Casino de Paris, a theater restaurant on Fifty-fourth Street off Broadway, had revolutionized café entertainment since its opening on December 30, 1933. As the Fortune Gallo Theater it had been dark for seven years. As a night club, with no cover charge and a two-dollar-and-fifty-cent minimum for which the customer received an eight-course dinner and saw a ninety-minute show, it was grossing forty thousand dollars a week and showing a profit of fifteen thousand dollars.

This flamboyant playground for the medium-income group was conceived by Willy Galuppo, an erstwhile lieutenant in Lucky Luciano's organization; Knocky Schwartz, a Lansky-Siegel mob bravo; Three Finger Brown and several other knaves who were among the organizers of a beer company and wanted a prestige spot in which to promote their brew.

Broadway's Mighty Midget, Billy Rose, had been hired to fill the twelve hundred seats—and he had succeeded, with performers like Jimmy Durante, Ella Logan, Martha Raye, Gypsy Rose Lee, Jimmy Savo, Eleanor Powell, Gertrude Niesen, music by Brown and Henderson, and girls: a hundred girls, mostly walking girls, incapable of dancing, even by Willy Galuppo-Knocky Schwartz standards. A nude girl in a fish bowl reduced to six inches in height netted twenty-eight hundred dollars a week.

On the stage, that summer of 1934, Eva whirled around her flame twice a night, at eight-thirty and twelve-thirty. Beneath the stage, Mike controlled the gas machine; he trusted no one else. After the show he sat with the cognoscenti of night life, the buyers and the bought, the lonely and the unloved. He listened in awe and envy as they drew red circles around their yesterdays. It mattered little that some of the legends may have been apocryphal, in this world only the unreal was real; and, as Philip Mass used to quote Walpole, since it is impossible to have the truth about life anyway, who is to say that the pleasant hallucinations are not as true as the others?

Like Richard II, they sat and told sad stories of the death of kings. . . .

"Al Woods, there was a producer! One year he had twenty road shows. He was smart, he stashed a million in a safe-deposit vault. Then he gave a duplicate key to a pal. The pal emptied it during the Crash. Al went into bankruptcy."

"How about Arthur Hammerstein? He made over two and a half million on *Rose Marie* and blew every dime building a theater so his father's name could be in lights."

"They were small change. The Shuberts took a bath for *eight* mill, the creditors got less than a cent on the dollar."

"I'll take Ziegfeld. How about the time he hired a private railroad car for a three-hour trip?"

"And the time he put on a private party and spent ten G's just for entertainment."

"How about the time he dressed his whole chorus in Irish lace petticoats that cost six hundred apiece? They wore 'em under big bouffant skirts and the audience didn't see a hand-stitched hem. When one of the backers beefed, Flo smiled and said, 'My girls know they're wearing Irish lace and it does something to the way they walk.'"

"Ziggy went big. When he died he owed the newsboy outside his theater eighteen hundred bucks for newspapers, at a penny apiece."

Mike's eyes sparkled. He had discovered the key to fame on Broadway. Failure was success if you went big enough.

Billy Rose had the combination. In the early twenties he made a hundred thousand dollars a year as a song writer, coming up with hits like "Barney Google," and he had gone through every nickel. He lost a new stake on his first Broadway show,

Crazy Quilt. He parlayed that disaster into *The Great Magoo*, a play by Ben Hecht and Gene Fowler, which lasted one week. Now, with the Casino de Paris doing capacity business, he had taken off for Europe on a four-month vacation.

Mike took Eva and her mother on the road, from Montreal to Mexico City, wherever he could get a booking. The Flame Dance was doubly hazardous in outdoor carnivals—the slightest change in wind was enough to burn her body—but true to her word, Muriel eagerly went through fire for Mike.

He thought of Bertha only in relation to Michael Junior. He felt sorry for her, she was a good girl who did not deserve this kind of life, but he could not help it. They were strangers. She had married Avrom Goldbogen and he was Mike Todd. It wasn't a matter of love but boredom. Bertha's world was safe, virtuous and dull. He was a hustler, he had to gamble to stay alive. Eva? She was a pretty thing, delightful and exciting, and, unlike Bertha, she did not destroy the illusion by talking. It gave him a sense of power to know he had created her. It never occurred to him that she might have created him: that she might be the flame and he the moth. As for Bertha, he was incapable of thinking about two women at the same time.

He went home as often as he could, to see his son. Each time the boy was an inch taller, each time he spoke more clearly and fluently, each time he came closer, in Mike's eyes, to his own image.

To his son alone did he give the full measure of his love. He never raised his voice or hand to him, not even the day Junior locked him in his room, out of pique, because Mike had been too busy to read the Sunday comics, and then had been afraid to let him out. Mike just laughed, leaving Junior's disciplining to Bertha.

"Are you going to stay in show business?" Bertha asked.

The question surprised him. He thought of himself solely as a salesman. Instead of newspapers, shoeshines, bluing, pants pressers, vegetables, drug-store gin, shoes, window displays, bricklaying or real estate, he was peddling entertainment. The products changed but the means of selling them remained the same. Only his technique improved.

Expediency, not desire, had brought him into show business. He probably would still be in the construction business had it not been for the Depression. People could not afford to buy houses, but the more hard up they were, the more desperate they were for amusement. He was a salesman and he sold what was salable.

There was an artistry involved: the skill of salesmanship. Everything else, including the product, was secondary. He was selling *himself*. Every prospective customer was a challenge. Every transaction was a new source of wonderment and delight to him. He had been a showman long before he met Eva. Conceiving an immense tube of toothpaste that covered an entire window of the Logan Drug Store was showmanship. He had not learned it. He was born to show off.

Most men lived by a pattern. In show business there was no pattern. He had no pattern except the first principle of the gambler: parlay.

One act was not enough for his soaring ambitions. He had to parlay it into a show.

"What are you sweatin' over?" he asked Danny Goldberg, lighting a cigar and planking his feet on Danny's desk in the *Variety* office.

"*Peggy's Progress*," Danny groaned; he pulled the sheet of paper from his typewriter, crumpled it and hurled it onto the ankle-deep pile at his feet.

Claude Binyon, a *Variety* mug who immortalized the stock-market crash in a headline, "WALL ST. LAYS EGG," had created *Peggy*, the weekly adventures of a naïve nude who worked for a peep show. It caught on. But Binyon was tapped by a Hollywood studio, and Danny, who had no interest in carnys, regardless of sex, inherited *Peggy*.

"I wrote myself out in two weeks," Danny sighed sadly.

"You ought to do some research," Mike suggested.

Danny shot him a caustic look.

Mike leaned back and blew a series of smoke circles. "Remember Paris Peggy?" he recalled.

"The talker?" Danny asked.

"Best pitchman on the strip first year of the Exposition," Mike said with authority. "I wonder what happened to her."

Danny let out a moan. "I got my *own* Peggy, I got a deadline, and if you don't . . ."

"She begged me to write an act for her," Mike broke in.

"Will you *shut up,* Mike? I have to get *Peggy* out in half an hour and I haven't an idea in my head."

"Tell you what I'll do, Danny," Mike said magnanimously, removing his feet from the desk. "I'll write your *Peggy* if you'll find my Peggy."

For the next several months Mike ghosted and collaborated with Danny, and *Peggy's Progress*, by unanimous opinion, was considerably swifter and spicier. "Dear Benny," each installment began in the form of a letter to her confidant. "How lucky I am!" she would exclaim. "Other people in show business have to do three or four shows a day. I only have one, from four P.M. until midnight, and all I have to do is lay on my back."

Each week a different rake tried to seduce *Peggy,* but virtue always triumphed in the end, though not until she had simpered through half a column of the raciest prose since Frank Harris' autobiography.

Danny came up with Paris Peggy, Coffin by surname, who was more anxious than ever to quit her job as a spieler and become a performer. Mike wrote a vaudeville act for her, a satire on the Exposition, which had a little bit of everything, including two midgets and three normal-size comedians attired in colonial hoop skirts and powdered wigs, a live seal, dogs, mice, turtles, goldfish and a variety of props: baseballs, basketballs, golf balls, brooms, balloons, skates, skis, snowshoes and beds.

Todd had range, if nothing else.

As a barker, Peggy was the best on the Midway. Before the same audience, as a performer, she could not speak lucidly. It was tragic and catastrophic. Mike did not have time or money to substitute; he had booked the act as a unit at the vaudeville houses he had played with Eva, and he had to take it out.

The unit lasted six weeks. It had too much talk and not enough legs, Mike concluded. He knew how to fix that. He had cased the Casino de Paris for thirty weeks. He had seen the hot-eyed hicks in the sticks when Eva's costume burned off. And he remembered the traditional battle cry at every smoker and burlesque show, "Bring on the dames!" It was fundamental, as Aristophanes had discovered in the fifth century—give 'em high dames and low comedy.

Securing eight lovely show girls capable of walking across a stage, and twenty-four beautifully formed chorus girls who did not have to move, was not difficult. Selling them was the problem. Almost all merchandise was sold to the public via the libido: alluring pictures of young girls, gorgeous girls, usually in one-piece bathing suits. They sold everything from breakfast food to roller bearings—but, the question plagued Mike, how do you sell *them?* He was going into the hinterland, he was taking a New York show to people who could not afford to go to New York. He had no intention of running a stag or catering to the few husbands who could sneak out for a night. There were more who could not. He had to sell the wives as well as give the men an excuse for going to a girlie show. You had to have a front, innocuous but entertaining.

Why not an animal act? He would have liked an elephant herd but he couldn't afford a flea circus. He found the solution in a newspaper, a photograph of Admiral Richard E. Byrd and friends at Little America. A bird by any name that could make the front page of the New York *Times* was good enough for him, but, unfortunately, he could not find a penguin in the United States.

In desperation he was about to cable Admiral Byrd, when Lou Wolfson of the William Morris Agency, its reputation for representing talent of every feather at stake, informed him that its vice-president in charge of aviaries, Harry Foster, had found a penguin on Tottingham Road, London.

"BRING PENGUIN IMMEDIATELY," Mike cabled Foster.

Foster booked passage on the *Ile de France* and Mike cabled him aboard ship: "DRESS HIM."

"This is Pete, the Personality Penguin," Mike introduced the bird, dressed in Foster's best white tie and top hat, to the battery of press photographers and reporters he had gathered at the gangplank.

"Mitt da profile!" said Jimmy Durante, chairman of the welcoming committee, and nuzzled close to Pete. The penguin, a hostile fellow, promptly bit a chunk out of Durante's celebrated proboscis. Schnozzola threatened to strangle him and sue Todd for a million dollars, as dozens of flash bulbs exploded. Mike respected Admiral Byrd, but going all the way to the South Pole to get his picture with a penguin in the newspapers, as the front pages of the following morning's editions attested, was doing it the hard way.

The words of Doc, the pitchman, came back to him. "Sell the sizzle, not the steak. Sell the bubbles, not the champagne. Sell the whiff, not the coffee." Mike was ready for his safari. He had his Flame Girl, eight show girls and twenty-four chorus girls, but he was going to sell the penguin, not the girls. He rented a bus, and the thirty-three girls, plus Eva's mother, went aboard, followed by Personality Pete and a comedian named Harry Savoy.

Todd's first show, *Bring on the Dames*, was on the road. He opened it in the Middle West and headed East.

On his first day at Isador Rappaport's Hippodrome in Baltimore, Pete was more perverse than personable. He would do nothing beyond being a penguin, and not even that for the

audience. The show went on but he wouldn't. He was unmoved
by pleas, threats and cajolery.

"Sorry, Mr. Rappaport, but Pete has stage fright," Mike explained during the intermission.

"The *star* of the show?" Rappaport was aghast and adamant.
"You promised a Personality Penguin and I advertised him.
Deliver him the next act . . . or else."

Savoy came out for the second act, and one step behind him
waddled the formally attired penguin. Whenever Savoy turned,
Pete wheeled with him; wherever Savoy went, Pete obediently
followed, the band maintaining its beat to his step. Pete stopped
the show.

Mike was gratified that his faith in animals and the teachings
of Doc, the pitchman, had been vindicated. "Consider how
much a little dog can express with just one woof, one tail to
wag," Doc had told him.

"Mister, you're a genius!" Rappaport told Mike in honest admiration. "How did you do it?"

"Psychology," said Mike enigmatically.

"Greatest animal act I ever saw." Rappaport suddenly grimaced. "But the smell! Worse than a camel!"

"I didn't smell a thing," said Mike. What was to be gained
by revealing that he had gulled the penguin into following
Savoy by secreting a smelt in the tail of the comedian's coat?
The odor would not be so oppressive in colder weather, he
hoped.

Colder weather came—ice, snow and sleet—and the bus rolled
through the sub-zero Middle West. There were many close
calls, one closer than the others. The bus skidded on a steep,
ice-covered hill and careened from side to side, out of control.
Everyone screamed as the driver clung helplessly to the wheel,
everyone but Mike.

"Hold on to the seats," he ordered in a calm, reassuring voice,
walking among them.

The bus plummeted on, missing cars by inches, at last left

the road and piled up on an embankment. Miraculously no one was hurt.

One of Mike's arms was wrapped protectively around Eva, the other clutched the penguin.

He was never satisfied with the show and did not stop improving it. Savoy reluctantly tried each new piece of business Mike invented for him and the penguin, and, to his amazement, almost every one was successful. In one skit Savoy, on one knee, proposed to a girl. Every few seconds the penguin interrupted him by tugging on his coat tail and looking at him. To the customers the sad-eyed expression meant, "Don't be a sucker, pal." To Savoy it said, "Slip me a smelt, Harry."

The big show that summer was the Texas Centennial Exposition at Fort Worth. Billy Rose was running it and Mike promoted a booking.

"You're coming up in the world, kid," Rose remarked, noting that he had parlayed one girl into a cast of thirty-five.

"You ain't doing so bad yourself," Mike conceded. Billy, he knew, was getting a thousand dollars a day.

Mike enjoyed the carnival atmosphere. He made many new friends and renewed acquaintance with some old ones, among them Joe Rogers, a saloonkeeper from Chicago, who was the self-appointed Mayor of the Midway, which meant running a card game for concessionaires.

In the hurly-burly of the vast amusement area Rogers had found a single oasis of comfort and safety, Admiral Byrd's Little America, a walk-through educational exhibit that had not even drawn Mike's penguin. A running pinochle game continued day and night, uninterrupted by a customer; but as the Labor Day week end approached, Joe feared that a trickle of holiday visitors might drive his guests from their sanctuary.

Mike came to his rescue. He convinced the owner of the exhibit that the card players could be an asset, and during the week end the guide led patrons through Little America, pointing out the impedimenta of Admiral Byrd's expedition to the South Pole.

"These are the Eskimo dogs, the fur-lined sleeping bags, the radio equipment, the stuffed musk ox from the frozen steppes and this . . ." Here he would pause at a table surrounded by seven silent, intense men playing cards from noon to dawn. "This is the way the men spent their idle hours during the long winter nights in the Arctic Circle."

"I'm bored with the show," Mike told Danny on his return to Chicago. "I'm closing it."

"You can't fold a winner!" Danny said. "You've run a solid year."

"Fourteen months," Mike corrected him.

"You can run another fourteen months. You'll be one of the big men in the business!"

"Like Will Harris, A. B. Marcus and Al Boardie?"

"Why not?"

"I'd rather be kayoed by Jack Dempsey than flatten Al Bunyak."

Goldberg was puzzled. "I don't get it."

"It's better to be a flop on Broadway, and be with the Shuberts, Max Gordon and Sam Harris. than to be King of the Vaudeville Units with A. B. Marcus, Al Boardie *and* Will Harris."

Broadway was the Big Street. All the rest were alleys. He had walked them.

Goldberg shook his head. "A flop is a flop anywhere."

Mike was impatient with Danny. "But you have a ticket in the Handicap, even if you pull up lame. That's better than copping a claiming race with a plater."

Danny knew Mike too well to argue with him. "Is it finished with Eva too?"

"She's going to do her own act, without the Flame Dance, at the Latin Quarter in New York and other top clubs. As

Mademoiselle Bastian—that's her mother's maiden name—until I have a show for her."

"Then it isn't finished?"

"You weren't listening, Danny. I said I was bored with the *show.*"

The Cold Mikado

He had learned many things in his wanderings, among them that *The Mikado* was the most durable of shows. He had read in *Variety* that as far back as 1886 the Gilbert and Sullivan musical was played one hundred and seventy times in a single evening by an equal number of companies scattered throughout the country, thanks to the lack of an Anglo-American copyright treaty that made it public domain. As recently as 1932, the Savoy Comic Opera Troupe had burlesqued it successfully in New York. In the late twenties, a nameless German producer had the mad idea of producing a jazz version, with choreography featuring the Charleston, at the Grosse Schauspielhaus in Berlin, and still it survived.

The Mikado deserved a dignified revival, Mike decided, and persuaded Mary McCormic of the Chicago Civic Opera Company to be his Yum-Yum. She was fading, but still second only to Mary Garden. The noted diva had hardly learned the lyrics when the Lord High Executioner, played by a bona-fide sheriff, closed the show during a tryout at South Bend, Indiana. It was a flop with honor. It was a good production and took in from $3,500 to $4,250 per week, showing a paper profit of $1,000, but failed for lack of operating cash.

Mike was disappointed, only because his invasion of Broadway would be postponed until he came up with a new bankroll. That meant going back to vaudeville, a detour he detested. And he had disbanded his tab show: Eva was booked for the year, Savoy had caught on with another show, and he didn't even know his penguin's address. His only assets were the costumes and scenery he had lingoed out of the sheriff.

He had to take another chance on *The Mikado*, this time without dignity. That unknown German producer *had* something: Gilbert and Sullivan were satirists, their words and music were meant to be re-created by each succeeding generation. It was clear to him that he had failed them by *not* souping up the show, and that was why he had been punished. He would streamline the production, add a chorus of dancing girls, update the lyrics and upjazz the music.

When it was done he called it *The Hot Mikado,* and took it on the road. It was successful but gave him no satisfaction. He knew he could make a living in the sticks, but that didn't prove anything. He had to beat the Big Street.

"I'm square with the board," he told Danny in Chicago. "Now for New York!"

Danny insisted on being logical. "Do you have a show?" he asked.

"I have an *idea* for a show!"

Danny groaned. His elder half-brother, Joe Sherman, old Stick and Slug, came in and embraced Mike. He liked Todd for the very characteristics others disliked.

"Joe, do me a favor," Mike asked.

"It's done," Joe said.

"Danny and I have to go away for the week end. Big business deal." Danny let out a cry of protest, but Mike ignored it. "Would you take Junior to the ball game Sunday?"

It was done.

They stood at the ticket window in Dearborn Station. Mike emptied his pockets and counted his wealth.

"What's all this about?" Danny demanded.

"You are my guest for the week end," Mike said and turned to the ticket seller. "How far can we go on fifteen bucks?"

"Green Lake, Wisconsin," came the reply after a moment's pause.

"Ring it up," Mike said and pushed his total assets under the grille.

Mike let Danny suffer until they were settled at Green Lake. He had learned that the simplest declaration, if withheld long enough—merely hinted or partly revealed, like an expert stripper *not* revealing an ordinary body—can, by mounting suspense, gain excitement and importance.

"We're going to do a play," he whispered confidently at last. Danny was aghast. "But we haven't got a play."

"We'll write one," Mike said airily.

"I've never written a play!" Danny exclaimed.

"Neither have I," Mike said. "We're even. I got an idea. This producer, a hustler type like Will Harris, is trying to keep a bedroom farce, a real turkey, going long enough to get a bite from Hollywood. He starts on a shoestring and loses the string. His actors walk out and his creditors walk in. All the action takes place backstage and onstage, so we won't need any sets. How does it sound?"

"Ghastly," said Danny.

"But I haven't told you the story yet! It's funnier than *Once in a Lifetime*. The play—that is, the play this producer is putting on—is called *Three in a Bed*. Do you follow me?"

"No," said Danny, knowing it made no difference to Mike.

"Like I told you, he's trying to keep the play alive until a movie studio buys it. Do you know what happens?"

"No," said Danny.

"A *bed* company buys it for advertising purposes."

"A bed company should buy both plays," said Danny dourly.

"I don't think you understand, Danny. This is a play within a play."

"You mean a play without a play."

Mike gazed across the lake to the horizon. "Call me Ziggy," he said softly.

"I don't know you that well, Mr. Ziegfeld," Danny mocked.

Mike glared at him. "That's the title of our play, Mr. Author!"

They wrote for two and a half days. Danny ran out of eating money and they finished the last act on the train.

Sherman took Michael Junior to the ball game, as he had promised, an exhibition between the Cubs and White Sox.

"Best game I ever saw," enthused Junior with the authority of his six years.

"I heard part of it on the radio," said his mother. "All that commotion, when the man kicked a bunt and . . ."

"Dragged a bunt, Mother," Junior amended her respectfully.

"What happened? I heard that someone in the grandstand ran out on the field and picked up the ball before any player could reach it. Did you see that, Michael?"

Michael nodded. "Yes, Mother."

"I'll say he did!" Sherman chortled proudly. "*He* was the one who did it! The official scorer decided it was a hit and the Cubs won the game! The White Sox wanted to hit Junior with a baseball bat but the Cubs protected him!"

That night Mike and Sherman celebrated Junior's future career as first baseman of the Chicago Cubs.

"I hope you got that crazy notion out of your head," said Sherman, "about giving up the tab show."

"That's finished," said Mike. He was obsessed with the fear of boredom. Action was the only therapy for it, change the sole catharsis.

"You're out of your mind."

Mike looked at him with forbearance. Poor Stick and Slug didn't savvy. There was no wonderment in his life. Maybe the fight ring had knocked it out of him. Maybe he never had it. Few did. Stick and Slug knew him no better than Bertha did. Play it safe, that was their religion. How can you play it safe in an unsafe world? How can you stand still when the world is moving? Failure was better than repetition. He had acquired a philosophy, without knowing that a man named Machiavelli had put it into words, that it is better to act and be sorry than not to act and be sorry. He could not look back on anything he had done, good or bad, he was too busy wondering what he was going to see or do next. He had to know and be known. People like Joe and Bertha didn't get it. They weren't restless. They didn't make things happen. Things happened *to* them. That was their trouble. You can't win if you haven't got a ticket.

"Hi-yo, *Silver!*" Junior charged into the room.

Sherman had one more arrow. "A Broadway show isn't a tab show," he said. "It takes money."

Mike did not take his eyes off Junior. As the size-seven Masked Rider of the Plains galloped into the kitchen with a triumphant "The Lone Ranger rides again!" Mike knew where he would find his angel. The Lone Ranger, a two-gun Robin Hood, was the biggest thing on radio. No respectable family that believed in preserving law and order, especially among their offspring, dared eat anything but Lone Ranger bread troweled with Lone Ranger peanut butter.

Every red-blooded American boy knew the Lone Ranger's voice, the hoofbeats of his faithful steed, Silver, and the grunt of his loyal Tonto, but, Mike smiled shrewdly, they had never *seen* him.

A man named King, who owned the rights to the Lone Ranger, listened avidly as Mike foretold the riches he would reap from a personal appearance tour.

"I played fifty-six weeks from coast to coast, from Canada to Mexico, with a no-talent penguin!" Mike said. "The Lone Ranger can go on forever!"

Mike left with a long-term contract and a forty-eight-state itinerary that would begin in the nearby community of Streator, Illinois.

The theater was filled to capacity with shrieking youngsters an hour before the performance began. At last the familiar hoofbeats were heard and a masked rider appeared on his white charger.

"Hi-yo, *Silver!*" he shouted as his horse reared before wheeling onto the treadmill in center stage.

"The Lone Ranger rides again!" Michael Todd, Jr., and more than two thousand other youngsters shouted.

The Lone Ranger rode on, and, at last, in response to the tumultuous applause, he removed his hat and his mask.

There was silence, total and ominous.

Then came a cry. Other wails followed. In a moment they swelled to a screaming, howling symphony of anger and disillusionment. Everything that could be thrown was hurled at the astonished Lone Ranger and his equally dumfounded horse.

"Fake! Fake!" the kids hooted. The instant he lifted his mask they knew he was an impostor: he was not the Lone Ranger *they* had conceived.

Backstage, King, terror-stricken, ordered the curtain rung down. "It's all your fault!" he raged at Mike. "You've *ruined* the Lone Ranger!"

"Don't get panicky," Mike tried to calm him. "Streator is a small town, it doesn't mean anything. Tomorrow we play Joliet, then Springfield, then . . ."

"Tomorrow the Lone Ranger rides on the radio and *nowhere* else!" King said.

"But I have a contract," Mike insisted.

"I'll make a settlement," said King. "Anything within reason."

Mike had him over a barrel, but he did not take advantage —he sold back the contract.

The harrowing experience taught him a lesson, the old truth that illusion is the first of pleasures and no tree in the world is as beautiful as the tree in your mind.

Call Me Ziggy

He did not hear the blind man's violin or the sad castanets, the moocher's pitch or the crackpot's prophecy of doom. These gaudy, raucous streets were cantharides to cheap souls but not to him. He did not see the pinched, frightened faces of the beaten and the lost, he saw only lights, lights that beckoned and enchanted him.

Booth Theater—Sam Harris Presents YOU CAN'T TAKE IT WITH YOU, by Moss Hart and George S. Kaufman

Ethel Barrymore Theater—Max Gordon Presents THE WOMEN, by Clare Booth

Winter Garden—The Shuberts Present THE SHOW IS ON, with Beatrice Lillie and Bert Lahr, Music by Rodgers and Hart

Music Box—Sam Harris Presents STAGE DOOR, by Edna Ferber and George S. Kaufman, with Margaret Sullavan

Shubert Theater—Alfred Lunt and Lynn Fontanne in Robert Sherwood's IDIOT'S DELIGHT

National Theater—Noel Coward and Gertrude Lawrence in TONIGHT AT 8:30

Martin Beck Theater—Guthrie McClintock Presents Maxwell Anderson's HIGH TOR, with Burgess Meredith

Biltmore Theater—George Abbott Presents BROTHER RAT

44th Street Theater—Paul Green's JOHNNY JOHNSON, with Jules Garfield, Luther Adler, Lee Cobb, Elia Kazan

Morosco Theater—George M. Cohan in FULTON OF OAK FALLS

New Amsterdam Theater—Walter Huston in OTHELLO

Broadhurst Theater—Helen Hayes in VICTORIA REGINA

As he walked, he gazed up at the marquees with reverence and envy. These were his cathedrals, and his gods, and he would soon be one of them.

He stopped at the Longacre, a Shubert theater, where an electrician was shuffling the bulbs on the marquee from HOWDY, STRANGER, Starring Frank Parker, to Michael Todd Presents CALL ME ZIGGY, a Farce in Three Acts, by Dan Goldberg.

"A very modest title," a slender young man watching the operation a few steps away commented sardonically.

"Maybe you know a better one," Mike snapped.

"I do," the critic smiled and held out his hand. "*Howdy, Stranger.* I'm Bob Goldstein, one of the producers. Shubert is moving us to the 46th Street Theater to make room for you."

"Nothing personal," Mike said. "Mr. Lee [Shubert] *insisted* I take it over."

Goldstein was disdainful of the rakish angle of Mike's derby, his checkered vest and the cigar he manipulated in his fierce jaw, but he was impressed by what these obvious props attempted to conceal.

His arrival had been noted in the New York *Times*, December 30, 1936, in a sentence. "The Sardi Building has a new tenant, Michael Todd, a Chicago producer."

He had moved into a small room at the St. Moritz. It was better to have a second-class room at a first-class hotel, he reasoned, than vice versa.

As his star, he had chosen Joseph Buloff, a comedian in the Yiddish theater, as unknown on Broadway as himself. Rehearsals were held in the flat of his friend, Lew Brown. There was no money for an out-of-town tryout. He had gone through his bankroll of ten thousand dollars, the seven thousand he had received from a grateful King for the return of his Lone Ranger, and three thousand he had lugged from his friends—Harold Costello, who was associated with the Oriental Theater in Chicago, and Robert O. Farrell, his lawyer.

Call Me Ziggy opened February 12, 1937.

"Many people who cannot write plays," Brooks Atkinson recorded in the *Times*, "cannot resist the temptation to write plays about plays. Although this one affects a highly facetious attitude toward the shoestring theater, it is no high-button boot itself. It is every bit as witless as the quack theater it pretends to satirize.

"Joseph Buloff is intoxicated with the true comic spirit. He is every inch an actor, imaginative, effervescent and inventive, but the play is destitute of merit."

George Jean Nathan had finished writing his notice before the first-act curtain. He dismissed the plot, cast, direction and settings in a withering sentence, and devoted several lucid paragraphs to the sartorial elegance of the producer.

Danny Goldberg read the notices and held his head. "Nobody will come now," he groaned.

"Sure they will," said Mike. "We'll give out passes."

"Give carfare with the passes," Danny added.

"*Call Me Ziggy* is definitely bad," wrote Robert Benchley, "and twice bad because it is a *bad play within a bad play*. But it does enlist the services of a real Jewish comedian making his second appearance on the English-speaking stage. I can hardly wait for his third appearance, but I have a hunch it will be in a picture from Hollywood in which he plays the part of the Duke of Alba."

Benchley's verdict was published in the *New Yorker* posthumously. The play closed after three performances.

As he read his obituaries, Mike noticed that *The Mikado* was playing at Stetson's Fifth Avenue Theater.

"I need a play, Danny," Mike told Goldberg.

"I don't," said Danny.

"This time we take no chances, no ideas by you or me."

"How about Shakespeare?"

"What was that French story Buloff liked?"

Danny had taken an oath never to permit Mike to con him into writing another word, but he knew, in the end, he would. Mike could talk anyone into or out of anything.

"What was the story line, Danny?"

"Typical French farce, too thin for a play, actually it's only one act."

"Give."

Danny knew it was futile to hold out. "You know it, Mike. About the mousy little government clerk in Budapest who is married to a fat slob who doesn't let him spend a *pengo* on himself. One day he buys a dress suit, on the q.t."

"And on time," Mike interjected.

"Once a month he goes over the wall, puts on his tails and hits the joints, posing as a man-about-town. He meets a lonely kid named Leni at the Café Rudolph, romances her and convinces her he's a poet. He throws a few odes and tells her he can bring her great happiness. By the time she comes out of the spell, Istvan, that's the hero's name, is gone."

"Can't miss," Mike exclaimed. "Cinderella in reverse. Go ahead."

"Leni traces Istvan to his flat, meets his wife, and, disillusioned, she returns to her first love. It sounds worse every time I tell it."

"It's a wonderful story, Danny! It isn't Istvan, it's *every man* who's trying to escape from the monotonous routine of his life; it's every man trying to break away or break out from what he *is*."

"But he winds up with the same old bag."

"You missed the point, Danny." Mike became solemn. "Maybe he can't get rid of his old self; maybe it will be with him until he dies. Maybe he can't go anywhere, not *really*, but he still has his *dream* . . . and his dress suit."

Goldberg had little hope. "It's so slight, Mike. Your only chance, if there is a chance, would be if you had a star to play it."

"I have! Joe Buloff."

Goldberg was too weak to argue. "Try to get George S. Kaufman to write it."

"I don't need George S. Kaufman. I got you."

"You, Buloff and me? That's what was the matter with *Call Me Ziggy!*"

Mike did not hear him. "I want a first draft a week from Monday."

He convinced Costello and Farrell that the only way they could get even on *Ziggy* was to invest in his new play. He put the bite on them, and a few friendly bookies, for seventeen thousand dollars.

The Man from Cairo, a so-called comedy in three acts by Danny Goldberg, adapted from the French play by Yvon Noe, produced by Michael Todd, starring Joseph Buloff and directed by a man with the improbable name of Harry Wagstaff Gribble, opened at the Wilbur Theater in Boston, mid-April, 1938.

It received excellent notices, while the tryout of another play at the Colonial Theater, *I Married an Angel*, with Dennis King and Vera Zorina, was panned unmercifully.

Mike felt genuinely sorry for the *I Married an Angel* company and expressed his feelings to the producer and cast.

The Man from Cairo moved into New York on May 4 to begin what Mike confidently expected would be a two-year run at the Broadhurst Theater.

"It is yesterday's cocktail," Atkinson reported in the *Times*. "Nothing this department can do can discourage people from shaking it up again and pouring it with the mechanical elegance of a bar steward on a cabin liner. Joseph Buloff is master of the tricks of pace, gesture and grimace that can make a hackneyed part uncommonly funny. A friendly audience thoroughly enjoyed it."

George Jean Nathan remained until the end of the first act and reported that, while the play was a catastrophe, he was pleased to note that Mike had toned down his flamboyant apparel and had worn a simple tuxedo.

"This is a dining-room comedy with the principals eating their way through three acts," *Time* stated. "There were those in the opening-night audience who wondered whether they shouldn't have been provided menus rather than programs."

The Man from Cairo was seven times more successful than *Call Me Ziggy*. It lasted twenty-two performances.

They walked on and off Broadway.

Danny heard the blind man's violin and the sad castanets, the moocher's pitch and the crackpot's prophecy of doom. He saw the pinched, frightened faces of the beaten and the lost.

Mike did not see or hear them, his eyes were lifted to the stars, his stars.

Henry Miller Theater—Jed Harris Presents OUR TOWN, by Thornton Wilder, Starring Frank Craven

Alvin Theater—Sam Harris presents I'D RATHER BE RIGHT, by George S. Kaufman and Moss Hart, Music by Richard Rodgers and Lorenz Hart, starring George M. Cohan

Winter Garden—The Shuberts Present HOORAY FOR WHAT?, Starring Ed Wynn, Music by E. Y. Harburg

Plymouth Theater—John Golden presents SUSAN AND GOD, with Gertrude Lawrence

Belasco Theater—GOLDEN BOY by Clifford Odets, with Jules Garfield

Music Box—Sam Harris Presents OF MICE AND MEN, with Broderick Crawford and Wallace Ford

Mercury Theater—JULIUS CAESAR, with Orson Welles

TOBACCO ROAD—Fifth Year!

And *I Married an Angel,* starring Dennis King and Vera Zorina, that he had felt sorry for in Boston, was a tremendous hit, sold out for months.

"I'll never write another play," said Danny, who was to keep his word.

"I'll hit it next time," said Mike.

For the first time in the years he had known Todd, Danny began to understand him. The flop of *The Man from Cairo* had made no more of an impression on him than that of *Call Me Ziggy*—it had not left a scar. Mike had no interest in anything that had been lived. He was never nostalgic or remorseful. He accepted human error as a necessity of life: mistakes were normal, to be made and forgotten. Winning *or* losing was of secondary importance to him, his thrill was in the struggle, the gamble. Mike had no fear of failure because he was immune to fear.

* **10** *

Joyeux Noël

It was Junior's ninth and most glorious Christmas. Marshall Field's son did not have as many toys as he did. Neither did Marshall Field's Toy Department. He had three complete sets of electric trains in operation, more than three thousand dollars' worth of equipment that filled every inch of the Todd apartment. Bertha, unable to get in or out of the kitchen, threatened to throw everything out if one more drum arrived.

Junior gazed at his father in awe. No question about it, he was the greatest man in the world.

The idea had been germinating in Mike's brain for five years, ever since he first saw the nude girl in a fish bowl at the Chicago Exposition and later at the Casino de Paris. One day a little boy had squirmed through the crowd and peered into the forbidden peephole. A clout on the ear interrupted the youngster's concentration. "Don't ever look in there again!" ordered the clouter, his father, who sneaked a fast peek. The expression on the little boy's face remained etched on Mike's memory. This year, having no show, he elected to do something about it.

Peepholes, he felt, should be confined to the enjoyment of children. He remembered his own youth and Doc, the pitchman, and his Magic Eye. But you can't have a peel-act for kids unless they're Dead End Kids. And they wouldn't be satisfied with miniatures. There must be a substitute, he was sure.

The fish-bowl illusion was produced, of course, by trick mirrors. Mirrors were expensive and cumbersome. How could it be done cheaply and simply? Mike knew enough about photography to realize that a reducing lens would achieve the same result. He found a warehouse full of lenses, long forgotten in U.S. Army surplus, some from World War I, others dating to the Spanish-American War. Next he found a bankroll, by name Yermi Stern. They bought the lenses, originally valued at $400 each, for ninety cents apiece, hired a loft and set two refugees to work.

"He lives! He breathes! He's *three inches* high!" Mike Todd, the barker, was giving a demonstration for the general manager of Marshall Field's store.

The manager stared at the miniature house the size of a bread box, within it a human St. Nicholas busy in his workshop, surrounded by his handiwork. Mike picked up a phone and dialed a number. Inside, Santa Claus picked up a telephone on his workbench and answered with a hearty "Hello!" Mike handed the receiver to the startled manager.

"Every child will be able to talk to Santa privately as they watch him," Mike went on. "Do you realize what this is, sir? Phonevision—and it isn't invented yet!"

"Hello—Santa," the manager said in bewilderment.

"Hello, Johnny!" Santa's voice came over the phone. "What do you want for Christmas and where do you live?"

The manager gulped.

"Don't be bashful, Johnny. How about a Flexible Flyer or an Ajax football or a Bulldog bicycle?"

"How does it work?" the manager asked Mike.

"With reducing lenses. Your Santa Claus is behind the curtain over there. He takes down the names and addresses. The next day the store can write or call the parents and tell them what their children want. It will be in stock, of course. And it's

absolutely free, sir. I don't want a nickel if you don't tell me
that our Kute Kris Kringle is the greatest attraction in the
history of Marshall Field's Toy House."

"How much?" the manager asked.

"They're not for sale. I can only rent them from Thanksgiving to Christmas for the introductory bargain offer of six hundred dollars each."

He leased 480 Kute Kris Kringles to department stores and
theaters, splitting with Yermi Stern a profit of approximately
$200,000.

He bought Bertha a mink wrap and a diamond choker, her
first expensive piece of jewelry. And he bought his mother
a coat which she would never wear.

"You're wasting your money buying mink for Mom," Frank
told him.

Mike shrugged. Jewish mothers fell into two general cate-
gories: those who wanted to show off, particularly the successes
of their children, and those who persecuted themselves. Sophia
Goldbogen, given a vacation at a summer resort, would insist
on taking a small inside room on the fourth floor instead of the
suite on the first floor reserved for her by Mike.

"He *lives!* He *breathes!* He's *three inches* high!" Junior chortled as he gave the spiel his father had taught him and gazed
at his own Kute Kris Kringle.

Christmas had never meant anything to Mike before. Now,
as Junior fell asleep in his arms, he felt a glow of satisfaction.
He would give his son many things in his life, but he wondered
if Junior would ever be happier than he was now, the day his
old man *proved* there was a Santa Claus.

His eyes met Bertha's. Had it been twelve years, almost
thirteen? Why, after all this time, couldn't he talk to her? Why
couldn't he tell her?

*Let go, Bertha, please. It's finished. I'm not your husband,
except in your imagination. We haven't lived together as man*

and wife for a long time. I never meant to hurt you, I never wanted to hurt anyone, but man is a hurting animal. I didn't betray you, not deliberately. If I betrayed anyone it was myself, the boy in the gondola behind the Villa Venice, and I couldn't help it. I didn't plan it this way, I didn't know it would be this way, but it is this way. I'm not the sixteen-year-old boy who married you. I'm someone else, a stranger. I have to be on the move. I can't stay home. I have no home. It wasn't your fault. I take all the blame, but that doesn't help matters. Your idea of security is owning something tangible, like a grocery store. Because one of your uncles has three grocery stores and makes twenty-five bucks apiece from them every week. I've had a million dollars on paper and not a hundred in the bank. I don't need that kind of security. I don't understand it and I don't think I ever will. Just as you don't understand my way of thinking, and never will. Why stay married then? Get a divorce. You're only thirty. You're a beautiful woman. Give yourself a chance. You deserve happiness, not this. I have to be honest. We never had very much between us, but what little there was, is gone. Let go, Bertha, please.

She knew his thoughts and the knowledge could not change her own.

You were the first, Avrom, and you will be the last. I gave myself to you and I cannot take myself back. I may not be your wife but no one else will be either. Call me jealous, possessive or foolish, but I cannot help being what I am any more than you can, I cannot change because you did. Where did you go, Avrom? We were so close when we had nothing but each other. Now you buy us everything and we have nothing, nothing at all. I love you, Avrom, I always will. The rabbi joined us "until death do ye part" and that is the way it will be.

He said nothing and he would do nothing, for Junior's sake.

He picked up the receiver and dialed a number.

"Take the rest of the day off, Tim," he said softly.

"Thanks, Mike," said the person on the other end of the phone, a fat man with a white beard and a red suit in the adjoining apartment. "And a Merry Christmas to you and your family!"

A moment later, Junior's Kute Kris Kringle was empty.

THE
THIRD
LIFE

"I can't spell good

but I know what I want."

* 11 *

Uncle Todd's Cabin

"He'll be all right in *The Mikado*," Mike said offhandedly as Bill Robinson strutted off the floor of the Cotton Club.

Jack Dietz, owner of the club, measured the handsome broad-shouldered young man with coal-black hair, puffing on a nickel cigar with the label off. Dietz always checked out-of-town hustlers, and his informant in Chicago had reported that Todd was "a hard-luck punk."

"Bojangles isn't for you," Dietz said brusquely.

"I'll make a star of him."

Dietz bristled. Bill Robinson was the star of the Cotton Club show; he had just finished his fourth picture with Shirley Temple; at sixty he was still the greatest tap dancer in the world.

"Can I get you Ethel Merman as Mrs. Mikado?" Dietz taunted.

"Can't use her," Mike said. "This is an all-Negro cast."

The man, Dietz concluded, was *meshuggah.*

Mike blew a cloud of smoke and his volatile face became radiant. "I'll dress him in gold. Gold derby, gold suit, gold cane, incandescent gold shoes. I'll build a special bakelite floor for him to dance on and . . ." Mike's eyes glittered. "I'll build a waterfall of soap bubbles on stage, forty feet high, and a volcano that really erupts."

The expression of disdain left Dietz's face. Maybe this punk was cracked, but, listening to him, Jack *saw* Robinson in his gold outfit, the waterfall and the volcano. At last reason returned.

"You were knocked out of the box the first two times," he reminded Mike.

"Because I went for buttons. It'll never happen again." It was the closest he had ever come to expressing regret but it was over in an instant. "If you're going to promote something, promote it *big.* This time I'm getting the best director, the best designer, the best choreographer and the best press agent on Broadway."

"While you're at it," Dietz said, "you better get the best angel."

"I have." He had seen the gleam in Dietz's eyes. He knew he would get Bill Robinson *and* the money from him.

He took Sammy Lambert, an experienced theater manager, from J. J. Shubert, and made him stage manager. He lured Nat Karson from Radio City Music Hall, to design the settings and the costumes; he also borrowed Charles L. Cooke from the Music Hall, to translate the traditional music of Gilbert and Sullivan into modern tempos. Cooke accomplished the feat in four weeks, working night and day with ten copyists *and* Todd. They were ready for rehearsals.

"I want the best jazzmen you can find," Mike instructed his musical conductor, William Parson, a former associate of Walter Damrosch.

Two weeks later, in the orchestra pit, Parson lifted his baton for the first rehearsal. He had raided Harlem, from the Rhythm Club to Connie's Inn, from the Garden of Joy to the Bucket of Blood, and he had rounded up the greatest aggregation of cats this side of Duke Ellington. Each musician was a solid virtuoso.

Mike sat out front expectantly.

Parson waited for quiet, then brought down his baton for the opening beat of, "A Wand'ring Minstrel, I."

Never, in its more than half a century of history, had the Minstrel wand'red so far. It was not Sullivan or Cooke, it was bedlam, every man for himself. Not a single cat looked at the music sheet on the stand in front of him, and for a valid reason. They ate music, they dreamed music, they *lived* music—but *not one of them could read a note.*

Mike's retinue grew. He hired Joe Glick, a Broadway-wise box-office man, as his general manager; Bill Doll, a bright young man scratching around on the *Herald Tribune,* as his press agent; and Eddie Jaffee, a shrewd little gadfly, as his secretary.

Eva was around, waiting patiently every night, never a complaint through the long rehearsals and interminable conferences that went into the early hours. All she wanted was to be close to Mike, even in the waiting room outside his office. Like Bertha, she had become accustomed to waiting.

"The knockers say you're fronting for Chicago hoodlums," Doll reported.

"It's not true," said Mike. "Santa Claus is backing the show." He told him of his Kute Kris Kringle killing; Doll planted the story in the newspapers and Broadway continued to believe that a gangster syndicate was behind him.

More Philistines were en route. Bernard Ullrich, a Chicago producer, announced that he was bringing the W.P.A. Federal production of *The Swing Mikado* from Chicago to the 44th Street Theater, across the street from *The Hot Mikado,* at $2.20 tops to Todd's $3.30.

Mike immediately dictated a protest in poetry of pure ire. For more than a year, he stated, he had made several offers to buy the W.P.A. *Mikado* and had been informed that it was not for sale. Recently, on learning that the government had decided to sell it, he had placed a bid. It had been turned down; and now that he had produced a swing *Mikado* of his own, the government, his government, was competing with instead of encouraging private enterprise.

"Is this the New Deal?" he demanded. "Is this why I, as a taxpayer, am supporting the Federal Theater, so it can try to break me with cut-price competition on the same street?"

He wired the four-page diatribe to President Roosevelt. The White House did not intercede.

Mike stood outside the Broadhurst Theater with Doll, watching the electricians spell *The Swing Mikado* on the marquee across the street. "I want a flag made," he said. "The biggest you can get. With an arrow pointing to our theater." Mike's eyes traveled up the façade of the Sardi Building next door. "Hang it there," he said, pointing to a window on the fourth floor, lettered DE MIRJIAN STUDIO OF PHOTOGRAPHY.

"Mr. De Mirjian," Doll addressed the tenant, "Mr. Todd is very much impressed with your work and wants to appoint you as official photographer of our production."

De Mirjian thanked him profusely.

"By the way," Doll said offhandedly as he left, "I don't suppose you would mind if we hung a little banner from a flagpole out of your window?"

The flag was an effective signpost for the Broadhurst Theater; and, as Mike had precisely calculated, in size and location, it completely concealed the marquee of *The Swing Mikado* from the view of anyone traveling east on Forty-fourth Street.

Ten days before the opening, advertised for March 16, Mike held the first run-through and, to his chagrin, the guests he had invited were laughing at the wrong places. He promptly announced a postponement of one week, which was followed by the customary rumors of disaster.

Mike *knew* he had a good show, possibly a great one. Having a good show, he was convinced, was not enough. The critics had to be told it was good. He did not trust their eyes and ears: they were human, they had prejudices.

How would the critics react to the scene in which the moon talks back to the Mikado with a barking *Wow-Wow*? It would get a big laugh from the audience, he was certain, but it was four to one that the critics would dismiss it as a cheap gadget-gag that belonged in a Todd vaudeville unit, not on Broadway.

He had no illusions where he stood with them. He did not belong to The Theater, he was an interloper, a brash carnival-barker. "Who is the chic-est musical director on Broadway?" he asked.

"Hassard Short," he was told, "but he's dated . . ."

"I asked who was the *chic-est!*"

"Hassard Short." He was the darling of the smart set, an elegant Englishman who had staged such hits as *Jubilee, As Thousands Cheer, Roberta, The Band Wagon, Sunny, The Great Waltz, Face the Music* and three editions of *The Music Box Revue.*

"He's my man," Mike said without hesitation. Hassard Short was a Name. He would be Mike's front.

Short watched his first run-through and winced. The pain heightened in the scene in which one of the characters made a seemingly endless inventory of his talents and titles.

"What is you *ain't,* man?" came the listener's ultimate response during a pause for breath.

"Mr. Todd," Short said loftily, "that is *un*grammatical."

"You're right, Has," Mike said. "But just for fun, let's see how it plays."

The handful of opinion-makers who determined the life or death of a show would damn him as a vulgarian for a line they would cheer if Hassard Short's name was on the marquee.

Even Dietz was impressed with his name and went for a second set of costumes Mike had asked for but could not get until Short said it was necessary.

The Hot Mikado opened at the Broadhurst Theater, March 23, 1939, with Bill Robinson as the Mikado, Gwendolyn Reyde as Yum-Yum, Rose Brown as Katisha, Robert Parrish as Nanki-Poo, Maurice Ellis as Pooh-Bah, sixty girls, and, as he had told Dietz, a waterfall of soap bubbles forty feet high and a volcano that actually erupted.

Mike was so nervous he remained outside, opening and closing the doors of the taxis and limousines until curtain time. He was opening cold, he could not afford a tryout.

At 11:05 P.M., Lee Shubert, the veteran showman, tapped him on the shoulder. "I'll pay the whole cost of production for half of the profits," he said.

It was a tempting proposition. Mike was in hock, he had chucked everything, including a heavy loan from Dietz, into the show. And he was bucking another jazz *Mikado* across the street that was a good show and a dollar-ten cheaper. A nod and he would have all his money back and fifty percent of the profits with no risk, even if the show folded the next day.

"You get a free ride, you *can't* lose!" Shubert said impatiently. "Deal?"

Mike took out a coin. "Heads I keep it, tails you're in," he said and flipped. It came up heads, and, without a change of expression, he tossed it over his shoulder. It was his last fifty cents.

Shubert, the most astute dealer on the Street, was more than twice his age but his parchment face crinkled in a smile of genuine respect. The boy was a true gambler. He preferred the excitement of spinning his last coin *for* a quarter of a million dollars to *having* the quarter of a million. It was not an act, the old man could tell. Todd was as indifferent now as he had been ten months previously when Shubert had seen him walk out of the same theater after the catastrophic opening of *The Man from Cairo*. Ziegfeld and Sam Harris in their boldest days couldn't fade this boy. He should have been a Shubert.

"Michael Todd has dressed *The Hot Mikado* beautifully, cast it expertly and staged it with such perfect timing and excellent taste," Burns Mantle wrote in the New York *Daily News*, "that it stands absolutely unrivaled so far as my play-going experience is concerned."

"Our man is hooked now," Jaffee told Doll. "A rave notice is like marijuana."

"Opium," said Doll.

Mantle's paean became a symphony as the critics were compelled to take sides in the battle of the *Mikados*.

"Multiplication is the enemy of novelty," George Jean Nathan wrote in *Newsweek*, "but Todd's *Mikado* is a decidedly better job in almost every respect than the Federal Theater's version."

"As a show, the *Hot Mikado* wins hands down over the *Swing Mikado*," *Time* magazine agreed. "It is gaudy, glittering, foot-wise and fast. Todd kisses Gilbert and Sullivan good-bye at about the eighth bar of the first song, then turns Titipu into a dance hall before late-comers are in their seats, makes Yum-Yum, Pitti-Sing and Peep-Bo carry on like three maids from reform school and finishes in an uproar when Katisha, no hatchet-faced termagant but an eye-rolling, hip-shaking, torch-swinging red-hot mama, busts in."

"As the Mikado," John Mason Brown wrote, "Bill Robinson is the most articulate man of our time. Bojangles is more than mortal. He is a titan, not of literature but with his feet, a superb master."

Robinson shook his head. "I ain't been so happy since I been colored," he sighed.

Mike had revolutionized the hoary operetta, and not by accident. This was his fourth *Mikado*. He had staged his first one almost twenty years previously as a boy at Bloomington Consolidated Grade School. Mary McCormic's debacle and the tab versions were tryouts for this one.

The artistic conception, inspired and brilliant as it was, was of subordinate satisfaction to him. His chief gratification, as always, came from the selling. Selling himself. That was his only fulfillment. He had found no leader worthier of following than Doc, the pitchman.

He had the formula now. He knew the combination. Hassard Short had a lifetime job with him, solely for his name. The critics would buy Dr. Todd's Snake Oil as long as Hassard Short's name was on the label. That made it *chi-chi*.

Mike overlooked no means of communication. He conceived an ingenious, animated sign, a precursor of the shadowgraph spectaculars on Times Square, at the northeast corner of Forty-sixth Street. On it danced the silhouette of Bill Robinson.

Bojangles stood on the corner, enchanted by his image performing his inimitable stair dance. In a moment his legs were moving in rhythm. He could not help it, and, anyway, a couple had recognized him. He would dance if he could get one person to watch him. In a few minutes he was arrested for blocking traffic.

Robinson appeared in court the next day in attire that made his spangled costume in *The Hot Mikado* look like a single-breasted sackcloth and ashes. Every inch of his coat was adorned with badges, gold or silver stars, that had been presented to him by sheriffs from coast to coast when he had been sworn in as an honorary deputy. He was weighted down with more than fifty pounds of lustrous authority, including a diamond-studded insignia as Special Deputy Sheriff of New York State and a gold-inlaid pearl-handled .32 caliber revolver given him by the police of the Harlem station. In his pocket was a personal card from his friend and *aficionado*, J. Edgar Hoover, the F.B.I. chief, who had come from Washington for the opening.

Bojangles pleaded to the music of *The Mikado:*

My object all sublime,
Is to be copesettic all the time.
So, Pooh-Bah—pardon, I mean, yo' Honor,
LET THE PUNISHMENT FIT THE CRIME.

The judge was nonplused by the display and blinded by the explosions of flash bulbs by a corps of press photographers that, of course, had been alerted. *The Hot Mikado* made the front pages and all New York was laughing over the arrest of Bill Robinson for the crime of watching himself dance.

More news about Mike and his show leaked out—or in his words, leaked in—to the newspapers, usually on page one, than his competitors received at space rates.

To commemorate Robinson's sixty-first birthday, Bojangles was dressed in a top hat, cutaway coat and spats, then danced from Sixty-first Street to the Broadhurst Theater, seventeen blocks downtown, a band running alongside playing the score from the show.

Bojangles was stretched out in his dressing room, recovering from his amazing feat, when Mike came in.

"You were good, Bill," said Mike, a shadow crossing his face. "Too good. You danced so fast—fifteen minutes faster than Bill Doll figured—that several press photographers he had assigned to corners in the Forties missed you."

"Get me my hat," Robinson called to his valet, got on his feet and went out in the street to dance the seventeen blocks over again.

Cole Porter saw the show seven times, the elite of Broadway congratulated him but Robinson was disappointed.

"Ah cain't unnerstan'," he told Mike, "why them boys what wrote the show ain't even stopped by to say, 'Hi!' "

The Hot Mikado was getting the publicity and *The Swing Mikado,* $1.10 cheaper, was making the profits. Mike's show was doing extremely well by current standards, $14,000 a week, but many weeks there was not enough to pay Robinson's $2,000 salary.

"You got to cut, Mike," Dietz and his other associates told him.

"I will not cut the quality of the show, not by one chorus

girl," he said adamantly, a precedent he would not break as long as he was in show business.

"You *have* to cut," his associates repeated.

Mike shook his head. He would not compromise on quality or principle. When he could not come up with Robinson's salary, which was almost every week, he gave him a percentage of the show in lieu of the $2,000 he had coming. Robinson's manager for more than thirty years, Marty Forkins, a graduate of Notre Dame, a lawyer and a manager of five boxing champions before he discovered his star in Richmond, Virginia (Bojangles, a waiter, had spilled gravy on his shirt), had little faith in ever seeing any money but he had no alternative or immediate bookings.

Every payday found Mike lashed to the railroad tracks and the train coming around the bend with the sheriff aboard. The show was staggering through its seventh and seemingly certain last disastrous week when Mike remembered the words of Marshal Foch during the first Battle of the Marne, that he, as a five-year-old boy, and his pals, brandishing wooden swords, had echoed in the Battle of Girard Avenue, *My center gives way, my right recedes: the situation is excellent, I shall attack!*

He did not have a nickel in the till to pay the week's salary, his credit was exhausted, he was going down for the third and perhaps the last time as a Broadway producer: *the situation is excellent, I'll take on Billy Rose!*

Rose had come far in the five years since he had been muscled out of the Casino de Paris. He had erected a huge electric sign on Broadway, spelling out two words: BILLY ROSE. He had given Texas a new dimension in its Centennial Exposition. He had used Lake Erie as a backdrop for his show at the Great Lakes Exposition. He had produced *Jumbo*, written by Ben Hecht and Charles MacArthur, with a score by Richard Rodgers and Lorenz Hart, starring Jimmy Durante and Paul Whiteman, and financed largely by John Hay (Jock) Whitney.

"The show will make Rose or break Whitney," a Broadway

prophet remarked. It cost two hundred and eighty thousand dollars and lost one hundred and twenty thousand, making a deficit of two hundred and seventy-five thousand dollars on Rose's first three productions. Unlike Mike, the little man had lost big, he had parlayed *his* failures into becoming ringmaster of a one-hundred-and-fifty-million-dollar circus, the New York World's Fair.

Mike had cased it. He and Noah Braunstein, a smart criminal lawyer, had gone the route, including a drop in the captive parachute. They came down, just in time. The equipment jammed and the next couple was stuck aloft for hours.

Now he made an entrance at Flushing Meadows worthy of the president of the Fair, the elegant and formidable Grover A. Whalen. A liveried chauffeur drove him to the Administration Building in a Pierce Arrow limousine, bulletproof, that Dietz had hustled from a hood who owed him money.

"Pretty dead around here," Mike commented, gazing out the window of the president's private office. "You need someone like me to liven up the joint."

Whalen was aghast at his impertinence. "Mr. Rose is doing that adequately," he said bluntly. "He is filling the ten thousand seats at the Aquacade as many times as the people can be herded in and out."

"There ain't any water in your Hall of Music and no customers either," snapped Mike. "One of the most beautiful buildings at the Fair, and the only ones who go to the concerts and recitals are the musicians. Face it, Grove, it's a white elephant."

Whalen blanched. His had been a liturgical life, from the pomp and ceremony of his career as New York's official greeter to his tenure as Police Commissioner. Formality was his watchword; he would as lief be caught without his pants, striped or unstriped, as violate ritual. Everyone addressed him as Mr. Whalen, his own brother would not dare call him *Grove*!

"You're running a carnival but you're not a carnival man," Mike went on. "I am. Because I'm part hick. You got to be a great showman. Sophistication ruins many who might have been great. You know those hams who show great emotion by lifting an eyebrow? They make a show reek of turkey. I don't want it. Maybe the carriage trade does. The carriage trade is good for only six weeks' business. The public wants broad theater, meat and potatoes at a low tap. Don't get too subtle. I can't spell good, Grove, but I know what I want."

Whalen looked down. He was astounded that his boutonniere had not wilted.

"What do you want?" Whalen heard, to his surprise, his own voice asking.

"I don't want anything. *You're* the one who needs help. But you can stop worrying, pal. I'll pull your chestnuts out of the Hall of Music and fill it night and day."

"With what?"

"With the hottest hit on Broadway, *The Hot Mikado.*"

Whalen eyed him skeptically. "Why should you close what you claim is a Broadway hit and bring it out here? It doesn't make sense."

"Show business doesn't make sense, that's why it's fun. Everybody will say I'm clanky, but I'm a gambler and a gambler has to parlay. You got more seats."

Whalen was not convinced. "People won't come all the way to Flushing Meadows to see any *Mikado*," he said.

"If you got something good, they'll swim a river of crocodiles to get it. Not at $3.30 a head but at forty cents to a buck. I mean ninety-nine cents. Always price your seats so the customer gets some change back. That's the trouble with your Midway. Coming in, I noticed several shows charge fifteen cents. Never price a ducat at fifteen cents. It means a quarter plus a nickel for two seats—and eighty percent of all tickets are sold in pairs—it smells expensive. If the customer gives you a quarter, give him back a nickel. Remember that, Grove."

Whalen was mesmerized by his impudence and his knowledge. "You can deliver Bill Robinson at forty cents to a dollar . . . I mean ninety-nine cents?"

"*And* the original cast. Of course, I'll have to forfeit a few months' rent and there are other expenses," Mike said casually. "No more than ten G's, I'll take it out of petty cash."

"*Mr.* Todd," Whalen said grandly, "why not let the Fair advance you the ten—thousand?"

Mike weighed the offer a long moment. "I would rather not be under any obligation to the Fair," he said, then shrugged magnanimously. "But if that's the way *you* want it, Grove, I won't fight you."

"I insist you take it, Mr. Todd," said Whalen.

That night Glick and Doll were sitting the death watch in the office when Mike walked in carrying a brown paper sack. He turned the bag upside down and a rain of bills, ten thousand dollars' worth, dropped gently on the desk.

"Tonight we eat," he said.

Glick and Doll stared at the currency in disbelief. "Who did you hold up?" Glick asked.

Mike gave him a hurt look. "Nobody," he said. "I just bailed out Grove Whalen. He was in big trouble."

The World's Fair was spread over 1,216 acres, hardly enough for Billy Rose *and* Mike Todd.

Rose's Aquacade, starring his wife, Eleanor Holm, with Johnny Weissmuller, Gertrude Ederle, Morton Downey and a cast of five hundred, called "the greatest spectacle in the history of show business" by *Variety*, had no competition and he aimed to keep it that way. Todd was no competition yet but he was coming up fast.

They met over a herring at Lindy's Restaurant.

"Mr. Whalen neglected to mention," Rose said loftily, "that my contract with the Fair forbids the presence of any other new and original musical show in the amusement area. The *Mikado* is out."

"The *Mikado* ain't been new since 1885, so it's in," Mike retorted. "What's more, I'm thinking of putting a box office in the back of the Hall of Music, facing your Aquacade. And I'm afraid, pal, I'm mighty afraid that's going to mean loud-speakers, very loud, right in your pretty ear, before and *during* every show."

Rose's jaw went slack. "But that wouldn't be . . ." Rose choked on his cheese cake.

"It would be for me," said Mike. "I've got a closed house and yours is open. But if you'd like to co-operate by giving me a plug from time to time, I might be persuaded to forget it."

The basement Barnum knew when he was licked. He capitulated in a pact known to the Broadway *landsleit* as the Treaty of Lindy's. Audiences leaving the Aquacade heard over the loud-speakers, "Billy Rose thanks you for coming and suggests that you visit Mike Todd's *The Hot Mikado,* the greatest musical of our time."

Not to be outdone, Mike issued a signed message in all *Hot Mikado* programs: "Although I have no financial interest in Billy Rose's Aquacade (How I wish I did have!), I want to whole-heartedly recommend it as the greatest spectacle of all time. I have witnessed Mr. Rose's super-production at least ten times and I mean to see it ten more times before the end of the summer. Something like the Aquacade comes along only once in a lifetime. I feel that it is my responsibility to call your attention to Billy Rose's unparalleled masterpiece of showmanship."

One night he relieved his ticket seller at the box office. All the forty-cent seats were sold and thirty-two ninety-nine-cent seats were left. He turned away three hundred customers who requested cheaper seats before he sold out.

"Nobody has to rub my nose in a fact like that twice," he told Glick. "Thirty-two times ninety-nine cents is $31.68, but three hundred times forty cents is $120. Keep your price low and set one price for the whole house, that's the answer."

"You *can't* charge the same for orchestra seats as you do for the balcony!"

"Is there a law against it? Precedent is the toughest thing in the world, Joe; habit is a horrible thing. I repeat, why not?"

"The people in the balcony will squawk."

Mike shook his head. "We're all show-offs. We don't mind sitting in the balcony if the doll with us knows it cost just the same as the orchestra. The most important thing is, it costs just the same to run a show whether it plays to eight people or eight thousand. Nobody ever went broke handling crowds."

On the week end of July Fourth he handled a record crowd of twenty-four thousand customers and promptly began smoking fifty-cent cigars.

On Monday morning a representative of the Actors Equity Association called on him. "You're putting on four performances a day," he said gravely, "and paying your cast the same as you did for *one* show at the Broadhurst. You can't get away with it, Todd! From now on, all salaries are quadrupled, and it will be retroactive."

"Are you nuts or a disappointed ingénue?" Mike raged. "I can't pay the cast on a basis of Broadway performances because I'm charging forty cents to ninety-nine-cent tops, not $3.30."

"That's no excuse. You will obey Equity regulations."

"Ekkity ain't running my business!" Mike shouted, but "Ekkity" did. For a few weeks, until he could convince an arbitration board that he should be granted a concession until the patrons and the payroll would balance, he was compelled to pay chorus girls two hundred dollars a week, unheard of in 1939. It created many problems, including space, for within a week each of the chorus girls from Harlem had at least one maid of her own.

Sam Zolotow of the New York *Times* was puzzled. "Your auditor says the show is losing money," he said to Mike, "and your publicity man says it is breaking records. How do you reconcile this discrepancy?"

"All I can say," Mike replied, "is that both departments are functioning perfectly."

The Fair closed after Labor Day and the show went on the road. Mike did not go along. He was confident that Forkins would stand sentinel at the box office no less zealously than he could. Also, the ardor of his friendship with Forkins had diminished in direct ratio to his ownership of the show. By the time the *Mikado* reached Dallas, Mike and Forkins were equal partners and no longer spoke to each other.

"Mike Todd is tempestuous, erratic and often incorrigible," the *Times* commented, "but he is probably the hardest-punching producer who ever came down the pike. Mike is a natural showman; he is tough and soft, good and bad. He can drive a granite bargain but, at the same time, he is known to his pals as a soft touch and on occasion has been observed in Lindy's weeping over his bagels for some reason or sentiment.

"*The Hot Mikado* would surely have long since been relegated to the warehouse under less hardy sponsorship. Old-timers who have watched Todd swimming for dear life in a torrent of red ink contend that there has been no one like him in show business for twenty years."

The legend was born.

"You found a home," Dietz said as they looked down over the city from Mike's apartment at 25 Central Park West this night late in December.

Was this home? Mike wondered. *It's a fake, Broadway, it's a phony,* Durante sang the song by Sid Skolsky, *but it's my street, the heart of the world.* You take the world as others created it or you imagine one yourself. This was the one he had dreamed, at least the start of it. No telling where it would lead. Back to Bertha? Never. She was the mother of his son, nothing else. Would it be with Eva, waiting loyally downstairs? No. One day she would tire of waiting, or he would tire of her. Someone else would come along, someone fresh and exciting. If she didn't he would create her. Life is like the movies, you produce your own show. Have fun and make a buck. What else is there? Use yourself. Use others. Use everything. That's what everything is for. Take chances. Danger is the test of a man. It's your duty to keep alive and fight the most seductive of emotions, fear.

"I'm going to Europe, Jack," he confided.

"What's the swindle?"

"Diplomatic mission."

"What's the swindle?" Dietz repeated.

"I have to get government renewals for a second year of exhibits at the Fair."

"I thought Whalen was still president of the Fair."

"He's over there but he's gotten lost or something."

Dietz had one remaining question. "How much will it cost me?"

"It all depends how much I have to pay Chevalier."

"*Maurice* Chevalier?"

Mike nodded. "I started in *The Streets of Paris* in Chicago. Now I'm going to put it on right, with real Frenchmen."

That day, while drumbeating the show in Washington, D.C., on a second swing east, Doll received a wire from Mike: IMPERATIVE YOU MEET ME IN NEW YORK TEN TONIGHT. AM LEAVING FOR LISBON.

Doll made it to Mike's office by ten.

"Know any good numbers in Lisbon?" Mike greeted him.

Doll shook his head. He was too breathless to speak.

Mike crammed two fistfuls of cigars into a bulging Gladstone and, without another word, left.

* 12 *

The Day He Chartered the Rex

The Frenchman in the adjoining seat said he was a millionaire and he was in trouble. Would Mike do him a favor and carry his money across the border?

"How hot is it?"

"Body temperature."

Mike's chivalry was at stake. He could never set foot in Barney Greengrass' Delicatessen again if word got out that he had failed to rescue a millionaire in distress, let alone that he had refused to take *anyone* else's ready across a border.

He pocketed the sheaf of banknotes as the train pulled into Hendaye, a French village on the frontier of Spain, and declared it with his own money.

"You have violated the law, Señor Todd," a Spanish customs official said gravely after he had counted and recounted the small bale of currency.

Mike braced for the blow.

"You have falsified your declaration," the customs man continued. "It is seven dollars short."

Mike stopped sweating. "Is that all?" he asked, realizing he had made an honest but slight mistake.

"I am sorry," said the official, "but I must detain you until you have filled out a new declaration."

"Forget it," said Mike impatiently, eager to join his pal, Abe Aronsohn, who operated the Embassy Club in London, the Frenchman and the other passengers whose passports had already been stamped. "Keep the seven bucks and let's get the show on the road."

The customs official's face hardened, he tooted a whistle, and almost immediately Mike's arms were pinioned by two members of the military police. "Señor Todd," said the customs man, "you are under arrest."

"What for?" Mike shouted.

"Attempting to bribe an official of the Spanish government," said the customs man, joining an endless list of skeptics who had and would misconstrue his motives, particularly when they were guileless.

Mike spent the night behind bars until he convinced his captors that the letter of introduction he carried as an ambassador without portfolio from Grover Whalen to Generalissimo Franco's brother-in-law was bona fide. The following day they unlocked his cell and gave him a gold key to the city.

The Frenchman had gone to Biarritz, and Mike, as a favor, carried his bundle over another border, into Portugal.

Lisbon, that winter of 1940, was the crossroads of a world spinning on a Hitler-Stalin axis. Clippers were piled up, ten loads behind. Priorities were meaningless. Pan-American World Airways, faced with a $5,000 government penalty for every day the mail was late, filled all available planes with mail bags.

Passengers were lined up three-deep at the airport, among them Ingrid Bergman, Anna Morgan, Ferenc Molnár and Chaim Weizmann. Mike checked the Italian Lines and learned that the last *Rex* had sailed from Genoa but would not stop at Lisbon.

"Why not?" Mike demanded of the manager.

"It is not on the schedule," the manager replied.

"It will be this trip," said Mike. "My friend and I have to get back to the States."

The manager controlled his Latin temper. "The *Rex* cannot stop for two passengers, sir."

"How many will it stop for?"

The manager was bewildered. No one had ever asked such a question before.

Mike took charge. "I'm chartering the *Rex* from Lisbon to New York. Cable the captain."

"But I cannot . . ." the manager sputtered.

"I'll make a deal with you. I'll guarantee fifty—no, I'll make it seventy—passengers. Start cabling. And it better stop here or your line will have to answer to Generalissimo Franco, the New York World's Fair *and* Michael Todd."

The *Rex* made an unscheduled stop at Lisbon for Mike and his party of seventy people whom he had persuaded to turn in their airplane tickets—except for Molnár, who had neither ticket nor money, only an order for transportation.

"Don't worry," Mike assured Hungary's most celebrated playwright, "I'll pick up the tab."

Molnár was intrigued by Todd, and the second day out, at breakfast in the royal suite, which Mike occupied by divine right, he insisted on granting him first refusal rights on all of his literary properties for five thousand dollars cash.

"I have a new play, only one act so far, but it's for you," Molnár said and told him the story.

"It's too delicate," Mike said.

"Thank you," said Molnár, "I'll call it *The Delicate Story*."

"Give it to Jed Harris," Mike said. "I'll take *Liliom* and make a musical out of it."

A musical out of a tragedy, the redemption of a scoundrel after death? It was unthinkable, and Molnár dismissed it as another of Mike's jests or pipe dreams.

In his first interview Molnár revealed that he had had to learn two English languages, one en route and one on his arrival.

"I prefer the first," he said. "It is not so much English as Todd Americanese."

"Where's Chevalier?" Dietz asked Mike.

He had been unable to make a deal with Chevalier, whose demands, to Mike, sounded like the French war debt.

Dietz was disappointed. "But you said we were putting on a *real* French show!"

"It'll be *better* this way," said Mike, master of improvisation. "If I had gone to Tokyo and brought back Japan's greatest entertainer I couldn't have done *The Mikado.*" Jack wasn't with him, he would have to explain. "*The Hot Mikado* is Harlem's conception of Japan, Pooh-Bah with a thousand medals. The *popular* idea, that's what draws, Jack. *Not too much realism.* You got to keep one step ahead of mass audiences. That's what's wrong with most creative artists. Do you know where I'm going to get my French show? On Forty-fourth Street, at the Shubert Theater. We don't even have to change the name, it's called *The Streets of Paris.* Couple funny boys in it, Abbott and Costello."

Dietz was dumfounded. "Then why the devil did you go to Europe?" he asked.

Mike looked at Dietz and realized that Jack didn't know him and never would. Why had he gone to Europe? He had never been to Europe, he *had* to see it. But a war was on, it was almost impossible to get a passport, transportation, a priority. He had heard of the possible diplomatic mission for the Fair, he had moved in and grabbed it. All the tumult he had created, for the Fair and for his own future productions, was an official excuse for making the trip. For most, activity was a means to an end. For him *it* was the end, its own result. To stop was to die, or worse, slide into the pit of anonymity.

Direction? All paths led to the grave. His sole interest was the journey, to make it as exciting as possible. That meant variety. Ceaseless, frenetic variety. Dietz could not understand, Mike did not know who could understand, because most people were concerned with getting *somewhere.* They made no sense to him. The thrill was in the chase, not in the capture, for the quarry *or* the captor. He would not attempt to tell Jack what he had done in Europe. It would not have made any sense to him. Life made sense to Jack. He was not born to tumult.

"I'm going to do a show about New Orleans too," he said. "I've never been there either. Got the idea from O'Henry's story, 'A Municipal Report.' And a recording of the 'Beale Street Blues.'"

Why tell him, Dietz reasoned in silence, that "A Municipal Report" concerned Nashville, and Beale Street was in Memphis? Mike wouldn't believe it, and it made no difference anyway. In his world logic was a liability and madness an asset.

"Brought back a great carny act from Portugal, Greco the Great. Jumps from a hundred-foot pole with a thirty-foot rope around his neck. Wait till you see him dangle!"

"You got your ass in too many chairs," Dietz demurred.

Mike fished in his pockets. "Give me a piece of paper," he said. Dietz found a business card. A moment later Mike handed it back to him. On the back he had scrawled:

> *February 2, 1940*
> *If I don't make a net $50,000 by fall, 1940, I quit show biz.*
> M. TODD

* 13 *

Fairest of the Fair

Mike puffed semicontentedly on his fifty-five-cent heater.

His Gay New Orleans, a ten-acre replica of the Vieux Carré, was the foremost attraction at the Fair. The year before, under

other management, the concession had been called Little Old
New York, and had failed.

His *Streets of Paris,* with Abbott and Costello and Gypsy
Rose Lee, was packing the Hall of Music, which, until he had
moved in, had been unable to pay the light bill.

His Dancing Campus, featuring Harry James' and Les
Brown's bands, Gene Krupa and an unknown singer, Doris
Day, another named Gordon MacRae, was jumping with as
many as 12,000 jitterbugs a night in the same place where
Merrie England, under other auspices, had been anything but
merrie the previous season.

His Old Op'ry House was playing to standing room only,
where, the year before, the Shakespeare Theater had flopped.

"This," he proudly told Harvey Gibson, the new president of
the Fair, pointing to a new building under construction, "com-
pletes our traffic control plan."

Gibson, making his first tour of inspection, was impressed and
disturbed. "Mr. Todd," he observed, "you seem to have closed
the exits that previously opened toward the Aquacade."

"That *is* our traffic control plan, Harve," Mike said. He had
surrounded Billy Rose. It was inevitable. He was more resourceful than Billy, he had more ideas, more energy and more
brass. One night Mike took Eleanor Holm on a personally conducted tour of his empire and entertained her so charmingly,
with her favorite vintage of champagne, that Mrs. Rose was late
for her performance at the Aquacade.

The armistice ended that night.

"When Todd is broke," Rose sent word via diplomatic
courier, "there will always be a job for him with me."

The Treaty of Lindy's was a scrap of sturgeon.

Mike did not actually own any of the shows, he was running
them for the Fair at a salary and a percentage of the profits, but
he strode the Midway as if they were his, and, in a sense, they
were. He conceived them, he sold them and he ran them. On
every marquee, billboard and advertisement the top line, above

all other credits, was as it always had been and always would be, MICHAEL TODD PRESENTS. Front was all that mattered, to him and to those he wanted to impress. This time he was fronting for a hundred-and-fifty-million-dollar World of Tomorrow. If the people thought he owned all the shows that bore his name, it was as good as if he did. The old Walpole Theory of Pleasant Hallucinations. Bill Doll trumpeted him as the biggest man on the Midway, and he did not deny it. Others provided the money but he alone spent it, prodigally, accounting only to his own discernment. He had no interest in accumulating money, only in spending it.

He wanted an exact reproduction of the Original Absinthe House in New Orleans and he got it—dusty and musty, replete with calling cards covering every inch of the walls and ceiling, the drip fountain, the Original's bartender, Lucian Casbonne, and free-loading newspapermen. "Even the bar is genuine wormwood," he boasted.

He wanted a bona-fide New Orleans restaurant—and he got it, a white-columned plantation mansion, with magnolias on the terrace—that served pompano and other Louisiana delicacies flown daily by special plane from the Gulf and prepared by the chef he had imported from the Hotel Roosevelt in New Orleans.

Famed eating houses established at the Fair grounds a whole year were unable to compete with him. On learning that a convention of three hundred bankers was asking bids for a dinner, he told Gibson, "I'll give them the lowest price, dollars under anyone else. That ain't all, I'll give each a cocktail free at my Sazarac Bar with the cost of the meal." No one could match his bid. The bankers, almost to a man, never left the bar or its chief attraction, Mike's reliable nude girl in a fish bowl. Their bar check was considerably larger than the dinner tab.

He wanted to burlesque Bob Ripley and he did, with a Believe It or Nuts exhibition of oddities, including a Gold Brick (painted), the World's Largest Midget (a man six feet

tall), the Girl without a Head (a mirror illusion) and a Chastity
Belt (with a quotation allegedly from Shakespeare, "Love
laughs at locksmiths").

He claimed, dead-pan, that he had installed fifty thousand
steel springs under the floor of his Dancing Campus so it would
give under the thousands of jitterbugs. An investigator for
Popular Mechanics, which published the item, came around
every night for months, requesting permission to tear up the
floor for proof. Mike outlasted him.

He yielded, with some reluctance, to Hassard Short's aes-
theticism and permitted him to dismiss Greco the Great after
one almost-fatal jump when his "safety" device failed to oper-
ate, and, in his place, hired Joseph Spah, an acrobat, who had
made a miraculous escape from the Zeppelin *Hindenburg* on
its last tragic flight. Spah, who worked under the name of Ben
Dova, did a comic drunk act while clinging to the top of a rock-
ing lamppost. In the late show, the lamppost was replaced with
a scantily clad girl, fifteen feet high, of papier-mâché.

He needed a blow-off act to clear the crowd for the next performance, so he hired Carrie Finnell, an elderly woman of remarkable muscle control who did a mammary St. Vitus Dance.

Atkinson of the *Times* raved about her performance. Bill
Bloeth of the *World-Telegram* was baffled. "The secret of Carrie's success will remain forever locked in her bosom," he wrote.

Mike installed Carrie as the hostess of the Do Bust Inn, the
entrance through a cutout facsimile of her, as abundantly en-
dowed.

Eva was still around, quietly waiting until all the others left.
She did her Flame Dance once a day in the midnight show at
the Gay New Orleans. She had hoped to be the star of the
Streets of Paris, but Gypsy Rose Lee had moved in.

For a twenty-five-cent ticket, a customer was entitled to
three full-length shows and a series of side shows at Gay New
Orleans.

One night, in the big scene from *Ben Hur*, two beautiful horses, one black and one white, driven by a Flushing Meadows Roman in a chariot, pounded across the great stage to the tune of a song called "Gone with the Breeze," when the floor gave way. The audience thought it was part of the act until the curtain was rung down.

Mike arrived backstage as a stagehand was loading a gun to put a merciful end to the black horse trapped helplessly below the stage floor where he had fallen.

"Nobody's going to shoot any horse in *my* show!" shouted Mike, who blanched at a finger sliver.

"We haven't any choice," said the stage manager. "That poor horse *can't* be moved."

Mike threw him a look of scorn and ordered nothing to be moved until he returned.

He ran out, found the acrobat, the Great Greco, doing his act on the Midway and hired him, not for his act but for his rigging. He had Greco's derrick and winch moved to the Gay New Orleans, and within moments, utilizing his knowledge of levers and fulcrums from his days as a construction man, superintended the rescue.

Mike pulled out the horse unscathed in time for the next performance.

He subdivided himself like his shows. Gypsy, at the moment, fascinated him most. She was smart, tough and had a sense of humor. And she didn't speak to Billy Rose either. Her feud with Rose had begun six years previously in the Casino de Paris, when she had refused to work in a tableau.

Rose was incredulous. "You, who have been arrested twice with Minsky, won't pose nude?"

"I wasn't exactly nude," she said. "I had my red bows glued on. Besides, I was getting more money."

"Aha, so your modesty is monetary!" Rose rasped, and another speaking acquaintance wasn't.

"I am not a stripper," she told Mike the day she met him,

through her sister June Havoc, who was working at the Fair. "A stripper is a woman who puts on a sex spectacle. My act is straight comedy."

"I don't care what you call it," he said, "as long as you zip."

Gypsy bristled. "I never use a zipper," she said. "A zipper is cheap and vulgar. And suppose one got stuck? I use ordinary straight pins. I used to toss 'em into the bell of a brass tuba in the band; they would go ping every time I hit the target. But it was too expensive, the guy wanted union wages."

THE BEST UNDRESSED WOMAN IN AMERICA, Mike billed her, WHO PROVED THAT THE G-STRING IS MORE THAN PART OF A BANJO.

The second day he knocked on the door of her dressing room at the Hall of Music. "Can't you read?" he asked, pointing to a sign on the wall: NO COOKING. THIS MEANS YOU.

"I like to cook," she said, "and it saves money."

"But the odor fills the theater! What *are* you cooking?"

"Knockwurst."

"It better be good, I'm a *maven* [connoisseur]." He sat down and ate heartily, after tearing down the sign. He loved knockwurst but hated hypocrisy.

His code of ethics, as everything else about him, was unique and inflexible. He had no compunctions about show-business larceny, "honest larceny" he called it, the small, harmless deceit, trick or flourish that adds gaiety to the world. Like the two shrill-voiced spinsters who let out horrendous screams as Gypsy reached for the fastening of the last stitch she wore.

"I suspect Mr. Todd knows the names of the ladies," Mantle wrote in the *Daily News*, "and it would not surprise me to see and hear them when I go back next time." He would not be disappointed, Mike had hired the lady plants for the summer. "Miss Lee is abiding by the rules of the art as laid down by the Fair authorities," Mantle assured his readers. "She is very careful not to take off more than she has on."

Gypsy was Queen of the Midway. Abbott and Costello objected to her billing, and, to placate them, Mike erected a blow-

up photograph of them, forty feet high, equal to hers, outside
the theater. Withal, they would not be with him long. Dietz, as
the spokesman for Nate Blumberg, a producer at Universal
Pictures and a brother-in-law of William Fox, asked Mike to
spring them so they could make a motion picture.

Mike had a contract with them, but, he rationalized, round
comics (comedians on the stage as differentiated from flat comics, those on film) were not box-office and he released them from
their obligation. They went to Hollywood and became, in their
first picture, the most successful comedy team in film history.

He created other stars by omission. He turned down a viva-
cious young singer named Betty Hutton because he didn't think
she was worth a hundred dollars a week. He also passed up an
unknown young man named Cornel Wilde. He was playing
percentage, he couldn't catch them all.

Mike hired Joey Fay at two hundred dollars a week to replace
Abbott and Costello, who had received eighteen hundred weekly. In addition, Fay was to receive twenty-five dollars for every
day it didn't rain. It poured sixteen consecutive days.

It was the last inning of the Era of Wonderful Nonsense.
There were fourteen bars in his domain. He was not a drinker,
a Drambuie after dinner was his limit; two slugs and he started
crying, for no reason except that he had had more than one—but
he enjoyed operating all those saloons, his friends could get
drunk in half a dozen languages.

He thrived on problems. When Doll reported that the Fair's
Artistic Approval Board had refused to grant permission to display his garish placards, Mike told him to have a rubber stamp
made, lettered OFFICIAL POSTING.

"People believe anything marked 'Official,'" said Mike. "You
could put a tollgate on Fifth Avenue and no one would question
it as long as you put up a sign, 'Official Gate.'"

Doll followed instructions, and his placards were prominent-
ly displayed inside and outside every *official* building on the
Fair grounds.

His old friend from Chicago and the Fort Worth Exposition, Joe Rogers, also became tangled in official red tape when he applied for a permit to build a bar on the Midway. One night, after months of patient waiting, Joe conferred with Mike. The *next* day, concessionaires and visitors were astounded to see a new and attractive gin mill, Joe Rogers' Rendevoo, on a lot that had been vacant the previous day. The miracle had been performed by several hundred roustabouts rounded up and supervised by the erstwhile president of the Atlantic and Pacific Ready Cut Houses, Inc.

Thereafter, Rogers was the Mayor of the Midway.

"How," President Gibson asked his executive board, "can we convince the public that there is no gouging at the Fair and that everything, entertainment and food, is reasonable?"

Mike heard about his problem and promptly posed Gypsy with two seedy Skid Row bums slopping over three plates of spaghetti under a Fair sign, "15 CENTS." The picture made all the newspapers, and Gibson was horrified.

Every newspaperman and accredited free-loader received a coin the size of a quarter. On one side was a likeness of George Washington, save that the features under the wig were Mike's and there was a cigar in his teeth. Beneath it was the lettering IN TODD WE TRUST, and on the back, "A Quarter Is All You Can Spend at a Michael Todd Show."

The holders of "Todd quarters" were entitled to admission to all of his shows, as well as free food and drinks at his restaurants and bars.

"They will advertise the low admission in their columns," he said prophetically. Without the arresting reminder, he knew, they would not mention the cost. Not obligated to pay for anything, they were not conscious of price.

Formal attire was mandatory at Harvey Gibson's major functions; for one of them, Mike rented a top hat, white tie and tails. Doll told Dick Williams, his photographer, to take a shot of the boss.

"No pictures!" Mike bellowed. He was self-conscious and suspected, rightfully, that he looked like Mandrake the Magician with a cigar.

Williams snapped the shutter as Mike shook a menacing finger at him. Doll had a life-size enlargement made, and, as a gag, erected the figure in front of the *Streets of Paris,* Mike's finger directed to the box office.

Joe Rogers appropriated the cutout and installed it in his pub, placing it so that Mike's finger formally pointed to the men's room.

Mike was furious and tried in vain to remove it. Rogers had taken the precaution of hammering it to the wall with hundreds of nails. Doll planted the story in the New York *Times,* illustrated with the photograph of Mike, in white tie and tails, directing traffic to the Rendevoo gent's room.

Todd's switchboard was flooded with calls, most of them beginning, "Hey, send me my suit back!"

"You sabotaged me, Bill," Mike said, deeply hurt, and fired him, for two days.

"And you, Joe"— he turned to Rogers — "how could you do it to *me?*"

Rogers remembered Little America, begged Mike's forgiveness and was granted amnesty.

The *New Yorker* discovered him. "I'm not terrific and I ain't no cheese," it quoted him. "I'd rather be lucky than smart." Max Gendel, one of Mike's press agents, provided the postscript: "Todd is half smart to everything."

He was rolling. His wardrobe was filled with custom-tailored suits by Wolfson, haberdashery from Sulka, Tripler and Orry Kelly, shoes from a personal London booter. A Cadillac limousine and liveried chauffeur awaited him night and day. He ate at the Colony and "21." He had the royal suite at the Ritz Carlton, and refused to give it up even upon the request of the Prince of Wales.

The legend grew. J. Bryan III wrote an article about him in *Collier's*, titled "Cut-Rate Showman." Bryan, obviously infected by his subject's unrestraint, described him as a Verbal Vandal, the Rhomboid Rhetorician and the Nizam of Necromantic Nudity.

"He is a short, burly, broad-shouldered young man, with a bear-trap jaw that has locked on a huge cigar for want of a bear," Bryan wrote. "He is addicted to bright green raiment ('clothes' would be a pallid word). He has a felonious contempt for the laws of grammar. He is also, and primarily, a showman."

Mike smiled sardonically as he read about himself. He was a mug by choice. By nature, he hated the tawdry, the blatant and the pretentious. He respected the humble dignity of his father but he was not willing to pay the price of poverty for it. He had chosen, for good or for bad, a gaudy business. He sold tinsel, perhaps better than anyone since Barnum, that was why *Collier's* illustrated the piece with a four-color photograph of him, coat off, sleeves rolled up, tie loosened, collar open, pointing his barker's cane to a bevy of gorgeous girls sharing his side-show platform. At a time when most people wanted to shut their ears to the ranting of the dictators and the cries of their victims, they listened intently to his "Step inside, folks!" He allayed their fears by being oblivious of them. There was no violence, no cruelty, no starvation in his world of beauty, gaiety, color, song and laughter. He was, from the provocative gleam in his eyes to the promissory note in his voice, his friend Molnár's beloved rogue, Liliom, come to life.

Mike had few illusions, none about himself. Show business was a guessing business and, consequently, a jackpot business. His luck was running and he was making the most of it. He enjoyed a fifty-five-cent cigar and smoked twenty to thirty a day, from his own locker at Dunhill's. All true cigar smokers are successful, he figured, because they can't stand to smoke cheap cigars: they keep in the chips so they can afford ropes that will not asphyxiate them. To stay on the safe side, he switched back to nickel cigars every so often to remind himself how it would be when he went broke.

He did not want to go broke but he was afraid of getting rich, too; it might go to his head. He went to the Friars Club regularly for two reasons, to play cards and to remind himself not to lose interest in his business and get sloppy. Someone always put the bite on him for a saw and it was invariably someone who had had top billing a couple years ago, until he lost interest in his work and got sloppy. He didn't mind the bite, he considered it a warning, a cheap investment.

The flourishing legend gratified *and* amused him. All was illusion, even his notorious green suits. He had given several of them to the Salvation Army, according to Earl Wilson's column. He did not deny it, but Gypsy was on to him.

"You give the *impression* of wearing a green suit when you don't," she said. "I'll bet you never wore a green suit in your life."

He had to admit she was right.

"I knew it," she said. "Even your Charvet ties with the purple cubes and red elephants are rather reserved."

He played the role of Mike Todd to the hilt. He didn't mind *Collier's* crack about his "felonious" syntax. It, like his mispronunciation of words and addiction to "ain't," was deliberate. It made others feel superior and lulled them into underestimating him, at least for one deal. Alone, while others were reading scratch sheets, he was studying history, literature and philosophy.

One morning, every employee on his payroll, from his executives to his ushers, received a book by Elbert Hubbard.

"*A Message to Garcia* FROM MICHAEL TODD!" read his printed memorandum with each volume. "READ IT!"

It was his way of telling them that theirs was not to reason why but only to carry out his orders on schedule, without alibis, like the immortal Lieutenant Rowan's mission to Calixto Garcia.

He read for knowledge, as his father had before him, from the classics, encyclopedias and almanacs.

"Man is neither angel nor brute," he learned from a thinker named Pascal, "and every attempt to raise him to the level of the former sinks him to that of the latter." That made sense, especially in his relationship with Bertha.

"Have success and there will always be fools to say you have talent." He had forgotten the author but he hoped he would never forget the line.

"He did what he did because he was what he was." It was supposed to be Lincoln's philosophy, and that was good enough for him.

He read everything he could lay his hands on. It would be different for Junior. He would not have to get his education *à la carte*, he would go to the best university in the country.

"Today we're flying a kite," Mike announced to his son one afternoon.

Everything his father ever did for him became a "production," and this day was no exception. It was the greatest kite he, or anyone else, had ever seen above Central Park. Up it went, more than fifteen hundred feet. It did not come down.

"That's kites for you," Mike said and took Junior to his Fair. He had a surprise: Junior would have the employees' soda-pop concession during his summer vacation.

"We're partners, son, and always will be." Mike shook Junior's small hand. For him it was a sacred moment.

Todd and Todd made an inspection of their realm.

At the Rendevoo, Rogers pointed to an elderly man seated near the door. "See that geezer? That's my uncle. He gets fifty-five bucks a week and doesn't do a damned thing but sit there."

"If he was my uncle," said Mike, "he'd get the fifty-five and he *wouldn't* have to sit there."

Junior looked up at his father proudly.

"Win a French kewpie doll!" shouted a white-haired barker

on the Midway. "Three balls for a dime, ten cents, one tenth of . . ." He stopped as he saw Mike. "Good evening, Boss!" he greeted him deferentially.

"Hiya, Duke," Mike said and introduced Junior.

The barker shook his hand and measured him. "I got a job for a boy your size."

"Thanks," said Junior, "but I have a job."

"If you're half as smart as your old man," the barker chuckled, "heaven help the suckers!"

"More people have seen Michael Todd's productions at the Fair," *Collier's* reported on September 7, 1940, six weeks before the World of Tomorrow became a carnival of yesterday, "than the total audience of any other producer."

By dint of uncommon frugality and, for him, extraordinary self-denial, he managed to save, from his four successful shows at the Fair, restaurants and fourteen bars, several sets of costumes, scenery and approximately fifty thousand dollars cash, half of his total profit. He was astounded that he was not in debt. So was Dietz, whose twenty-five percent of the concessions had netted him $75,000.

It would not be easy for Mike to recover from this stroke of prosperity.

THE
FOURTH
LIFE

"Money is only important

if you haven't got it."

* 14 *

The Sucker

He was back in Chicago, managing the Oriental Theater with one eye and looking for action with the other.

Difficult as it was to find an adequate stage show for the Oriental, Balaban and Katz having tied up practically all the available vaudeville talent for their chain, the selection of films was even more onerous for Mike. He looked at three or four features daily and was appalled by the preponderance of unmitigated junk. The lords of Hollywood should change their basic conception of picture making, he was convinced: they should try to make bad pictures *deliberately* and, employing the same skill and efforts, he was certain they would not produce such a high percentage of blanks.

After the opening of a particularly dismal show, he invited the critics to his office and proceeded to pan it more sulphurously than any of them had intended doing. He apologized for wasting their time and promised that, rather than lay an egg like it again, he would close the theater "For Repairs," as the marquee always announced, not for the imaginary renovation of the building but for actual repairs on his brain.

The critics were disarmed by his candor and gave the show compassionate notices, as he knew they would. It was good for only one week but that was enough, the next time he would think of something else.

He was in Palm Springs when his lawyer, Robert Farrell, called him about a location that might interest him.

It was a deserted and dilapidated jai alai *frontón* on North Clark Street, but its magnitude fascinated him, the 12,284 square feet on the ground floor in addition to the 4,000 square feet in the balcony.

Here was a proscenium of Toddian dimensions; and, as he stared into space, he envisioned a modern Circus Maximus that would make Billy Rose's old Casino de Paris look like a backroom speak.

It couldn't be done, he was told by architects, contractors, show-business friends and especially by prospective investors. The barn was too big, they insisted, not even the Rainbow Gardens Ballroom could make a go of it.

Mike studied the vast structure with the practical experience of a builder and the imagination of a showman.

"I want the stage over the dance floor," he said, "sixty feet across and twenty-four feet deep. The balcony will take a four-hundred-foot bar. We should be able to seat eight thousand people."

"You mean eight hundred," his friend, Joe Sherman, corrected.

"I mean eight thousand."

Sherman stared at him. "This is Chicago, Mike, a crummy joint on the North Side, not the World's Fair. How can you draw eight—no, *one* thousand out here to a *night* club?"

"By charging only four bits to get in and *no* cover charge, by giving them a first-class dinner for seventy-five cents, by serving champagne cocktails for two bits, by selling five-cent Cokes for a nickel and cigarettes at the same price they get them for at drug stores, by *not* having any B-girls, hostesses, 26-games or dice boxes . . . oh yes, and *not* charging for checking hats and coats. And another thing, no waiters. I'm putting in waitresses."

"Now you're off the trolley," said Sherman. "The union says you *got* to have waiters."

"No waiters!" Mike screamed. "My customers would be afraid of guys in full-dress suits. I'll handle the unions."

Sherman shook his head. Mike wasn't making any sense.

"Theodor Herzl said, 'If you want it, it's no longer a dream,' " Mike quoted his most recent teacher.

The biggest, gaudiest and most incredible theater-restaurant in history was no longer a dream because he wanted it.

"What this country needs is a good fifty-cent night club," he said. "I'll give 'em two dance bands, a hundred entertainers, two hundred waitresses, the *works*."

"What kind of décor do you want?" Watson Barratt, his scenic designer from the Fair, asked.

Mike picked up a guest-soap wrapper he had just opened from the Hotel Sherman and handed it to Barratt. "This shade of blue."

He imported an interior decorator from New York, a refugee who had been touted as a genius. He produced nothing the first ten days except classical black circles under his eyes. "I can't sleep in my hotel room," he shrilled, stamping a graceful foot. "The drapes! I can't *stand* the frightful color!"

"That's a reasonable complaint," Mike said and ordered a new set of drapes, of material, shade and design that would make him happy, to be hung immediately.

He had four hundred painters transforming the *frontón* into a phantasy of red, white and blue on a field of silver stars, when he received an SOS from Bill Doll in New York.

"WHAT ARE YOU TRYING TO DO, GIVE ME AN INFERIORITY COM-PLEX?" Mike replied by return wire. "I'M GETTING A JOB FOR YOU AND YOU WANT ME TO STOP EVERYTHING FOR RAILROAD FARE BACK HERE."

All his money was gone and he was hustling around town looking for $100,000 to pay for the equipment.

Joe Miller, owner of the 885 Club, agreed to put up fifty percent of the money for twenty-five percent of the action. The proposition had a secondary appeal for Mike: Miller was an experienced café owner and could handle the food-and-drink end of the business, leaving Mike free to run the show.

Miller came up with the $70,000 Mike needed to open. It was not Miller's money. He had parceled it off to investors whose identity would not be disclosed, even to Todd, for some time.

Mike was to receive $1,000 a week salary, $300 expenses and twenty-five percent of the profits. And it was stipulated in writing, as it would be in every show with which he would ever be identified, that sole control of policy was invested in Todd.

The Michael Todd Theater Café opened on Christmas Day, 1940, with a sixty-foot stage full of pretty girls, singers, dancers, acrobats and animal acts, featuring the vaudeville comedy team of Willie, West and McGinty from Billy Rose's Aquacade, the hilariously mad carpenters who nearly wreck themselves in the process of building a house on stage; a Ben-Hur chariot race and the Gay New Orleans revue, direct from 2,500 performances at the World's Fair, with Gypsy Rose Lee *and* the Flame Girl. Every one of the eight thousand seats was filled.

"At least a few folds of the mantle of P. T. Barnum now flow over the tough shoulders of Showman Mike Todd," *Time* reported on January 6, 1941. "Previous wearer of the whole mantle was Showman Billy Rose, but if Showman Rose has not been forced to relinquish it entirely, Showman Todd has at least forced him to share it."

The first show was five P.M., as unprecedented as everything else about the operation. It was run, as Mike put it, on the principles of Andrew Jackson and Abraham Lincoln: for the common people, for Elmer and his wife and the kids—and the hell with café society. The white-tie set could come for the midnight show if it wanted to, but no one was asking them. From four P.M. on, they came on streetcars, many in overalls and sleeves rolled up, with their families. The kids chinned themselves on the metal railing around the huge circular balcony that had a commanding view of the stage, and they watched the extravaganza in wonderment.

Throughout the performances, at each end of the stage, stood a Todd talisman, a penguin. Not Pete or a relative but a stationary penguin that seemed to be stuffed. As the final curtain came down, to the surprise of the customers and the delight of the children, the inert penguins came to life and strutted off stage.

At the end of the first week, the stage manager requested Todd's permission to fire the penguins.

"What have you got against penguins?" Mike asked.

"Nothing," said the stage manager, "but I just got information that the two Bavarian midgets in those penguin suits are Nazis!"

Mike weighed the charge. "They're such *little* Nazis," he sighed, "they can't do much harm."

Junior was growing up, dark and handsome like his father, quiet and well-mannered unlike his father. One night, after the early show, he knocked on Gypsy's dressing-room door. She was expecting Mike; they had a date for dinner.

"My father was unavoidably detained," said Junior. "He has asked me to take you to dinner."

Junior was an impeccable host, ordered expertly, even to her favorite champagne, and conversed wittily. At the end of the dinner he said, "Dad is paying for the dinner, Miss Lee, but your split of champagne, that's on me."

Mike was living alone at the Drake Hotel, and every night, after the last show, he had his chauffeur take Gypsy in his Cadillac to the Ambassador, where she had an apartment.

On January 11, Mike's limousine was leaving the rear entrance of the café, on its nightly trip after the last show, when three masked hoodlums jumped on the running boards, guns drawn.

"This is a snatch," the leader said and climbed in. One of his men took the wheel, and the car shot away. Another pistol-whipped the chauffeur, William Corbett, insensible and dropped him in an alley. After they were safely away from the lights of the business district, the leader turned to the two women huddled in the back seat. He grabbed the purse of the younger, Miss Carol Hathaway, Mike's accountant.

"Hey!" he exclaimed. "Where's Gypsy Rose Lee?"

"In her dressing room," Miss Hathaway replied.

"Vas ist mit you?" asked her companion.

"Good Christ!" said the hoodlum, seeing the white-haired, gentle little woman in her seventies. "Stop the car!"

The discovery of Corbett's battered body brought, at Mike's demand, a swarm of police to the café and an all-points alarm. In the midst of the tumult, the white-haired elderly woman companion of Miss Hathaway walked into the café. She was calm but weary from her walk; it had taken her more than an hour to get back.

"Why didn't you take a taxi?" Mike demanded.

"I had no money," she replied.

"No money! You went out of the house without a dollar?"

"Avrumele," Mike's mother said forbearingly, "I was your guest. Does a lady bring money when she is your guest?"

Mike was shocked. He had thought, naïvely, that the strong-arm era had ended with Capone. His total disillusionment was yet to come.

He went to Palm Springs for a vacation.

When he came back he found what Billy Rose had found at the Casino de Paris after his vacation in Europe.

The prices had been raised and the salaries had been slashed. There was a cover charge *and* a minimum. The 26-game girls had been moved in. Boxes were rattling with loaded dice.

"What the hell is this?" Mike demanded.

"You weren't getting the strength out of the joint," Joe Miller answered.

"You're insane!" Mike shrilled. "This cannot—this *will not* happen in any place that has *my* name out front."

"Face it, Mike," Miller said realistically, "you got only twenty-five percent of the say."

"Look at the contract! *I* control the show, without interference."

"Mike," Miller pleaded, "the show is costing too much. You had it up to eight-five-o-o. Now that we're established we can cut down. That goes for the advertising too. We don't need it. You can't get the strength out of the joint if you don't cut down."

He had been hearing this ceaseless cry since *The Hot Mikado*. He could not cut. It went against his nature. He sold extravagance. Without it his trademark would be gone, he would have nothing to peddle.

"You're right, Joe," he said icily. "When I left, we were taking in only eight thousand a night, fifteen on a week end. One week we took in a mere ninety *G's*. Just jai alai players who happened to stumble in by mistake, no doubt."

Miller could not answer Mike's words or meet his eyes.

"It isn't me, Mike . . ." he said, his voice trailing.

"Who is it?" Mike demanded.

"The Boys," Miller said. "I didn't have seventy G's of my own."

Mike did not hesitate. "Pay me off," he said. "You and the Boys run it."

"What about the name?" Miller asked.

"Is your name Mike Todd?" he replied.

A medium-sized, conservatively dressed man, with a short black mustache—flanked by two husky men in long overcoats, long sleeves, velvet collars, pockets that bulged at the expected places—walked into Mike Todd's office at 32 West Randolph Street in the Oriental Theater. One look at them and Mike dismissed his secretary, Ann Rosenthal.

Avrom Goldbogen faced the man who had earned the proudest and most lethal *nom de guerre* in Chicago gangsterdom: Frank Nitti, the *Enforcer*.

Todd looked at Nitti's bodyguards. "You've seen too many Warner Brothers pictures," he said.

Nitti explained his position. His money was in the Michael Todd Café. It was news to Mike, but, as Nitti expounded, the picture became clear. Todd blamed no one, not even Miller, who had gone to Nitti and Joe Fusco, once a beer foreman for Al Capone in the twenties, currently the liquor boss for Nitti, Capone's successor. They were the banks.

"Fusco went good for the equipment," Nitti said. "We put up the dough on *your* name, not Miller's. The word's out that you're being muscled out—and *we* don't like it."

"I'm *not* being muscled out," Mike said. "I'm walking because *I* want to walk."

Nitti did not believe him. Todd, he was certain, was holding out for a deal.

"Your name *has* to be out front," Nitti said tonelessly. It was an order.

Mike looked at the Enforcer without flinching. "When I walk out," he said, "my name goes with me: every sign that's lettered 'Michael Todd.'"

The most feared commander of Chicago's underworld fixed his eyes on Mike. "What do you want?" he asked.

Mike stared out the window at Randolph Street, where he had roamed as a kid.

"*Chicken . . . Aren't you one of the boys?*" The old cries echoed through his brain. It was a moment of decision, what Hemingway called "the moment of truth."

It's easy to nod. Most people do. Most people are afraid. I can stall. No, I can't stall. If I say, "I'll think about it," or, "I'll let you know," or, "Let's talk tomorrow," I'm dead. Surrender is surrender whenever you say it. But the money. He asked, "What do you want?" That means the limit.

Wait a minute! If I go for it, I'm one of the Boys, one of them. I'm not one of them, no matter how much the price. I have dreams. I'm not one of them.

Why not, Avrumele?

What if—what when—something goes wrong? It always does. You can't yell copper when you're one of them. You're a citizen of the lawless. You'll never be Somebody, really, except in the columns you buy. You won't be respected, not by your family and the friends who knew you when. You won't get invited to the right people's homes, you'll be an outsider the rest of your life.

If I don't go, what? To a mobster nothing is worse than something that's legitimate, something that's true, someone who can't be bought. All they worry about is the few guys who won't stand for the arm. Where am I if I'm part of the arm?

The alternative? The percentage of legitimate guys that get killed is less than those in the rackets, and I play percentage. But . . . this is Opportunity. With the Mob behind me I can be the biggest man in show business. And what's the use of kidding, I want to be the biggest man in show business, bigger than Billy Rose. All I have to do is nod.

"I'm walking," Mike Todd told Frank Nitti.

The Enforcer stared at him in amazement. "Do you know what you're doing?"

He knew what he was doing. He was turning his back on the men in power, the hoods. He was being, as they called him years ago, *chicken*. Because now, as then, he was not one of them. It was not a question of principle, on his side *or* theirs, but of self-preservation. If he said yes and later changed his mind and ran out, then he *would* be killed. He would rather chance a going-over now than cement shoes later.

There was something else . . . something between *chicken* and *greed*. Belonging. What side *was* he on? On their side, he gave orders and did not take them. On their side, he took as much off the top of the sheet—off the *gross*—as he wanted. On their side he was a *right* guy. *One of the mob*. He would *belong*.

But he did not belong. Never had. That, in a sense, was his trouble, his problem. If you *belonged*, you had a gang behind you, in glory or grief. Back-slappers, hand-holders, defenders. How do you rate with Toots Shor? How do you stand with Winchell? Toots and Winchell were the Dun and Bradstreet of Broadway: they made you with a smile and unmade you with a frown. By *their* standards you were a right guy or a wrongo. Like it or not, that was the acid test on Broadway: what tables, if any, you rated at "21," the Stork Club and Shor's. Most guys he knew, especially the ones who had *made it,* had to have a feeling of belonging. They would rather belong to Shor's Inner Circle than have Money, Fame, Women and what went with them. Toots was the Father of the Belongers or the *Belongless*.

Mike didn't know the password. Or he had forgotten it. He had no one to confide in, no one to ask, "What shall I do?" He was at the big crossroads: he had to make *the most important decision of his life* and he had to do it in a matter of seconds.

He was torn. He had one god and he bent his knee to him: instinct.

"I'm walking out," he repeated. If he had to belong to the

Boys, he belonged to no one, especially to himself. He wanted the world to know him and love him and envy him, but he would not pay Nitti's price. He could not prophesy what he might do on some future day, but now, at *this* moment of truth, he preferred the dignity of being alone.

Nitti was not easily surprised, he had bought too many men. Todd had to know that, with a nod, he could take seven-five-o-o off the top, he could finance any play, any film, any dame, any *thing.*

Avrom Goldbogen did not waver.

"I don't know if you're the dumbest guy or the smartest," Nitti said, his face hardening. "I don't know if you got moxie or you don't have moxie, but . . ."

"You aren't going to kill me, Nitti," Mike said evenly. He wasted no *ain'ts* on hoods. "I'm dealing myself out."

One of Nitti's bodyguards pulled back his arm to smash Todd.

"Don't be big guys," Nitti snapped, intercepting the blow. "Who asked you?"

In the presence of class, Nitti had class.

Mike watched from his window as the three men left the building. He would have been one of them if he had nodded. A man had to make his stand so many times, and he had to be right or he was dead. It was frightening if you thought about it. He didn't.

The word got around how Mike had stood up to the Enforcer, and his reputation as a guy with guts was established forever. He was the Pin-Up Boy of gangsterdom, but he had to go.

After lawyers battled for six weeks, a compromise was reached: Todd would be given notes for the sum of $65,000. In return, he would permit the place to be operated thereafter as THE THEATER CAFÉ and, in smaller letters, *Formerly Mike Todd's.*

The Theater Café was raided the first week that Mike was

out. "Selling liquor to a minor," was the complaint, a charge that can close any bar in the country that the authorities want to be closed. It is the easiest rap to hang on a joint, the most difficult to defend. The Theater Café deserved to be raided for many reasons and, ironically, was knocked over for a violation of which it was innocent.

Police Commissioner James P. Allman recommended to Mayor Edward J. Kelly that its license be revoked. It was unnecessary. Todd had taken his magic with him. The café went into bankruptcy in less than two weeks.

"Todd should have known better," Mike's lawyer, Farrell, testified at the bankruptcy hearings. "I'm sure I didn't know his partners had Capone or Nitti affiliations; possibly he didn't either. They owed him a lot of money, but he has abandoned it and has no complaints. He just packed up and left town because he wanted to keep his good name."

Mike was proud of the name he shared with his son, and on June 22, his thirty-second birthday, he had it legally changed from Goldbogen. He was officially Michael Todd. But who was Michael Todd? He was, according to the New York *Times*, "the hardest-punching producer ever to come down the Pike," and, according to *Time* magazine, the heir to Barnum's mantle as America's greatest showman. He was adroit and cunning, a wise guy in a world of suckers.

He was so astute that in eight years of show business, he had parlayed the Flame Dance into *Bring on the Dames* to *The Hot Mikado* to four smash shows at the World's Fair to the most spectacular theater café in history to getting the stench of hoodlums on him.

"We still have the act, Mike," Eva said. She had not stopped waiting.

The man who was supposed to be half smart to everything had parlayed himself back to where he had started with her in 1933. He had no illusions about being on the turf. As Uncle

Elya used to say, poverty is no disgrace but no great honor either.

He felt good for a better reason. When he had to make the *big* decision, he knew he had acted as his father would have.

* 15 *

Operation Hate

He had taken Joe Fusco as a partner without knowing what he was doing. Now he joined Gerald L. K. Smith's organization and he knew what he was doing. He did not attend meetings in New York, where he might be recognized, but he donated an occasional fifty dollars when he could afford it, and remained a member in good standing.

Mike was in Detroit, looking for a theater location, when he met Smith's advance man, who was there for the same purpose. There were shortages in everything; it was becoming increasingly difficult to find halls, for tab shows or hatemongering.

"They just canceled an auditorium I had lined up in Chicago," Smith's advance man said dejectedly. "Unlesss I come up with a place this week, we'll have to pass it this trip. The Old Man won't like that." He shook his head fearfully.

"I know every barn in Chicago that seats more than ten people," said Mike. "Maybe I can help you."

"I'll be indebted to you for life if you do," said Smith's man. "So will the Old Man."

"Quit worrying," said Mike, "I'll find a place."

They shook hands.

"By the way," Smith's man said as an afterthought, "do you know Winchell?"

"I've met him two or three times in night clubs," Mike said.

"Isn't there *any* way of getting him off our backs?"

Mike shook his head doubtfully. "Lots of people have tried. He's got too much muscle."

"Did you hear last Sunday's broadcast? He murdered us! Where the hell does he get that information?"

Mike shrugged. "He knows the right keyholes."

"If you find any way of getting to him, let me know."

Mike nodded.

Emotions were running high in Chicago. All efforts to prevent Smith from appearing at Kimball Hall that night seemingly had failed. A petition of protest signed by the Jewish tenants of the building, as well as sympathetic neighbors, convinced the landlord he had made a mistake. Smith was out.

"I'll get you another place," Mike promised Smith.

The opposition was tremendous but, with the assistance of his old friend and backer, Harold Costello, he succeeded in renting the Masonic Hall in the Oriental Theater Building. Costello, building manager of the Oriental, could not say no to Mike, unsympathetic as he was to Smith's ideology. It took all of Todd's entreaties to make him stick to his bargain after a Jewish-owned restaurant on the basement floor threatened to break its lease if Smith was allowed to use the premises. Mike held Costello to his word.

At 7:30 P.M., thirty minutes before the meeting was to start, Mike walked to the cigar counter in the building and bought a cigar. He was lighting up and did not see the three men walking toward him.

"Av Goldbogen!"

It had been a long time since he had been called by that name. He turned.

"America Firster!"

He saw three pairs of fists and three pairs of legs converge on him. In an instant he was stretched on the sidewalk, every inch of his body being pounded, kicked and spat upon.

"Let me up! I can . . ."

They kept pumping flesh and leather until the sidewalk was stained with his blood.

"This is—a—bum rap . . . I can prove . . ." he managed to gasp through swollen lips.

"How?" the spokesman asked.

"By—one of—the *boys* . . ." he struggled to say.

"Who'll stand up for you, *America Firster*?"

Through the pain he groped for a name and whispered it, a prominent ward politician.

The spokesman looked at him disdainfully. "You're lying, you rat bastard."

"Let's give him the benefit of the doubt," said one of the other two assailants.

They dragged him by the neck and sleeve-walked him to the Covenant Club. He was shocked, as they passed dozens of people, including two policemen, that no one stopped to inquire why he was being manhandled, why he was battered and bloody. You could be killed in the middle of Randolph Street, he thought, and no one would turn his head.

"You know this anti-Semitic bastard?" the spokesman asked the ward politician whose name Mike had mentioned, seated at his favorite table.

"It looks like Mike Todd," he said. "Let him go."

They released him reluctantly.

"I got to get cleaned up," said Mike, with an anxious glance at his watch, "or I'll be late for the meeting."

"What meeting?" the politician asked.

"Gerald L. K. Smith's."

Smith entered the Masonic Hall like a crusader. His coat was draped over his shoulders. Frenzied women fought zealously to kiss his hands. He strode triumphantly to the stage, where he was flanked by two U.S. Army soldiers in uniform.

Mike sat on an aisle seat in the second row, one eye half closed and the other narrowed in a hard glint.

"Franklin D. Rosenfeld and the Kike capitalists who put him in the White House . . ." Smith began.

A few minutes later he was interrupted by the arrival of police and the F.B.I.

"You got nothing on me!" Smith screamed.

"That's what you think," said one of the agents, removing a microphone that had been concealed in the curtains. "We finally got a tape on you."

Winchell had another exclusive that Sunday night, from an undercover operative who had been giving him information directly from Smith's inner council for three months, the same person who had hired and wired Masonic Hall and put Smith out of business for the duration of the war.

The three assailants who had almost killed him gave him a hero's welcome at the Covenant Club that night.

"How did you do it, Mike?" one asked in honest admiration.

"If you can't lick 'em, join 'em," Mike replied. *"Then* lick 'em."

He was surrounded by back-slappers.

"The moral is never to trust a Mike named Todd," he chortled. "He might be a Hebe named Avrom Goldbogen."

* 16 *

His Star, Her Garter

He was back with a vaudeville unit, thanks to the costumes he had salvaged from the café and thankful for the people to fill them, especially Gypsy.

Doll and Glick took the tab revue, remnants of the Gay New Orleans, on a tank tour, riding the day coaches to save money.

They arrived in Buffalo and discovered, to their dumfoundment, that not an advertisement, placard or publicity item on their engagement had been planted. Moreover, the owner of the theater they were supposed to play had no knowledge of their coming.

It had been an oversight: Mike had neglected to book the town.

"Having a wonderful time," Doll wrote him on a postcard from Niagara Falls. "Wish you were Sam Harris."

One night he called Doll for a report on the night's receipts.

"Where are you, Mike?" Doll asked.

"Why?"

"If you're in California I'll talk fast. If you're in New York I'll talk slow."

"I'm in Chicago," Mike said. "Talk medium."

In Milwaukee, an art student from Marquette University came backstage and asked Gypsy's permission to sculpt her. Gypsy was flattered to be selected as an *ouvrage d'art*, and, the same day, the young sculptor moved into her dressing room with a pail of clay.

"Miss Lee," he asked as he molded her celebrated figure, "what do you think of when you strip?"

"I sublimate nudity into an ascetic distraction," she said, "by singing detachedly of frustration, psychoanalysis and philosophy."

He gulped. "You ought to write a book," he said.

"I am writing one," she said.

Larry Lawrence of the Milwaukee *Journal* charitably ignored the show and wrote of Mike, prophetically: "What Todd will be doing in the amusement world before he reaches forty is anybody's guess, so just for fun I'll take my guess now. Mine is that he'll go broke a couple more times and have only a paltry million and forty-two ideas in his kick by the time he's forty."

The unit foundered for three months and collapsed. Mike was oblivious of its closing, he was working on *two* musicals.

He had been in New York for several months signing talent for a show called *And So to Bedlam.* Early one morning at Lindy's, after fourteen consecutive hours of haggling with actors' agents over what he felt were exorbitant demands, he shook his head sadly.

"Why are you shaking your head?" a flesh peddler asked.

"What's going to happen," Mike asked, "if the seat breaks?"

"What seat?"

"The one I'm going to make my profit on."

On the eve of rehearsals, after the final reading, he junked the production, took his loss and concentrated on his other show, *Beat the Band,* by George Marion, Jr., with music by Johnny Green, the composer of "Body and Soul" and "I Cover the Waterfront."

Beat the Band was the story of an Artie Shaw-type of orchestra leader who has a dispute with a hotel that hired him and in reprisal, through a freak clause in his contract, the management makes him play in the boiler room. In the third act he makes the boiler room the most popular club in town, and everyone loves happily ever after.

"Dick Powell could play it," Mike suggested.

"Dick Powell?" His advisers shook their heads. Powell was in limbo. His star as a song and dance man had waned, and he had not yet been discovered as a dramatic actor. And he had never been on a Broadway stage.

Mike brought him to New York. The first read-through was the last, for Mike and Powell. Both lost all interest in the show instantly.

The actor's wife, Joan Blondell, came up to console him. He introduced her to Mike.

"You've been away from Broadway a long time," Mike said.

"Ten years."

"Too long," Mike said. "Maybe I'll bring you back one of these days."

She graciously refrained from commenting; he had had enough punishment for one night.

Beat the Band was subsequently produced by George Abbott, with Joan Caulfield, Jerry Lester and Romo Vincent, at the 46th Street Theater. It lasted sixty-eight performances.

The big story in the morning papers was the legal ban on burlesque. In a three-thousand, five-hundred-word decision, Supreme Court Judge Aaron J. Levy branded burlesque "inartistic filth" and denied the application of Brothers Minsky for a court order to force the City Administration to renew their theater license.

As Mike read the obituary he decided this was the right time to produce a burlesque show with three graduates of burleycue —Gypsy Rose Lee, Bobby Clark and Carrie Finnell—at $4.40 tops.

"Sophisticated theatergoers won't pay that kind of money to watch old burleycue skits," Hassard Short said after Mike outlined the format.

Mike smiled. The burleycue skits were not old to a $4.40 audience, only to forty-cent audiences. Sophisticated theatergoers *and* the critics would accept burlesque as legitimate theater because Hassard Short's name was on the marquee. It would be unadulterated Minsky, but with Short as a front it would have the illusion of smartness.

"You take care of the art, Has, I'll put in the a-a-a-a-ah," he said. "I'm calling it *Star and Garter* and we open at the Music Box, June seventeenth."

"Impossible!" his director exclaimed. "That won't even give us time to take it out of town."

"Can't afford any tryouts," said Mike. "But I'll tell you what I will do for you, I'll invite an audience for a preview."

Short was nonplused. "A preview? When?"

"The night before the opening."

"That's wonderful!" Short shrilled. "And if anything needs fixing, we'll have the whole night to revise it!"

The preview was disastrous. Mike's panic-stricken backers held a council of war on the sidewalk outside the theater, and one of them, Herb Freezer, demanded the return of his ten thousand dollars that night.

"I hate angels," Mike said. "They usually have opinions."

Mike's "family"—Short, Glick, Dietz, Doll and Harry Bloomfield, a ticket hustler who had become an assistant—pleaded with him to cancel the opening and take it to Boston. In its present shape, all agreed, it would be murdered by the critics.

"It doesn't need a Boston tryout," Mike said. "It needs new songs, new skits and new scenery."

"And new money," Dietz added.

He could not raise a dollar. The word was out that *Star and Garter* was a bomb.

"I'm afraid we can't open," Mike said disconsolately in Gypsy's dressing room after his luckless safari.

"You *have* to open," Gypsy said. "I just paid a hundred twenty-five bucks to paint this dressing room and I bought two gallons of body paint. Two *gallons*, Mike. That's enough for years!"

"We need another week to fix the show," he said. "That's an extra week's expenses. Worst of all, one of my backers, Herb Freezer, wants his ten G's back. And I'm tapped out."

"I'll buy Freezer's interest," she said casually.

"I said G's, not G-strings."

"I heard you."

He was incredulous. She could not have that kind of money. "But that crummy tenement you live in . . ."

"I own the whole crummy building."

The salvage job began. He telephoned an agent in Los Angeles to have an act flown to New York. He ordered a new routine in which each chorus girl's costume would cost $386, something of a feat since the apparel consisted of a necklace, brassière, chastity belt and hat.

And he hunted for money. Before he could open he had to put up two weeks' salary guarantee for the company, a total of $25,000. This was the law of Actors Equity, the musicians' and stagehands' unions.

Mike could not raise a fraction of the $25,000. His credit was exhausted, his backers had run for the hills.

"I'll go for the guarantee," Gypsy said.

Gypsy Rose Lee had earned every dollar she had the hard way. She had been on the stage since she was four years old—a quarter of a century of cheap hotels, sometimes tents, night coaches, buses, brought up by a mother whose favorite aphorism was, "Do unto others before they do you." She had gone the route from carnivals to fraternal organizations; from Sid Grauman's stage shows in Hollywood to bit parts in two-reel comedies with Harold Lloyd and Bebe Daniels; from the Pantages vaudeville circuit and the Orpheum to George White's Scandals; from Minsky's to the Ziegfeld Follies to a tempestuous year with Mike at the Fair. She was the best in her profession but she was weary of the grind: she wanted to become an author.

Gypsy had money because of her innate Scandinavian frugality, because she lived in a thirty-dollar-a-month apartment, because she had never wasted or, until now, chanced a dollar. Why, she asked herself, was she willing—hell, eager—to gamble every cent she had on the most reckless promoter in show business and a burley that looked like a cinch to be closed the second night, by the critics or the police?

Mike stared at her in awe. "Twenty-five big ones, Gypsy. You can't dig up that kind of scratch in twenty-four hours."

"*One* hour," she said. She had money and bonds stashed all over town. She had been frightened by signs in banks that said deposits were insured only up to $5,000.

Within an hour the supposedly toughest businesswoman ever

to parade across a stage put $25,000 worth of bonds on the line.

"How much percentage do I get?" she asked when Mike brought a lawyer, William Fitelson, to draw the partnership agreement.

After an hour of legal-financial mumbo jumbo, Gypsy lost her patience. "Just cut the pie fairly!" she said.

Fitelson, lost in a sea of percentages, was bewildered.

"A pie!" Mike shouted, impatiently chomping on his cigar. "For God's sake, Bill, make her a pie or I'll make it myself. If she wants a pie, give it to her!"

Gypsy not only stripped her bank accounts for Mike, but, from her tremendous experience in burlesque, she gave him sketches, gags and bits of business which he rewrote in his own patois. They worked in her apartment every night until exhaustion and dawn caught up with them.

The week's reprieve was ended. The curtain went up on the night of June 24. He knew, without looking, that there were ridges on his fingernails. There always were at times of stress. They were his emotional calendar; like the rings on trees they marked the times of recent emotional crises. His colitis was distressing him too. He was a nervous Jew. *Everything* bothered him but no one else knew it. He was a better actor than any he hired.

On stage, in what was advertised as "a cast of 100 and a number of lovely young girls," Bobby Clark was playing Mike's version of Dan McGrew in the Malamute saloon.

"Where's the powder room?" he asked, staggering from the bar.

The bartender pointed outside. Clark opened the door and several stagehandfuls of snow were hurled in his face.

"It's too cold," he said, closing the door. "I'll wait till spring."

The sophisticated first-night audience roared with unrestrained laughter. Skits that had died one week previously were now, through some magical alchemy, belly laughs. He had transformed a flop into a hit.

"Likely it was the sight of those dark and shuttered houses along Forty-second Street that stirred in Mike Todd some dim, nostalgic memory of a far happier day," Lewis Nichols wrote in the *Times*.

"Mr. Todd has pulled no punches and only the trickier G-strings," Mantle wrote in the *Daily News*. "As burlesque, *Star and Garter* is a good show in a rich setting. Bobby Clark was never funnier."

"Burlesque, the fast and fallen woman of the theater," chronicled Louis Kronenberger in *PM*, "swept into the Music Box all done up in silks and ermine. A leg-and-laugh show with considerable lure and good filthy fun, it is fleshed with style rather than suggestiveness, and offers an entertaining evening."

Mike's intuition, to stage a burlesque of burlesque, had been unerring. The public, depressed by Allied reverses during the first six months of the war, craved escape entertainment. And he had it—the highest dames and the lowest comedy on Broadway. The show figured to run two years, and it ultimately did, for six hundred and nine performances.

There was standing room only at the Music Box, yet Mike could not meet his payroll. He grabbed the money out of the box office as fast as it came in, and, to save time, had I.O.U. pads printed in denominations ranging from $100 to $10,000. What he didn't spend he gambled—on horses, cards, anything with odds—or loaned, via his Don't Go to Strangers Department for needy friends, acquaintances and part-time enemies, which invariably exceeded its budget of $2,500 per week.

"Money is only important if you haven't got it" was one of his favorite maxims, and he lived by it.

To prevent the show from being closed while it was sold out for months in advance, Mike ultimately barred himself from the box office, evolved a complicated system of withdrawals that required a crew of auditors and gave Glick sole control of his money. Joe allotted him all personal funds, Joe paid all bills, Joe put away the savings, if any.

"Joe's got to be a real sumptuarian," Mike told friends. "There used to be a time he'd come over to mooch a cup of coffee off me. Now he has his penthouse at the St. Moritz and his maid to bring him his coffee on the terrace." It was a good-natured condescension of a master of sumptuous living to his apprentice. The extra syllables he added to convert an adjective to a noun were symptomatic of his knack for adding a flourish to everything he discussed.

It was late afternoon. Todd's favorite sign, ALL SEATS FOR TO-NIGHT'S PERFORMANCE SOLD OUT, had been hanging in front of the box office all day and a ticket seller was telling a customer how lucky he was to get two tickets *only* four months in advance. Mike was in a benevolent mood when two quietly dressed men walked into his office and informed him they were taking over the box office. Mike leaped out of his chair, fists knotted. The spokesman stuck an identification card under his nose and Mike sank back in silent resignation. He took on the whole world *except* the F.B.I.

For the next three hours, until curtain time, an uninterrupted series of arguments raged at the box office. Many irate customers presented receipts and other proof that they had paid for tickets to that night's performance, but the man behind the wicket insisted there must be some mistake, there were no tickets under their names for that night, and gave them the choice of a refund or a reservation for a later date.

Outraged protests and threats filled the lobby. Bedizened women and their escorts had come long distances and at great expense, many had considerable influence or contended they had—heads would roll for this, they promised, and the first would be Todd's.

More than sixty persons who had paid for bona-fide reservations at hotels and ticket agencies were sent away infuriated.

The curtain went up at eight-forty and the show was on. The

crowd was roaring at Clark's japery, Gypsy was coming on to prove that there is, after all, no substitute for a woman's body—and no one on stage or out front was aware of a grim drama being enacted in the fourteenth row of the orchestra.

Two plainly dressed couples were sitting in the middle of the fourteenth row, laughing loudly, when one of the men felt a tap on his shoulder. He turned. The man seated behind him gestured for him to leave. The man in the fourteenth row blanched, turned and whispered to his three companions.

They stopped laughing too.

In a moment the two couples rose, made their way to the aisle and left, with an escort. From the moment they had entered the theater, twenty minutes previously, they had been surrounded. The thirty couples on all sides of them appeared no different from any others present, but they were F.B.I. agents and their ladies. They had received a tip at five o'clock that afternoon that the two couples under surveillance were going to attend *Star and Garter*.

By moving into the box office and taking over these sixty seats, they were able, with the arrest of the four ringleaders, to break up the biggest Nazi espionage ring in the United States.

Mike couldn't understand their interest in Gypsy. She didn't have many secrets.

There was only one note of tranquillity in Mike's life: Junior. He permitted nothing to interfere with his visits to Junior's summer camp in Belgrade, Maine. He had a standing date with Izzy Rappaport of Baltimore, whose son was also at Belgrade, and they made the trip together every other week end.

On a Wednesday in August, Izzy came to New York and learned, to his surprise, that Mike had undergone an emergency appendectomy the previous day. He was granted permission to visit him but was adjured to remain only a short while and not to excite him.

Mike was sitting up, attired in a garish Hawaiian sports shirt and a tinted brown straw hat, a lighted cigar between his teeth, holding court with the chorus of the *Star and Garter,* when Izzy, on tiptoe, cautiously opened the door of his room at the Westside Hospital.

"Any message you want to send Junior this week end?" Izzy asked after the room was cleared.

"I'm going with you," said Mike.

Izzy was astounded. "You were operated on *yesterday!*"

"I'm going," Mike said with finality. When the train left Penn Station on Friday on the rugged day-long journey, Mike, still in stitches, was aboard, a present for Junior under one arm and a box of cigars under the other. It would take more than an appendectomy to keep him from seeing his son.

Two weeks later Mike brought Junior home in his new Cadillac convertible coupé. He cherished those hours. Junior was the only person he never interrupted, the one person he wanted to hear.

"You got a birthday coming up," Mike said. "How would you like a dog?"

"No animals."

"Why not?"

There was a long pause. "Remember the time in Chicago when Blackstone the Magician called me up on the stage?" Junior said at last.

Mike nodded. "You were about seven."

"Six. He gave me a rabbit . . ." Junior's eyes misted. "It died the next day. It was the greatest tragedy of my life, Dad . . . It bothered me for five years, up to a couple months ago."

Mike's face darkened. "What's gone is gone, son," he said solemnly. "Never waste a second on the past. There isn't time, and time is the most precious thing in life. Don't *ever* look back, only ahead."

Ahead, along the four-lane parkway, four or five miles of cars, as far as the eye could see, were piled up because of the heavy southbound traffic and road construction. The outside northbound lane was almost deserted.

Mike slowed down to an almost stop behind the stalled line, suddenly pulled out across the white line and into the northbound lane, still proceeding south.

"Get back in line, Dad!" Junior, now standing on the back seat, was yelling hysterically. "Hurry up and get back!"

Mike continued his course, Junior's hysteria mounting as they passed mile after mile of stopped cars. No more than one or two came from the opposite direction.

"We'll be pinched for sure!" Junior said.

"The cops will thank me, son," Mike assured him.

Speeding along majestically, they passed more than five hundred cars, and, at the head of the bottleneck, Mike waved at the two motorcycle policemen who were regulating traffic. The cops waved affably in return.

Junior looked at his father with new respect and envy. It was *natural* for him not to follow the crowd. It was natural for him to ignore the rules and do what made sense. He had no fear of the consequences because he was confident that what he was doing was right. Out of all those thousands of motorists piled up—and there must have been many smart men among them, Junior figured, doctors, lawyers, college professors—not one had *thought* of pulling out and taking the northbound lane that was not being used. If anyone did, he had lacked the courage to do it. Junior knew that he would not have done it, and he doubted if he ever could.

Mike confounded everyone he touched or who touched him, Junior included.

He was looking for action, and when his friends, Ben Peskay and Bob Goldstein, touted him on a new show the Theatre Guild was trying out in New Haven, he went along.

"It's a musical comedy without comedy," Goldstein told him, "but it may make it. You can get in for fifteen G's."

Mike watched the show but did not put up the money.

"It's a very good show," he said, "but I don't want any part of it. Because it isn't *mine*." He wanted to roll his own dice and gamble on his own talent.

The show was *Oklahoma!*—and it would gross more money than any musical in history, in excess of twelve million dollars. Mike would have a part of it, twelve years later, and it would have a pivotal influence on his life.

Mike expected to see his name in the columns almost daily because he worked at it, but he was not prepared for this item in Winchell's column:

"Gypsy Rose Lee, who recently shed her second, Arnold Mizzy, N.Y. manufacturer, and Mike Todd are on fire."

Gypsy had no desire to break up anyone's home, even one that was already broken. She found another man. His name was Alexander Kirkland and he was an actor who had attracted attention in *Men in White*. Gypsy married Kirkland, with a trained monkey as the ring bearer. Gypsy left the show, and Mike—for whom *Star and Garter*, like every other show he would ever produce, had no snap after opening night—looked for the second bet in his parlay.

* 17 *

Fade Me, Little World

Ethel Merman, Cole Porter, Herbert and Dorothy Fields glared at Mike. *He* was going to tell *them* how to put on a musical?

He was. Ethel Merman had been the star of Cole Porter's
Anything Goes when he was playing carnivals and fairs with
his Flame Girl, and Herbert and Dorothy Fields were among
the theater's foremost librettists, but they were working for
him now. He had picked up the show when Vinton Freedley
had dropped it; he had invested $62,500 of his own money
(advanced by Joe Schenck and Joseph Moskowitz of Twentieth-Century Fox), and that wasn't tin.

"I'm not just a bankroll guy," he said defiantly. "I'm the
producer—and I'm not going to be a nominal producer! I'll
junk the show right now *and* the sixty-two and a half before I
yield artistic control." He was not bluffing.

They were not challenging his position, Porter interjected
diplomatically, they were merely defending a scene they believed in.

"It reads well," said the Fieldses.

"It plays well," said Porter.

"It *feels* good," said Merman.

"It's *out*," Mike said.

"It's a great sketch," Merman insisted.

"The better it is, the worse off we are," Mike said. "If it
stops the show we have no show."

They were adamant. It was more than an argument over a
scene, it was a showdown to determine who was boss.

"Okay," said Mike indulgently, "I'll *prove* it and let *you* have
the pleasure of heaving it out. If I'm wrong I'd better go back
to selling shoes."

He ordered the costumes and had the sets built for the scene
in question, at a cost of five thousand dollars. They were used
once, for the dress rehearsal. The scene was thrown out, at the
request of Ethel Merman, Cole Porter and the Fieldses.

Mike never mentioned it. Five G's had been a cheap price
to establish the fact that *he* was the producer.

Between top-drawer Porter songs like "Hey, Good Looking!"
and "By the Mississinewah," *Something for the Boys* told the

lunatic story of three uninhibited cousins who inherit a Texas ranch next to Kelly Field, set up a boarding house for soldiers' wives and, in their spare time, make defense gadgets out of carborundum. The hostelry turns into a scandal and Ethel, by getting some carborundum in her teeth, turns into a radio receiving set. After that nothing even tried to make sense.

"Doesn't an opening-night crowd ever give you butterflies?" Merman was asked by a member of the cast as she was going on stage at the Alvin Theater on opening night, January 7, 1943.

Ethel laughed. "If they had what I got," the great pro said, "they'd be up here and I'd be down there. What have I got to be nervous about?"

The show ran late, and Burns Mantle of the *News* and Howard Barnes of the *Herald Tribune* were compelled to leave early in the third act to make their deadlines. They got as far as the door, where Mike stood sentinel like a Cerberus.

"Back to your seats, boys," Mike commanded. "You're not leaving."

"We'll miss our editions!" Mantle protested.

"You'll miss my bomber!" Mike shouted. He had conceived a special effect for his third-act climax, a spectacular illusion of an Army bomber, propellers spinning, taking off.

The ushers were under orders to stop all critics who attempted to take flight before the bomber. Nothing stopped the critics from speaking their minds the next day.

"My best advice," wrote Mantle, "is to run, not walk, to the nearest agency and reserve seats. Ethel Merman can thank Mike Todd for a happy overnight hit."

"The fabulous Mike Todd has brought in the musical comedy for which Broadway has been waiting a long, long time," Nichols reported in the *Times*. "Ethel Merman gives a performance that suggests all her performances before last night were simply practice."

"*Something for the Boys* made Broadway a better place to

laugh in," Richard Lockridge stated in the *Sun*. "We can thank
Mike Todd for this. Mr. Todd, always a lavish man, has been
lavish with everything."

"This should be the answer to playgoers' prayers for a long
time to come," Barnes predicted in the *Herald Tribune*.

Star and Garter and *Something for the Boys* were sold out
for months in advance. He could do nothing wrong. When
Merman was suddenly taken ill, Glick prepared an announcement to close the show. Mike stopped him.

"There's only one Merman," Glick said. "That's who they
pay to see and they won't take any substitute."

There was standing room only that night at eight-forty when
Bill Johnson, the leading man, came out to make a curtain
speech Mike had written.

"Ethel Merman is ill and cannot be with us tonight," he began. "We know that you in the audience join us in wishing her
a speedy recovery. Anyone who wishes his money back will
be refunded it cheerfully at the box office. But . . ."

He paused. "There is a little girl who has been waiting eleven
months to go on. Betty Garrett appears on Broadway for the
first time tonight and . . . it may be *a new star will be born!*"

The audience applauded hopefully.

Mike stood in the wings smiling. *This* was show business.
There was an air of *expectancy*. It charged the theater like an
electric current. Instead of being disappointed by Merman's
absence, the crowd considered itself fortunate. Years from now
Betty Garrett might be a great name and they could boast that
they were there the night she became a star.

A real showman created this climate of expectancy. The same
trick would not work twice, not as well. What was good yesterday is not good today. Producing this frame of mind, by psychology—the anxiety for the next moment or hour of entertainment—had been second nature to him since he absorbed the
teachings of Doc, the pitchman.

"How many refunds?" Mike asked Glick after the first act.

"One," Joe replied.

"Probably a cousin of Merman," said Mike.

Betty Garrett, a green understudy when the curtain went up, gave a brilliant performance of the girl with musical teeth and played the role a full week. It was her passport to stardom on Broadway and in Hollywood.

"I don't know how to thank you, Mr. Todd," she said.

"I'm the one who's grateful," he said truthfully. Nothing gratified him as much as pulling in a long shot.

He remodeled Freedley's office in the Alvin Theater and converted it into an oak-paneled Tudor suite.

"The baronial décor becomes you," Gypsy said on her first visit, "but that"—she pointed to the copper shield with crossed swords over the fireplace—"is *de trop*."

The following day Gypsy sent him a life-size painting of herself at work, and he hung it over the fireplace.

Gypsy was in the chips, thanks to *Star and Garter*. At Mike's insistence, she bought the three-story, twenty-six-room town house built by Anne Vanderbilt on East Sixty-third Street. Its five-thousand-dollar marble floor, fountained patio, seven baths and elevator were a considerable improvement over her thirty-dollar-a-month flat.

"Hold on to it," Mike counseled her, "and it will be worth ten times what you paid for it. I know real estate."

Gypsy had found new interests. And she was writing a book, a thinly disguised autobiography.

"It's a long way between a navel and a novel," Mike cautioned her.

The legend grew and grew. When Broadway wasn't quoting his wisecracks it was recounting his latest battles.

He had recently bought the Broadway Theater at Fifty-third Street for $400,000 and was now in the process of selling it to Lee Shubert for $430,000, an unprecedented feat.

"You're a chiseler!" Shubert screamed at one point in the sulphurous negotiation.

"Listen to what's talking," Mike roared. "Now I've been called a chiseler by the best of them. Remember the traveler?"

Mention of "the traveler" was sufficient to send Mr. Lee into a paroxysm of rage. The curtain in question belonged to Mike, a memento of an early show that had been lost in transit. It had cost him nine thousand dollars, but the insurance company allowed him only one third its original value. He was about to accept the three thousand dollars when he received a tip that the "lost" traveler was at the San Francisco World's Fair, in a show operated by J. J. Shubert. Mike received a check for nine thousand dollars promptly from Mr. Lee and did not bring up the painful subject again, except on special occasions like this.

"Next thing you'll be telling people you gave me money," Mike scorned.

"I gave you something more valuable than money," the crotchety theater titan countered. "I took your arm and walked across Forty-sixth Street with you when you were a penniless barker and your rear end was coming out of your pants. After that, everybody trusted you—that walk was worth a hundred thousand dollars. I *made* you, Mike Todd!"

"Another one! Okay, you're now an official member of the I Made Mike Todd Society. I'm making you vice-president in charge of the pickpocket concession."

Mr. Lee would not take such abuse from any other man on the Street and he would have been heartbroken if Mike had treated him with any greater reverence. Mr. Lee was the hardest dealer on Broadway and Mike could get more from him than his sweetheart. The old man worshiped his nerve and knew that, beneath the crust, was a stand-up guy whose word was as good as his own. Todd had one price and Mr. Lee paid it, $430,000.

Few could best Todd in a deal or a *mot*. Mike Jacobs, the fight promoter, was one of the few who outsnookered him. In appreciation for a pair of complimentary tickets he had received for a boxing show, Mike sent a salesman from Charvet et Fils to Jacobs' office with a case of ties. The salesman asked Jacobs to make his selection, customarily one or two ties, complimentary from Todd.

"I'll take 'em," Jacobs said, pretending to misunderstand, and grabbed the entire case, some *two hundred* cravats. Twenty dollars' worth of fight tickets had cost Todd twelve hundred dollars.

He got his money's worth: the incident leaked into the Broadway columns. Everything he did was to the end of getting himself talked about, but behind the gay show-off was a cunning trader, a calculating brain respected by the smartest dealers on the Street.

"I got a flop fight coming up," Jacobs confided to him one night at the boxing promoter's home in Red Bank, New Jersey. "Nobody worth a dime is available to fight Joe Louis, and I have to go with it. How can I sell it?"

"How much you charging?" Mike asked.

"Fifty bucks top and I hope I don't get arrested."

"They won't buy that turkey for fifty," Mike told him. "The only way you can sell it is by charging a *hundred bucks* ringside."

Jacobs took his advice, doubled the price and the fight was a financial success. Todd's knowledge of snob-appeal had paid off again.

"I'm getting old," Jacobs told him one night at his home. "Why don't you come in with me? You can take over."

Todd wanted no partners and no part of the fight racket. He was shooting for more exciting game. He was learning all the ways and means of the Big Street, fulfilling his boyhood ambition of having fun and making a buck.

His generosity was genuine, and the members of his own profession, the Friars, made him their Abbot. He immediately became the highest roller in the club's history. His game was gin rummy, no limit.

One night he beat Lou Walters of the Latin Quarter for fifty thousand dollars, then, to everyone's astonishment, stopped playing. "I can't go on," he told Walters, "I'd take your club."

"Don't worry about me," said Walters, a proud man.

"Maybe you can afford to lose the club," said Mike, rising from the table, "but I can't afford to lose a good gin partner."

He checked all sources to find out what players were traveling where, and made appointments to meet them for games aboard a plane or train. Once, learning that David O. Selznick was ducking a subpoena in Atlantic City, he met him there for a three-day game. He generally lost because, unconsciously, he had a compulsion to lose, *as if his zealous drive, his life force, would die if he were not broke.*

Every morning the gin players queued in front of the bank waiting for the doors to open so they could cash his checks, they hoped. Invariably it was a photo finish between them and Harry Bloomfield, Mike's pay-off man, to the teller.

One of his favorite players was Benny Davis. Benny was a worthy opponent, and, more important, at least twenty Friars were always ready to take a piece of his action against Mike. It saved time for Mike, playing one man but losing twenty times as much.

He was taking on Davis one night when Al Lackey, Sophie Tucker's former husband, showed up. Lackey was currently down on his luck and Mike had okayed him at the Hotel Edison. When the weekly bill was presented, Mike gave him the money to pay it. Lackey had not done so.

The hotel manager complained to Mike and Mike took it up with Lackey. "I gave you the money," he pleaded. "Pay the man."

"I don't feel like paying," Lackey said.

Now Mike watched in astonishment as Lackey took the rent money and bet it on Davis against *him.*

Mike's jaw hardened. "What are you doing, Al?" he demanded.

Lackey glared at him. "Look here, Todd, don't tell me what to do with *my* money."

Damon Runyon discovered him. The famed columnist envied Mike, everything about him. He envied his appearance. Damon was a peacock and had a wardrobe larger than the stock of many men's shops, but he could not match Mike's studied casualness of dress. He envied Mike's talent for spending money. Runyon had never learned how. And he envied Mike's popularity with beautiful girls. Damon had woman-trouble all his life and he drew Mike out on the subject, not that Mike ever needed encouragement to discourse on any topic for any length of time.

"If a friend's house is on fire or somebody steals his dough you warn him, but if someone has moved in on his wife you look the other way," Mike remarked one night. "I don't see that. A friend tells you.

"On the other hand, if someone took a girl I was going with, even if she happened to be married to me, *I'd* thank him—for showing up her character weakness. It's impossible to *steal* a man's girl, Damon. It just can't be done—if she doesn't want to be stolen."

He wasn't letting on that he had woman-trouble of his own; he had to preserve the illusion for Runyon's sake, as well as his own.

Damon was frustrated on many fronts. Even his lexicon, which had brought him his greatest celebrity, was a fraud, and in his heart he knew it. No bona-fide hoodlum ever spoke Runyonese; there were a few of his incense swingers who memorized his jargon *after* he wrote it. Mike's speech was pure, as original as the thoughts it expressed: he minted more picturesque phrases accidentally than Runyon and the rest of the professional wordsmiths did on purpose.

Mike's wit was a rapier as sharp as his judgment of character. He could spot a phony before he opened his mouth.

The moment a mooch began a lachrymose tale, Mike unbuttoned his collar. "For my lump in the throat," he explained.

The instant a counterfeiter made a too-clever ad lib obviously brewed in advance, Mike cracked, "Clever *prepartee*." When standard words were inadequate he created new ones: contractors' estimates thus became "guesstimates."

He threw telephone callers off balance by starting a conversation, "How come I never hear from you?" even though he had spoken to the party two minutes previously, or had not spoken to him for five years, invariably closing with, "Thanks for talking to me."

"Don't make a Dreyfus Case of it," he would stop a speaker from assuming *his* prerogative of elucidating a point at length, or, when someone was on too long, which meant the instant he wanted to expound, he would stop them with a "Take a listening part."

He could be terse when he wished. He would never turn down anyone in trouble—"calling from the police station" in his lingo—but an unsympathetic request would bring a "How do you want your no, fast or slow?"

He had a ready aphorism for every occasion.

"A man never went broke tipping lavishly or spending on women," he answered critics of his profligacy. "Dames who want diamonds, furs and paintings make guys work harder to *get* 'em."

"Poverty is a state of mind. When you start thinking with your wallet, you're always wondering what you *can't* do instead of what you can do, and you're never going to get off your back."

Runyon tried to put him down on paper but with indifferent success. Damon's ear was trained for the *unreal*, he could not capture Mike's exuberance and translate him into fiction, for the simple reason that Mike's life already *was* fictional.

"Mike Todd is the greatest natural gambler I've ever known and the most spectacular of all the many colorful figures that have passed through the Broadway producing scene in the past thirty years or more," Runyon wrote in his nationally syndicated column on February 1, 1943. "The majority of them, like the great Ziegfeld, favored a fancier stratum of society than the Big Street affords, and few of them were known by sight to the customers who read about them in the theatrical columns.

"Mike is strictly a Broadway fellow. He hangs out with the song writers and actors and band leaders and sporting men at Lindy's. He talks their language. He hates to go to bed and will stay up as long as he can find anyone to stay up with him. He is a gin-rummy fiend and will play until the cows come home.

"Todd is a bundle of energy and craves action. He has no illusions about the chancy nature of his business. He says going broke again would be no surprise or novelty to him. He is enormously good-natured, worldly-wise in every way and one of the mob, as the saying goes."

It was the highest accolade Broadway's official historian could bestow.

"He is . . . one of the mob." Mike smiled sardonically at the line. He was *not* one of the mob, any mob, never had been, he only gave the impression he was. He had fooled Runyon, who considered himself the wisest guy on the Street. Mike sent Runyon a vicuna coat. Damon already had three vicuna coats but he was a man who sought one more of everything.

Aside from his shows, Mike was the darling of the critics. Lloyd Lewis—author, historian, editor of the Chicago *Daily News*, Franklin D. Roosevelt's "conscience" who, perhaps more than any other adviser, made the President socially conscious—adopted Mike and wrote countless columns about him. Lewis exerted as much influence on Todd's life as on Roosevelt's.

"I'm a product of pen and ink," Mike admitted. "Lloyd

Lewis and Damon Runyon invented me." He did not add that he enjoyed living up to their romantic conceptions of him.

One Friday night, after dining at Lüchow's, Mike invited George Jean Nathan and a friend, an art dealer, to the fights at Madison Square Garden.

En route in the taxi, Mike's curiosity was aroused by a package the art dealer had been carrying all evening.

"What is it?" he asked at last.

"It is a very rare porcelain jar," the art dealer said proudly and named the maker and history of the piece.

"It's not authentic," Mike said flatly.

The art dealer was outraged. "I'll have you know, Mr. Todd, that I have been dealing in porcelain for thirty years and my reputation . . ."

"The package you're carrying could not possibly contain the piece you mention," Mike interrupted. "*That* was created exclusively for Queen Wilhelmina of the Netherlands and is slightly larger."

The art dealer indignantly opened his package, positive he would prove Mike did not know what he was talking about. He inspected the bottom of the jar, then, without a word, hastily and self-consciously rewrapped the package.

Mike took a long, eloquently silent pull on his cigar and looked out the window. Nathan smiled.

A few minutes later, in conversation, the art dealer quoted a passage from Shakespeare, "But all's brave that youth mounts and folly guides," and commented that, while it was one of the Bard's least repeated lines, it was his favorite speech from *Twelfth Night*.

"It's from *As You Like It*," Mike demurred.

"You're wrong this time, Todd"—the art dealer smiled—"it's from *Twelfth Night*."

"For how much?" Mike asked.

Nathan ended the dispute. "It's from *As You Like It*," he said.

"Act Three, Scene Four," Mike added accurately.

Madison Square Garden was a complete sellout, even the scalpers were out of tickets, but Mike Jacobs found room for Todd and his guests. He personally escorted them down the aisle to ringside, past the press section to the row on the apron of the ring. With a snap of his castanet-like store teeth, Jacobs rousted three hirelings who were holding the precious chairs against the possible last-minute arrivals of VIP's.

Nathan and the art dealer were astonished to watch the fights from such a vantage point. At last, between rounds, Nathan turned to his companion. "I always wondered who sat in these pre-press row seats. Now I know." He cast an eye toward Mike, chomping on his cigar and making a big bet loudly. "Porcelain experts and Shakespearian scholars."

A few days later Nathan wrote in a magazine article: "Todd is the greatest fraud I know. He is an Oxford man posing as a mug." The same day he sent Mike a copy of *The Dramatic Criticism of George Jean Nathan,* autographed, "From one Wonder Boy to another, just to make William Saroyan mad. George."

That spring, Wonder Boy Todd went to Dayton, Ohio, where Wonder Boy Private Saroyan was stationed, to discuss *Get Away, Old Man,* his mordant study of Hollywood.

"Why do you want to produce it?" Saroyan asked.

"I want to kid the genius racket," Mike said.

"That's good enough. First, let's eat. I've discovered a wonderful little Hungarian restaurant."

"Sounds good," Mike said. "I'm very fond of goulash."

"Nothing fancy," Saroyan warned him. "Simple food prepared by simple people. Every dish is as honest as the man who cooks it. The spirit of the nation, Todd, the American flag in cotton bunting."

"You sound like a Saroyan character," Mike remarked. He looked at the menu. It was exclusively Italian cuisine.

"Spaghetti and meatballs are our specialty," a girl said. "And the lasagne is very good."

Mike looked up into the pert Irish face of the waitress. "I thought you said this is a Hungarian restaurant!" he said to Saroyan.

"Wait until you see the owner," Saroyan said.

A moment later, the owner, a genial Swede, came up. "Order the spaghetti and meatballs," he advised them.

"See what I mean?" Saroyan said as they ate their spaghetti and meatballs. "The spirit of America, Todd! It's 'My Country 'Tis of Thee,' the melting pot. People from all nations praying on their knees in the open fields at sundown. If you're here tomorrow, I've got a real Armenian place I want to take you to. Fellow plays a Jew's harp like it was a Stradivarius violin."

They finally got to the play. Mike was en route to Hollywood. If he could cast it there, he said, he would produce it on Broadway in the fall.

Saroyan wished him good luck and ordered another plate of spaghetti.

It was high tide in the swimming-pool set. Thirty thousand members of the motion picture industry were in the armed services, but the second and third teams, making second- and third-class films, were smashing all box-office records. Ninety million people went to the movies every week, and their favorites stars were Abbott and Costello, closely followed by a frenetic young man named Mickey Rooney, a dog named Lassie and a horse named Flicka. It took a genius not to be a genius.

Twentieth Century-Fox Studio, having staked *Something for the Boys*, bought it for $265,000 and gave Mike a suite of offices, a few doors from Damon Runyon, who was proving that even a Broadway columnist could produce successful films.

Mike insisted it was only a hangout and he had no intention of making pictures.

"Me match wits with these geniuses out here?" he told the press, explaining that in his vocabulary a genius was a dope

who isn't too much of a dope because he's making dough while
other dopes stand around and wonder how he does it. "I'm
happy on Broadway. I don't want no part of this rat race. The
only reason I'm in Hollywood is to cast a couple shows."

He conducted his New York office, his two shows on Broadway and half a dozen others in work through his deskful of
phones at Twentieth. He was always on the lookout for new
acts.

"I just read about a talking horse down in Virginia," he told
Bill Doll one day. "Get her."

Mike moved in fast. He began playing gin rummy with
Runyon at Mike Lyman's Restaurant or Dave Chasen's tavern,
and graduated quickly to the company of Joe Schenck, Sid
Grauman, David O. Selznick and Charles Feldman at higher
stakes. Hollywood was the gin-rummy capital of the world and
they were its royalty.

Joe Glick was dead.

It was a hard blow for Mike. Glick was the most trustworthy
man he had. Joe was horse-crazy, always trying to get even on
the last race, but he would chop off his right hand before he
would dip into the tambourine.

"Joe Glick may have been a poor man in dollars and cents,"
the rabbi began his tribute at the funeral, "but he was wealthy
in friends, not the least of whom was Michael Todd." The rabbi,
grateful for a highly successful benefit show Mike had staged
for his synagogue at the Alvin Theater that week, devoted the
next fifteen minutes of his eulogy to an inventory of Todd's
virtues.

Jed Harris, the producer, listened. He had come to pay his
last respects to a man who had weathered many stormy years
in his employ. He smiled at the memory of the cards Glick had
sent to all friends and business associates when he joined Todd.

"I take pleasure in announcing that I am no longer associated with Jed Harris," read the cards, embellished with blue-birds.

The rabbi's voice droned on in praise of Mike.

Harris, who was partially deaf, at last looked up and shattered the silence with a strident shout: "Who died?" It broke up the funeral.

THE
FIFTH
LIFE

"You're a cynic, Brock: your eyesight

is so bad you see things

as they are, *not as they* ought *to be."*

* 18 *

Enter Joan Blondell

Mike was fearful and nettled. "Do you have to sit in the *first* row?" he asked.

Ethel Merman was serene and adamant. "I don't want to miss anything." She had come to Philadelphia to see *Something for the Boys* for the first time from out front, the opening of the road-show company starring Joan Blondell, and she was going to make the most of it.

"She hasn't been on the stage in eleven years," Mike pleaded.

"You're romancing her, Mike," Merman reminded him impassively and turned to the stage. "Go fill my costumes, Joanie," she said without animus, only professional pride. She had just won the New York Drama Critics Award for giving the year's best performance in the part.

Joan Blondell was a trouper. As a child she had toured the stages of Europe, China, Australia, and almost every tank town in the United States, before hitting in *The Trial of Mary Dugan*

and the *Ziegfeld Follies*. As a member of the Warner Brothers
Stock Company, where she met and married Dick Powell, she
starred in scores of films, most of which seemed to have been
shot from the same script: *Gold Diggers, Sinners Holiday,
Lady for a Night, Two Girls on Broadway, Three Girls About
Town, Three on a Match, et alii.* She had a new name in each
picture but she was always Joan Blondell.

She was a beautiful, delightful minx and she couldn't fill Merman's costumes. Her singing voice had but a single asset,
bravery.

"I'll find a play for you, sweetheart," Mike promised her after
the debacle.

The Naked Genius, a comedy by Gypsy Rose Lee and George
S. Kaufman, couldn't miss, on paper. Unfortunately, when it
was translated from paper to the stage, it was more naked than
genius.

"Who am I rooting for?" Mike groaned. He hated it. The
more it was fixed the more he hated it.

The Boston tryout audience hated it too and, while Kaufman
was making rewrites, Mike flew to Hollywood.

He was hardly off the plane before Steve Trilling, number
two man at Warner Brothers, asked him not to make any deal
for *Naked Genius* until his company had a chance to bid.

Within an hour, Frank Orsatti, one of the most influential
agents in the industry, was at Joe Schenck's home, where Mike
was staying.

"I've seen the confidential report on *Naked Genius* given to
L. B. Mayer and his advisory board," Orsatti whispered. "You
can name your price, Mike . . . but you have to give me your
word M.G.M. gets it. Please, Mike, I'm your friend."

"I can't rig the wheel, Frank," Mike said. "If Metro is the
highest bidder, it gets it." He didn't know how or why, but
he had a gold mine.

"Promise me this much, pal," Orsatti pleaded. "That you
won't make any deal before I get back to you Tuesday."

It was a fair request. This was Labor Day week end, no offices would be open until Tuesday. Mike agreed.

The following day he drove to Lake Arrowhead to visit Joe Schenck. Several calls were waiting for him.

"I don't want any more calls," Schenck ordered. "Don't make offices out of *all* my homes."

Mike explained that he had a turkey but, for some strange reason he didn't even want to know, every studio in Hollywood wanted it.

Schenck chortled. "Good!" he said. "Make those suckers pay!"

Mike grinned. "It's all teed up for Metro."

Schenck chuckled. He loved to see Mike outsmart Hollywood's top men. A few minutes later the phone rang, this time for Schenck.

Zanuck, his chief of production at Twentieth Century-Fox, was vexed. "I thought Todd was a friend of yours." Zanuck's voice was raised in anger.

"He is!" Schenck replied.

"A *fine* friend," Zanuck said scornfully. "He sold you out, Joe. Orsatti got to him and made a private deal with Metro for *Naked Genius*. We weren't even given a chance of making a bid."

Schenck put down the receiver and turned to Mike.

"I'm buying *Naked Genius*," he said.

Mike was mystified. "I told you it was a dog, Joe," he said. "One of the *worst* plays I've ever seen. I can't imagine the kind of report Mayer got on it but I'm the luckiest guy in the world to unload it—at a price."

"I said, *I'm* buying," Joe said sternly.

Mike appealed to his best friend. "Not you, Joe, after all you've done for me. I don't know what's going on but I couldn't face you again if you got stuck with this bomb."

Schenck smiled grimly. "Don't give me the reverse psychology, Mike, I'm the daddy, I *invented* it."

He held out his hand to seal the bargain. "You're getting $187,500 and ten percent."

"Please, Joe," Mike implored. "I swear on our friendship it's a stinker. *Please* back away."

"No more of your larceny and carny tricks," Schenck said, losing patience. "Shake!"

Mike surrendered reluctantly. "I gave L. B. Mayer my word I wouldn't make a deal until Tuesday."

"Keep your word," Schenck said. "Our deal is official Wednesday."

Mike returned East, positive he would never understand the workings of a Hollywood boss's mind. He regretted that his best friend had insisted on being *it*, for a selfish reason as well as the unselfish one. If Joe had not forced him into the deal, he would have gotten at least $250,000 out of M.G.M.

He took the play to Baltimore, and it looked worse, if possible, than it had in Boston. Kaufman continued to rewrite it, and the safari staggered into Pittsburgh for six weeks. The audience hated it.

"I've done everything *I* can," Kaufman delivered an ultimatum. "I've changed every line but it still won't play. You *can't* take it to New York, Mike. Close it."

"You were the guy who wanted to close *The Man Who Came to Dinner* on the road too," Mike shot back.

"George is right," Gypsy said. "The critics will slaughter us. Fold it, Mike."

"I'm taking it to New York," Mike said, and, for the next week, he and Gypsy sat up in her suite every night doctoring the script. A great stage effect, he was certain, might save the show. He remembered the sensation his soap-bubble waterfall and volcano had caused in *The Hot Mikado* and what the mock-up bomber had done for *Something for the Boys*.

"I got it!" he exclaimed early one morning. He took a sheet of paper and drew a model of an incredible wall clock which became a waterfall, with cherubs floating round and round, as it struck the hour.

"A waterfall gets 'em every time," he said, and, for insurance, being a sucker for animals, he wrote in a trained dog, a monkey and a rooster.

He beat the notices with advertisements that read: "GUARANTEED NOT TO WIN THE PULITZER PRIZE. IT AIN'T SHAKE-SPEARE BUT IT'S LAFFS."

The adventures of Honey Bee Carroll, a burlesque queen who has a book ghost-written for her and almost marries a rich, social publisher, were not as uproarious as Gypsy had lived them. Even the character of the young artist from Marquette University, who had actually moved into her dressing room for a week to sculpt her, was, on the stage, unbelievable.

"It hasn't a chance," Gypsy groaned.

"I'll remind you of that when I hand you your first royalty check," Mike said and gave her his opening night gift, a jeweled compact.

The show landed at the Plymouth Theater on October 21— and the verdict was unanimous.

"*Naked Genius* is very bad indeed," Barnes reported in the *Herald Tribune*. "It is dull whimsy, full of stale gags and inept performing. The material is never good and sometimes terrible."

"I can understand why Miss Lee and Mr. Kaufman wanted it to close last week on the road," Kronenberger commented in *PM*. "What I can't understand is why they didn't get out an injunction or mutilate the scenery or shanghai the cast. Mr. Kaufman's direction kept things moving but I could only pray they would stop."

"There were a few animals, but even the entire Ringling Brothers and Barnum and Bailey's circus could not have saved it," Waldorf sighed in the *Post*.

Mike was desolate. He had the two biggest hits on Broadway, he had Cole Porter and the Fieldses working on another surefire musical and he had six other shows in various stages of production, but nothing else and no one else mattered. He was in love with Joan.

She had let Mike persuade her, against her better judgment, to make her first Broadway appearance in twelve years. She had risked her career as a motion picture star on a play in which she had little confidence. She had received the most devastating notices of her career, and they made no difference to her. She was in love with Mike and, to her also, nothing else mattered.

No play ordinarily could survive two days after such a panning, but Todd was determined to keep it open. He had put Joan into it to unite them, and now he had to keep her East. He had to have her near him.

Gypsy called him the next morning, extremely disturbed.

"Why are *you* upset?" Mike asked. "You called the turn."

"It's not the notices," she said. "It's the lovely compact you gave me. I left it at Lindy's!"

"Meet me in an hour," he said, "and I'll replace it."

He led her to an impressive exhibition of paintings and told her to take her pick. She decided on a huge canvas, *La Toilette*, a nude by the French painter Bouguereau.

"It isn't bad," Mike commented, "but if I were you I'd take that one . . ." He pointed to a smaller canvas. "Or even that one over there."

Gypsy looked at Mike curiously. What did he take her for? The Bouguereau cost $3,765. The smaller paintings were $2,750 and $2,100. This wasn't like Mike, even his worst enemies couldn't call him petty.

He read her look. "Please go for one of the smaller ones," he begged, "and I'll give you the difference in cash."

She couldn't do that, she took her six-foot, $3,765 Bouguereau.

"You won't leave that at Lindy's," Mike cracked.

Gypsy's faith in her Bouguereau would be rewarded; it would increase greatly in value. The $2,100 and $2,750 canvases she passed up would increase even more: One was a Rousseau, the other a Gauguin.

The second night of *Naked Genius*, Kaufman telephoned to learn the worst.

Mike chuckled. "We had fourteen standees."

"Say that slowly," Kaufman snapped. "I know you must be hysterical."

"Fourteen standees," Mike said slowly.

"Send me the statement verified," Kaufman barked. "And if what you say is true, then I'll quit show business."

It was true, but Kaufman did not quit show business. *Naked Genius* grossed, by a miracle of exploitation, almost twenty thousand dollars a week for the first month. Gypsy received a royalty of twenty-five hundred dollars every Wednesday, and Mike a net profit of three thousand dollars.

He was not surprised. "Most of the customers are in the money because of defense factory employment," he explained at a press conference. "Most of 'em never saw a play before. They don't even know what a play is and they seem frightened by the thought. They wander up to the box office and ask what picture is showing. If they're not thrown by the information that it's a show, they ask if they can go right in: they think it's first come, first served for seats and keep moving until you find what you want. Our ushers have grown gray trying to explain that the curtain doesn't go up until eight-forty, that everything in the joint is reserved and there ain't no Mickey Mouse. This is the era of meat-and-potatoes drama. Give 'em the simple stuff, down to earth. That doesn't mean that the quality of your entertainment should suffer. The result is mediocrity. Unfortunately, even mediocrity is paying off; the public is so entertainment-hungry they'll look at anything. All you can do is hope your show somehow overcomes good notices."

His office at the Alvin Theater was the capital of show business.

He heard a warning buzzer over the ringing of three telephones and flipped a key in his private address system.

"She's on the way up, Mr. Todd," the voice of a lookout reported.

Mike nodded to his aides, Harry Bloomfield and James Colligan, who sprang to action. In a matter of seconds they removed the painting of Gypsy from over the fireplace and replaced it with the original copper shield and crossed swords, a standard procedure every time Bertha visited him. Her jealousy was unabated.

Their relationship was strictly monetary. He gave her jewelry and furs, more than she could wear but less than she seemed to need. He had anticipated her visit. "Here's some security," he said and handed her a life-insurance policy for one hundred thousand dollars. Bertha looked at it. She would have exchanged it happily for Mike and a little grocery store.

Naked Genius was playing to near-capacity houses and the advance sale remained brisk when, without warning, Mike closed the show after the thirty-sixth performance.

"The show was a mess which should have been confined to the drain," his friend, George Jean Nathan, reported the obsequies, "but the public shrugged its shoulders at the criticisms and rushed to the garbage in droves. Although playing to more than seventeen thousand dollars a week, Mr. Todd, in a miraculous sudden seizure of repentance, closed it.

"Mr. Todd, his face lighted with an angelic holy glow, said, 'In show business you can't please everyone, but I believe pleasing less than half is not a good percentage, therefore in my eagerness to please the public I am closing the show despite the fact it is earning a substantial profit. I believe the money I might be losing as a result is not as important as the good will of the people who might not like the show.' "

Mike neglected to mention that, in addition to his altruistic motives, he had sold the motion picture rights—and *that* was the reason he had not folded it in Boston, Baltimore or Pittsburgh. Under the terms of the Dramatists' Guild contract, the play had to run on Broadway a minimum of three weeks.

It was a sad defeat for Joan, and Mike felt guilty. "I'll make it up to you, sweetheart," he promised.

"I hope the picture turns out better"—she forced a brave smile—"but I doubt if the Hays Office will approve the title."

"So they'll change it to *The Half Naked Genius*," Mike said.

They changed it to *Doll Face*, with Carmen Miranda and Perry Como, and it was as dreadful as the play.

It was no solace that Saroyan's *Get Away, Old Man*, picked up by George Abbott after Mike had dropped it, died in December after thirteen performances at the Cort Theater, even with a fine cast headed by Richard Widmark and Edward Begley. That made two in a row for Abbott; he had also struck out on Mike's *Beat the Band*.

Mike derived no satisfaction from anyone else's failures as he felt no envy over their successes. He was preoccupied with himself, at the moment promoting financing for the most lavish musical Broadway had ever seen.

He would show everybody, especially Joan.

* 19 *

I Love You

Everything was going wrong in Boston.

A bass fiddle player in the pit slumped in his chair and fell to the floor during a rehearsal. Mike was the first to reach him. A moment later the musician died in his arms.

Superstitious stagehands shook their heads. It was a portent of calamity, the show would never open.

The tryout opening was postponed twice because the costumes and scenery did not arrive. When they came, the elaborate lace hoopskirts for the first-act finale were crushed.

"Seven hundred bucks apiece," Mike groaned, "and all we get is enough twisted wire to make pretzel molds for the whole world."

"It's impossible to replace them," his costume designer reported, "because of wartime shortages."

Mike ignored all interdictions. Offered cheaper substitutes, he threw them on the floor and screamed, "Mother Hubbards? For a Mike Todd show? Is this morale or ain't it? I give 'em music and laughs and dolls dressed up like platinum horses. And the show goes two hundred and twenty G's, it's *my* dough and that's the way it's gonna be." He had to have and he got lace hoopskirts that cost seven hundred dollars each, one hundred and fifty dollars more than Ziegfeld's legendary lace petticoats.

Cole Porter was unhappy about the score: he had not come up with a hit song.

"What's the most cliché title in the world?" Mike asked him.

" 'I Love You,' of course," Porter replied.

"I . . . love . . . you," Mike repeated slowly. "I'll bet you can take that title, use only *three* notes—one for each word— improvise a two-finger exercise and come up with a smash hit."

"You're crazy, Mike," said Porter.

"Bet me."

"Bet."

His scenic designer was unhappy too. "That character in the script, Riviera," he complained, "is supposed to paint a mural. I can't paint a mural, Mike."

"Get Riviera," Mike ordered.

"Riviera who?"

"Diego Riviera, the Mexican muralist. He's the best, ain't he?"

Diego Rivera was commissioned to do a "Riviera" for three thousand dollars.

The book, concerning Joe Bascom, alias Humphrey Fish, a racketeer hiding out from the F.B.I. in Mexico, who establishes a numbers lottery in competition with the government, was written for Victor Moore and William Gaxton. They agreed to play it for sixteen percent of the gross in lieu of salary. Mike promptly took Bobby Clark out of *Star and Garter* and gave him the starring role. Clark was not a Moore or a Gaxton by reputation or, in general opinion, by ability, but Mike thought he was the funniest man in the world. And he was a reasonable man: he worked for straight salary, no percentage.

For Montana, a lady bullfighter, he picked Gypsy's sister, June Havoc. To complete his polyglot cast of "stars" he resurrected George Givot, the Greek dialect comedian.

He wanted the biggest and most beautiful girl on Broadway and he got her. Her legs were seventy-one feet long. Traffic was hopelessly tied up for blocks during the ten days it took a crew of workmen to erect her reclining one-hundred-fifty-foot body, painted by Alberto Varga, the *Esquire* artist, on thirty sections of Flexboard above the Winter Garden.

Mike's eyes glistened. Ziegfeld had never spent ten G's for a sign.

There were eight carloads of scenery, enough electrical equipment for two musical shows, a cast of one hundred and fifteen, forty-one stagehands, thirty musicians, and fifteen wardrobe mistresses for six hundred costumes.

Mike grinned. Ziegfeld had never been so opulent.

Every rigging line, every inch of space backstage was filled with scenery, and only a fifteen-foot bar prop was left over. There was neither room to fly it aloft nor to let it remain stationary. Mike solved the problem by assigning the bar its own jockey, a stagehand who remained at its side the entire performance, trundling it from one spot to another in a series of twenty checkerboard moves strategically planned to keep it from encumbering subsequent scene changes.

Mike chuckled. He had the largest attraction ever housed in the Winter Garden, bigger than Ziegfeld's biggest.

The hoopskirts worn by the fifty show girls, singers and dancers in his first-act finale were so voluminous no dressing room could have accommodated them even without the girls. The feat of dressing was accomplished behind screens *on* stage, and should a stagehand with a Rabelaisian sense of humor raise a backdrop, the audience would witness a mass striptease of unprecedented proportions.

"Exclusive!" the gossip columnist's frenetic voice shrilled from a Hollywood radio station the night of January 10, 1944. "The seven-year 'perfect marriage' of Joan Blondell and Dick Powell is on the rocks! After the divorce, Joan will marry Mike Todd, the fabulous Broadway producer!"

The poorly kept secret was public. It was not news on Broadway or in Hollywood. Mike had never been able to conceal his romances. He had to share his emotions. And Joan was not ashamed of her love for Mike.

His daily telephone calls to Joan multiplied. Her studio was putting pressure on her to issue a denial. She needed his advice. She wanted to see him. It was impossible. Everything he owned and could borrow was riding on *Mexican Hayride,* opening in less than two weeks.

"Call Louella," Mike told her.

On January 12, Louella O. Parsons quoted Joan in her syndicated column for International News Service:

" 'The West Coast radio announcement that I am planning to marry Michael Todd is ridiculous. I am aware that there have been rumors about Mr. Todd and myself. Although I did not know him until I went East to appear in *The Naked Genius* three months ago, I have found him to be the greatest of considerate friends. I am proud of our friendship. I hope I shall never lose it. But any romantic attachment is emphatically denied.' "

Significantly, she did not deny that her marriage to Powell was finished.

Mexican Hayride opened at the Winter Garden, January 28, with an "All-Star Cast and a Corps of Female Alps." It was a hit from the moment the impish Bobby Clark of the sudden grrrr, the steady leer and the carousel-horse lope, pole-vaulted on stage with his cane, cracked his heels like a frisking lamb and changed into disguises ranging from a Mexican flute player to a buck-toothed Indian squaw.

June Havoc was a worthy transmitter of Porter's rhymed ruefulness:

> *When your body turned to dust is,*
> *They won't care how flat your bust is.*

A sample of the subtle humor was the scene in which a woman tourist, observing a dozen Mexicans sprawled upon the ground in a siesta, commented, "I wouldn't want a Mexican as a lover."

Her guide smiled indulgently. "How do you think they got that way?"

The critics unanimously approved.

It would run 504 performances.

The only columnist who did not pull out all the stops was Louis Sobol. A few days previously, after Sobol had admired a custom-tailored shirt he was wearing, Mike had sent him half a dozen. The day after he panned the show, Mike sent him half a dozen Charvet ties to go with the shirts.

Porter lost his bet to Mike. The three-note exercise with the most cliché title in the world, "I Love You," became the year's top song hit.

How did he do it? Broadway wanted to know the magic formula.

"How do you find so many beautiful girls for your choruses?" he was asked.

"I don't pick them in the dark the way so many producers do," he answered.

"Would you amplify that, Mr. Todd?" he was asked.

He would amplify anything. "The surest way to snarl up a show," he said, "is to start playing with the girls. If I single out one, the others are jealous. And the girl I single out, I can't criticize her work."

"Are you superstitious, Mr. Todd?"

"Yes, I never sleep thirteen in a bed."

His badinage was a part of the camouflage. They would not believe the truth anyway. It was too obvious.

You had to have ideas. He didn't know where they came from but they never stopped coming. You had to have safe-blower's fingers in picking the ideas to back and the ones to back away from. That was instinct, you couldn't learn it. You had to be a salesman. You had to believe in your product. You had to be convinced it was the greatest in the world. *If you can't sell yourself first, don't try to sell anyone else.* But make sure you have something good to sell. If you haven't the merchandise, no amount of advertising or publicity will help you.

Dramatize the sale. Capture people's imagination. That was showmanship, to him the most important thing in life. Without knowing it, he had been in show business since the day he was seven years old and stood on Hennepin Avenue with a knife in his neck. He had been the middle man between Doc, the pitchman, and the public. Now he was the pitchman.

Feinting was as essential as slugging. He leaned toward Sam Langford's strategy, which actually was a variation of Doc's teachings. "I put my head out, and when he hit me I took it away," Langford had recounted his fight with Iron Hague. "Then I put my head out again and repeated. Then I put my head out again, and when he hit at it I *stayed* right there. Naturally he hit right past me. I belted him out."

Mike's philosophy had not changed essentially since he was a boy. *Have fun and make a buck. Seek the strange and unusual. Act like a mug so people will say you're not a mug. Don't go by what a man says but by what he does. Recognize your mistakes. If you can correct a wrong, have the grace to do so; and if you cannot, have the wisdom to know the difference. Never argue, repeat your original assertion. Always concede the obvious, admit what the D.A. knows. When the judge says not guilty, don't applaud, leave the courtroom. Be a rebel when you're right. Only equals can hurt you. Life is a toy balloon among children armed with small pins. If you go to bat often enough you overcome poor judgment.*

He thought of himself as a rubber ball, the kind children wound of elastics, getting bigger and bigger, bouncing higher and higher.

Liberty magazine published an article, "The New Ziegfeld," by Earl Wilson, and epitomized Todd's philosophy: "I'm just a lucky bum. I'd rather be lucky than smart, because so many smart guys are broke."

"When he was unknown," Wilson recalled, "he would stamp around the offices of acquaintances shouting, 'I tell you, I'm a genius!' He would sometimes add that he was probably the greatest showman that had come along in fifty years.

"He has such gifts of persuasion. . . . Indeed, toilers who have gone to him to complain about not being paid have remained to lend him their life savings. Once he approved a hard-up employee's $27 expense account, then borrowed $25 of it, explaining that he had to entertain some important people at the Stork Club. He silences most of his employees at such dark times with an appeal to their loyalty. One man who felt he should be paid for weeks of work got from Mike a look that was eloquent with injury. 'What are you trying to do,' Todd asked the Judas, 'make me lose confidence in myself?' "

Mike was deeply hurt. He could not honestly recall ever having whispered, let alone shouted, that he was a genius. If there were any geniuses in the world, and he doubted it, he had not met one, certainly not in his mirror. He knew Wilson had not invented the item, it must have been planted by a jealous competitor. The charge that he did not pay his employees enraged him. If this were true, why did they remain with him? The same carpenters, electricians, stagehands and office staff who worked for him when he first came to New York were still with him on every show. How did they live if he did not pay them? The unions and state labor commissions would have put him out of business long ago if he had defaulted on even one week's salary.

The article puzzled him. It hailed him as the New Ziegfeld, the most lavish spender in the history of Broadway, and at the same time accused him of heisting his office boy's piggy-bank. It made no sense. He drove a hard bargain but an honest one. Only a sucker overpaid for *anything*. He was not ashamed of his relationships with his employees. He would match any showman on the Street for generosity. If Wilson had asked Bill Doll, he would have told him that he received his full salary every week during the years he was in the Army. Mike wanted no credit for it and he would not mention it.

Mike had taken Ziegfeld's place, had pulled off three of the biggest musicals in Broadway history, and he was frustrated. He did not have a ticket for the biggest show.

He pulled strings. The Undersecretary of the Navy, Adlai Stevenson, was a friend of his. So was Lloyd Lewis, whose publisher, Colonel W. F. Knox, was Secretary of the Navy. On March 9, 1944, he received orders from the U.S. Navy to report to Fort Jay.

He passed his first physical examination and failed his second. After four days of observation on Governors Island he was sent home. The Navy would not take a man of thirty-four who had had colitis for ten years, even if he was a pal of the Undersecretary of the Navy.

He staged shows for the U.S.O. at training camps but, for him, they were an inadequate substitute.

One night he took Gypsy, Bill Robinson, Benny Fields and Frank Fay to Fort Monmouth. On his arrival he found that the first fifteen rows had been roped off for Army officers and the town's notables. He told his assistant, Sammy Lambert, to take down the ropes.

A few minutes later Lambert reported that the Commanding Officer had countermanded his order.

"Are you working for me or him?" Mike asked.

Lambert returned some time later. The first fifteen rows were filled with brass and local notables, he said, and nothing could be done about it.

"That's what you think," Mike said.

It was nine P.M., half an hour after the show was supposed to start, and not a performer had appeared on stage. The crowd was stamping and whistling. Tension mounted.

"What is the meaning of this?" the Commanding Officer demanded of Mike.

"This is supposed to be for the Army, and that means *enlisted men*," Mike snapped. "This ain't any floor show for the country-club set. If they want it, it'll cost 'em a hundred thousand dollars. Clear out those fifteen rows—or else."

After several minutes of threats and pleas, Mike compromised and let the officers and notables have two of the fifteen rows. Only when the G.I.'s had taken over the other thirteen rows would he start the show.

Playing the U.S.O. Officers' Circuit was not his idea of doing his bit. Enraged, he enlisted in the Army and, while awaiting orders to go overseas, with two outstanding hits running, he accomplished the unprecedented feat of producing three additional shows on Broadway in eight months.

* 20 *

Noble Experiment

Elsa Shelley was a Russian actress who, when illness forced her from the stage, wrote a play. It was a perceptive and uncompromising study of a fifteen-year-old girl and juvenile delinquency.

Elizabeth, a timid young virgin, induced by an older and wayward friend, accompanies a sailor to a room over a saloon and is seduced. She has another assignation with the Navy, this time yielding from patriotic motives; then she takes up with a wealthy corrupter of adolescents and, after him, a noble young violinist. The consequences, within four months, include syphilis, an abortion, arrest on a morals charge and imprisonment.

Elizabeth Versus You and I was a fierce indictment of society, the first wartime problem play to reach the theater, and Mike was the least likely person to read it, let alone produce it.

"It says things that should be said," the master of high dames and low comedy told Burton Rascoe. "I'll organize a road show and play it in courtrooms all over the country for the benefit of judges, police and city officials."

"It would be most worthy," Rascoe said.

"And good showmanship," said Mike. "It wouldn't cost anything except the actors' salaries and transportation. The set is there."

"I'll have to do this with my left hand," he told his staff. "I'm cutting you in for the headaches, the credit and the profits.

First, I'll give you a new title. *Elizabeth Versus You and I* won't sell ten tickets. Call it *Pick-Up Girl.*"

Harry Bloomfield's first concern was a theater. It was almost impossible to rent a house, particularly for a questionable drama.

"Stop worrying," Mike said. "I just bought the 48th Street Theater out of petty cash."

Pick-Up Girl, "produced by Michael Todd's Staff: Harry Bloomfield, James Colligan and Harriet Kaplan," opened at the 48th Street Theater on May 3, and received the most eloquent notices in Todd's bulging scrapbooks.

"As a piece of reporting, it is grimly exhaustive," Barnes wrote in the *Herald Tribune.* "The writing is honest, the acting uniformly excellent and there are moments of dramatic depth and meaning. You may be shocked and even moved as the figures of the work disclose an enormous crime of contemporary society."

"I beg of you," Rascoe pleaded in the *World-Telegram,* "plan to see *Pick-Up Girl,* even if you have to start saving pennies in order to do so."

Gibbs disagreed with the premise that most sexual irregularities can be attributed to a bad economic system, and indicted the play as "a mixture of the trite and the moderately absurd, just the story that might be expected from a young and sentimental reporter after his first assignment in night court."

Another critic who did not share the general enthusiasm, Irving Hoffman of the *Hollywood Reporter,* wrote a murderous review. It was not published, for the good reason that it was never delivered to his editorial office, although he filed it with Western Union. He was unable to trace the notice and secured no proof of what had happened to it, but, after that, he put nothing past Mike.

Mike had produced his first problem play and he was proud that he had. He could not understand critics like Barnes, who carped because he had not offered "a resolution of the tragedy of juvenile delinquency." He thought that the presentation of a problem was sufficient. How could anyone presume that the theater would solve problems that man, through his laws, religions and philosophies, had been unable to resolve through the centuries?

The play that Rascoe said could not miss, the play that Mantle nominated as one of the ten best of 1944, the play Garland nominated for the Pulitzer Prize, lasted fifty-three performances.

* 21 *

Catherine Wasn't Great

Catherine II, the amorous Empress of Russia, embraced her last boudwarrior in the royal bedchamber at the Forrest Theater in Philadelphia.

Mike looked at Izzy Rappaport, one of his backers. Izzy looked at Jim Timony, Mae West's gentleman-in-waiting. Timony looked pale.

"Straighten her out, Jim," Rappaport said.

"Why me?" Timony asked. "Let the critics do it."

"I'll tell her," said Mike and went to her dressing room.

"Miss West," he said respectfully but firmly, "you got to play it broader, for laughs. This is supposed to be a comedy, not a tragedy, even in Philadelphia."

She knew what it was supposed to be. She had written it and she was playing it. It was not intended to be a burlesque; it was a sex drama. She knew what they wanted in Philadelphia. She had played the Model Theater here with a muscle dance and a trick dress with a break-away strap in 1912 when he was a two-year-old sucking his thumb in Minneapolis.

"If you want to change the whole conception," she said, "we'll have to postpone the Broadway opening for weeks, maybe months, to reconstruct it."

"We're opening at the Alvin Theater one week from tonight, Miss West," he said. "Let's get to work."

She sighed. He was so impatient, always in a hurry, and, as everyone knew, she liked a man who took his time.

There was a knock on the door. The young actor playing Lieutenant Bunin, Gene Barry, entered.

"Pardon me," he apologized when he saw Mike, and started to leave.

"That's all right, dear," Mae said and turned to Mike. "I've been dyeing his mustache," she explained. "The lampblack he had been using smeared all over my face every time he came close to me."

"Miss West . . ." Barry started to interrupt.

"The best dye in the world," she went on. "I use it myself."

"Miss West . . ."

"What is it, dear?" She looked up.

Barry pointed to his bare upper lip.

"Your mustache!" she exclaimed in horror. "Why did you shave it off?"

"I didn't," he said dolefully, turning to leave, "it fell out."

"I got a new scene for you," Mike said after Barry had gone.

"Another one?"

"Don't fight me, Miss West, we're only trying to improve the show."

"But there's a limit," she protested. "Like the new song you wanted to put in tonight. The writer finished composing it at a quarter past eight, fifteen minutes before the curtain! I couldn't learn it *that* fast!"

"I didn't expect you to, Miss West," he said. "I told you someone would give you the lyrics from behind the curtain. Now about this new scene . . ."

"What is it?" she sighed in resignation.

"You're receiving the ambassador from Turkey. You look him over and you like what you see. 'The Turkish situation interests me mightily,' you say, soft and sultry. 'Come into my boudoir and we'll talk turkey.'"

There was a pained expression on Mae's face. "You're trying to make a *caricature* of Catherine the Great!"

"Let's face it, Miss West, this isn't a Helen Hayes vehicle."

Mae bristled. "And who is Helen Hayes?" she demanded sternly.

"Okay, here's something more subtle. You're holding court. I'll dress up all the courtiers in skin-tight pants. You're inspecting 'em. You sashay among 'em head down, like this. Remember, keep your head down. After passing several of the boys, you pause momentarily and say, 'You're new here.'"

She looked at him and smiled. He had kept her so busy writing and rewriting the play that she had not had time to investigate him as a man. It had been strictly business. He even insisted on addressing her as Miss West.

"Mike," she said with the languid inflection of banked-fire carnality that was her trademark, "we don't have the proper vibrations."

"Miss West," he responded, "our friendship is more important." He was still self-conscious with famous women. Joan was the exception.

"I still say," Mae West's voice came from far away, "we ought to have the proper vibrations."

He was thinking of Joan. The week before, on July 15, she had sued for divorce.

She would be free to marry him in a year. He had to be free

by then too. He felt that his obligation to Junior was discharged. Junior would be fifteen years old in a couple months. There was no further justification for maintaining the pretense and hypocrisy of his marriage. It was right, until now, for Junior to live with his mother. Now he should see and hear love in his home, not jealousy. He *had* to convince Bertha she must consent to a divorce.

Mae West had been faithful to her concept of sex since she was chosen as the original Brinkley Girl in vaudeville back in 1914. She had fought with the censors of every medium—the stage, screen, books and radio—to preserve that concept. In 1927 she had gone to jail for writing and playing a red-light-district show, *Sex*. One year later she fearlessly returned to Broadway with *Pleasure Man,* a tract on homosexuals, which was raided by police on opening night. Nothing had deterred her. She had come back with *Diamond Lil,* the "C'mup an' see me sometime" temptress, which she wrote as a novel and a play, produced by and starring herself, three times on Broadway, once in England, and in a successful motion picture, *She Done Him Wrong.* She had been one of Hollywood's foremost stars, her salary of $480,833 in 1937 being the second highest in the country. She knew what she was doing and she had no intention of backing down for a Michael-come-lately like Todd.

He respected her and had been drawn to her by something critic Dick Watts had written: "Mae West is probably a great moral influence. She takes sex out in the open and kids it; she burlesques sin instead of making it desirable." Mike figured that *Catherine the Great*, with Mae West playing as a nymphomaniac with a sense of humor, would be a fun show. But she was playing the role *straight!*

"Mike, I'm not happy about my leading man," she said, a plaintive note in her voice. "I told you to find me the biggest, handsomest brutes in town."

"I did my best," he said, "but I warned you, the biggest, handsomest brutes in town are in the Army."

"I know one brute who isn't, and he would make a great leading man."

"Who?"

"Wee Willie Davis."

"*Who* is Wee Willie Davis?"

"He's the biggest, handsomest brute I know."

"Can he act?"

"Can he act? He's one of the best wrestlers on the Pacific Coast!"

Mike brought him to New York and tested him for the lead.

"He's a big, handsome brute all right, Miss West," Mike said, "but he seems incapable of reading difficult lines like 'Yes' and 'No.' Or is he going to grunt the part?"

It was August 1, the night before the New York opening. A dismal rain spattered the windows of Izzy Rappaport's office in Baltimore. He reread Mike's four-page telegram in disbelief.

"DEAR IZ," it began, "IN VIEW OF THE FACT I MISREPRESENTED THE PLAY AS A COMEDY, I HEREBY RELEASE YOU OF THE TEN THOUSAND DOLLAR COMMITMENT AND YOU HAVE NO OBLIGATION WHATEVER."

Izzy had been in show business a long time and had backed many shows, but nothing like this had ever happened to him, or, to his knowledge, to anyone else.

"I've had winners with you and losers with you," he told Mike on the phone a few minutes later. "I'm in for ten G's and I'm staying in."

"You're dealt out," Mike said.

He was not obligated legally or morally to let Rappaport off the hook, but he lived by an inflexible code of his own making that transcended laws and conventions. He would have had no compunctions about Iz's losing his ten thousand dollars on a certain flop *if* it were a flop comedy. But because he could not deliver the comedy he had promised, it was no sale. Mike was scrupulous about such things; to him no contract was as sacred as his word.

Catherine Was Great opened at the Shubert Theater on August 2, without Wee Willie Davis or Izzy Rappaport's ten G's, before a patriotic audience that had bought four million dollars' worth of war bonds for the privilege.

Barry, playing Lieutenant Bunin, was unaccustomed to carrying a sword, and in the second act, during an embrace, his scabbard came between him and his Empress.

A covert smile stole over Mae's face. "Lieutenant," she ad-libbed with a Westian leer, "is that your sword or are you just glad to see me?"

Unfortunately she digressed from the script insufficiently.

"Catherine had three hundred lovers," she apologized in a curtain speech. "I did the best I could in two hours."

Nathan damned the play as "a dirty-minded little girl's essay on the Russian Empress, played like a chatelaine of an old-time *maison de joie*. After Mae had rolled her hips for the two hundredth time and nasally droned her glandular intentions in respect to most of the males in the troupe, even the staunchest West disciple felt faintly surfeited and would have settled, with loud cheers, for Cornelia Otis Skinner in Bible readings."

"Mae West Slips on the Steppes!" shouted the headline in *PM* over Kronenberger's notice that began: "This morning the Siren of Sex lies self-slain by her own pen. Todd has staged the show in a mighty splurge of semi-barbaric splendor, and, while Mae's Catherine was not too bad an idea, it should have been turned into a fifteen-minute blackout in a revue and somebody else might better have written the script."

Time reported that Mae's dialogue "had the specific gravity of lead, and the results, when not merely sedative, were often crushing."

As a writer, Mike concluded, Mae wasn't any better than Gypsy.

"It's your own fault," Mae West chided him. "If we had only had the proper vibrations . . ."

His mind was vibrating and therein he required no collaboration.

* **22** *

Wunderkind

The idea had come to him in Boston during the tryout of *Mexican Hayride* the previous year. He had just read Dennis Lynch's book, *Boss Tweed and His Gang,* and he was intrigued by the astonishing record of political corruption.

William Marcy Tweed, Grand Sachem of Tammany Hall, bribed the Governor, the Legislature, the Mayor of New York City and countless lesser officials. He and his cronies stole two hundred million dollars in six years. Tweed's Ring was the quintessence of rapacity. It billed the City $7,500 for two thermometers. It charged $170,729.60 for forty chairs and tables. It made the City of New York pay $1,826,278.35 for plastering one city building and $3,852,196.75 for the carpets.

"He went big," Mike said with respect. He looked out of his hotel window onto the Common—and he had his setting.

"Let's do a musical on Tweed," he told Herbert and Dorothy Fields, "using Central Park as a background. You know, graft the thievery of Tammany Hall onto the nostalgia of Currier and Ives."

Up in Central Park, the most ambitious project he had ever staged, took form.

Mike's new office was a stately residential relic, designed by

Stanford White, at 10 West 56th Street, not far off Fifth Avenue. It had seven floors with quarters for a business staff of twenty-one employees, two large rehearsal rooms and an office the size of a ballroom, its vermilion walls covered with posters of old and current Todd shows.

"Never stay in this joint alone," Runyon warned him after his first inspection, "or they may find you some morning like they did Joe Elwell, as dead as a mackerel. It was in a house just like this, behind an Empire desk just like yours."

"Who would shoot me?" Mike asked.

"It might be someone who has seen one of your shows," Runyon said.

"I've got three going and five coming up," Mike boasted, then outlined his stupendous plans for *Up in Central Park.*

"You might as well know," Runyon said, "that you are no longer in my good books since I discovered you are at heart a snob."

Mike was shocked.

"When I was in Hollywood," Runyon went on, "you used to be glad of a welcome in my set. Then you somehow wedged your way into the Beverly Hills upper-crust with swells like Schenck, Feldman and Selznick, and from that time on all I got was the back of your thick neck. Back here, where you are a social outcast, you are eager to be seen with me. How do you plead?"

"Let's go around and see Mae West," said Todd, who was tone-deaf to complaints. "She is giving her hundredth performance of Catherine tonight, in spite of your pals in the fourth estate."

"I heard you weren't speaking to Mae West," Runyon said.

"I wasn't for a while," Mike admitted, "but we exchange hellos now. Small ones. You've got to hello anybody that runs a hundred nights, don't you?"

They made the rounds of Broadway until well past midnight.

"Todd," Runyon said at last, "you are a great man."

"What," Mike asked in surprise, "do you think I've been telling you since seven o'clock?"

Up in Central Park was going into the Century Theater. Mike did not have a drama ready for the smaller 48th Street Theater, on which he held a lease at one thousand dollars a week, and he agreed to rent it to Brock Pemberton, one of his early idols, at three thousand a week.

Mike watched the rehearsal of Pemberton's play.

"There's one thing wrong with it," he said. "That rabbit."

"That rabbit," Pemberton retorted disdainfully, "happens to be *the* play."

"You don't get it," Mike snapped.

Pemberton bristled. "I discovered this play by Mary Chase. I worked with her on it. I got Frank Fay and Josephine Hull to play it. I've put *my* money in it. And you say I don't get it!"

"You don't. It's a fantasy and you're playing it straight! Elwood P. Dowd—Fay—imagines he sees a rabbit. The public should too." He had not forgotten the Lone Ranger.

"Should too *what?*" Pemberton lost his patience.

"Each customer should *imagine* his own rabbit, like Elwood P. Dowd," Mike went on. "He shouldn't *actually* see it. Elwood is an idealist, not a cynic."

"Cynic? What *are* you talking about?"

"You. You're a cynic, Brock: your eyesight is so bad you see things as they *are*, not as they *ought* to be. Like Don Quixote, 'he saw what he desir'd to see.'"

"Stick to musicals, Mike," Pemberton snapped. "This is my business."

"And this my theater. I don't need any flops. But this one is a cinch to die if you insist on using that moth-eaten rabbit."

"*Moth-eaten?*" Pemberton exploded. "I'll have you know that rabbit is custom-made and set me back seven hundred and twenty dollars. The most *expensive* rabbit ever made!"

"It'll be a lot more expensive if you use it," Mike said.

Pemberton was adamant. "This play is about a rabbit . . ."

"An imaginary rabbit," Mike interjected.

"That rabbit cost me seven hundred twenty bucks and I'm getting my money out of him," Pemberton said.

Mike pulled out a roll of bills and counted out seven hundred and twenty dollars.

"Here." He handed the money to Pemberton. "I know you don't understand art, but I think you understand seven hundred and twenty dollars."

The play, *Harvey*, opened at the 48th Street Theater on November 1, with Frank Fay, Josephine Hull and an imaginary rabbit. It won the Pulitzer Prize, had the fifth longest run of any play in Broadway history and was sold to Universal-International Studios for $750,000.

What its fate would have been if Mike had not bought the rabbit's suit from Pemberton will, of course, never be known.

Up in Central Park was almost ready.

He offered a part in it to J. M. Kerrigan, the eminent Irish actor.

"If the schoundrel is an Irishman," Kerrigan said, "thin I won't play 'im."

"Let's not be anti-Semitic about the Irish," Mike counseled.

Some Philadelphia critics panned it, the others damned it with faint praise. Mike was *certain* he had a hit, but he was in trouble, he needed money to fix it. And because of hot tips and cold dice, he was deep in debt.

Matty Fox, a U.S. Army Major working on a high diplomatic level with General Walter Bedell Smith in Europe, commuted between New York, London and Paris weekly but found time between flights to listen to Mike and, more important, help him. Fox was a promoter in the finest tradition.

"A pal of mine, Mike Todd, needs a hundred and fifty G's to keep his show from folding," he told Arnold M. Grant, his lawyer and trustee. "If you can get a client to lend Todd the money, I'll guarantee it."

Grant raised the hundred and fifty thousand dollars, in return for which the investors, Boston financiers and Matty Fox, were given five percent of the show.

Two weeks later, on the eve of moving to New York, Mike called Grant to Philadelphia.

"I want an option," Mike told him, "to buy back your investors' interest. I'll give them forty thousand bucks profit."

"Forty thousand net of expenses," Grant interjected.

"Agreed," Mike said.

"On one condition, Todd. You must exercise the option two hours *before* your New York opening, not afterward when you know whether you have a hit or not. You can't have it two ways."

Mike measured the tall, lean man in his middle thirties, a portrait of self-assurance from his authoritative, modulated voice to his expensive, conservative clothes. Instinctively he did not like Grant, but he recognized a shrewd man. He had to be smart to represent Matty Fox. He felt that he and Grant would do business, a lot of business.

Armed with the option on Grant's terms, Mike went to Joe Schenck.

"I got a hit, Joe," he told his friend and occasional backer. "I also have an option to buy back the investment of the angels before the opening. If you'll give me a hundred and fifty G's, I can own my own show and get back on my feet for the first time."

Schenck gave him the money and Mike exercised his option, without giving a nickel in cash, agreeing to pay Grant's backers fifteen thousand dollars a week for ten weeks and then continue until the forty-thousand profit was discharged. Grant's fee of seven thousand five hundred dollars was to be paid by Todd, but never was.

"Mike Todd has so much faith in his show," a story leaked

in the newspapers, "that he wrote a check for $250,000 before the opening to clean up past obligations and buy all outside interests."

Mike's associates did not share his confidence. They had not forgotten the *Catherine* notices and feared the critics' bayonets.

"In that event," Mike said, "let's throw the greatest opening-night party in history."

That meant he would have to top Billy Rose's opening night of *The Seven Lively Arts* the previous year at twenty-four dollars per head, followed by champagne in the basement lounge. He was charging only twelve dollars a ticket, but he was determined to put on a Caesar's feast. He had some of Joe Schenck's hundred and fifty thousand left.

The mid-nineteenth century of Boss Tweed did not end when the curtain was rung down the following night. It carried on to the outside of the theater, where almost every horse-drawn carriage in New York—broughams, hansoms, barouches, victorias, landaus, tallyhos and *calèches*—awaited to convey the entire first-night audience along the snowy, moonlit paths of Central Park to a champagne and caviar party at the Tavern-on-the-Green.

"This is the finest blowout since the days of Diamond Jim Brady," ex-Mayor Jimmy Walker, an authority on parties, stated unequivocally.

The guests, among them Postmaster General James A. Farley, Democratic National Chairman Robert Hannegan and Herbert Bayard Swope, concurred.

Sigmund Romberg, who had composed the score, including its hit song, "Close as Pages in a Book," sidled up to Mike, an expression of anguish on his face. His beloved Danube was never bluer.

"My music!" he groaned. "You can't hear a note! If you don't order the orchestra to play louder—*much* louder—you must take my name off the show."

"I'll look into the matter," Mike promised, "and do the right thing."

A few minutes later he was cornered by Dorothy Fields. "Why did I write lyrics, *dear* Michael?" she hissed. "All you can hear is the *music!*"

It is an unhappy and illogical world, Mike was thinking, when Howard Bay, his scenic designer, grabbed his arm. "Eleven hundred, Mike," he protested. "Eleven hundred bucks for a pot-belly stove—and what happens? Actors stand in *front* of it the whole time!"

Mike turned to see Bertha giving Burton Rascoe of the *World-Telegram* a sisterly buss.

"No play is so bad a producer's wife has to kiss a critic," Mike growled, chewing hard on his cigar.

He wondered about the critics. It was his first operetta and his first try at a musical in period. He might have missed, but he did not think so. It was a Saturday night, too late for the reviewers to make the Sunday editions. That was why he had put on the party: he had gambled that, in the event they did not like his show, they would write about his ten-thousand-dollar party.

He could have saved the ten thousand.

"Just why Mr. Todd, whose show was a sufficiently good and sure-fire one, should have deemed it necessary to ingratiate himself with the reviewers I cannot understand," Nathan wrote.

"Todd has assembled a flawless production," Otis Guernsey wrote in the *Herald Tribune.*

"The over-all effect is one of beauty and charm," Morehouse wrote in the *Sun.*

"*Central Park* is about as big as its namesake and just as pretty to look at," Nichols wrote in the *Times.* "It is like a lace valentine or a Currier and Ives print."

Runyon devoted an entire column to the opening.

Earl Wilson of the *Post* spoke for those who attended the party.

"Everybody thought that the party was the biggest thing of all time in New York, with two orchestras and champagne at every table. When the guests left at four A.M., a cab awaited each one, and the doorman announced, 'The cab ride will be with the compliments of Mr. Todd.' I have attended Evalyn Walsh MacLean's lavish parties in Washington but she never paid her guests' way home."

Neither had "The Great" Ziegfeld.

Up in Central Park took in $311,292 the first six weeks, an all-time record for Broadway. It would run 504 performances, gross four million dollars in New York alone and show a net profit of twenty thousand dollars a week.

"What *chutzbah!*" his enemies said. "Todd's whole budget was a hundred and fifty G's. He gave Matty Fox a hard-luck story and got the one-five-o. Then he gave Joe Schenck a song and dance and conned him out of a hundred and fifty G's to buy out the angels. Schenck thought they got the customary *fifty* percent, that's the only reason he went for a hundred and fifty big ones. He didn't know Mike got their one-five-o for a stinking five percent, and Mike didn't tell him. What a highwayman!"

"What brains and guts!" his friends said. "He went into hock for a hundred and ninety thousand bucks and gave his backers forty thousand profit *before* the opening of a show that stood a chance of folding in three days. He winds up with a *hundred percent* of his own show without investing a nickel of his own, and he did it legally. He deserves to make a fortune on it because he had *faith* in it—more than his well-heeled backers who were glad to get out—plus the foresight and ability to buy them out *before* the red board went up. What maneuvering!"

Friend and foe had to admit he was the shrewdest operator on the Street.

He had picked up a copy of the *New Yorker,* Junior's, and begun reading a story about a Jewish family by Arthur Kober. One paragraph reminded him of his father, and instantly he knew what he wanted to do as his next play. He even had the title, *Bella's Got a Fella.*

The following day he collected several Kober stories and commissioned the author to write a comedy. In time he hired Elmer Rice of *Street Scene* fame as the director, rented the Wilbur Theater from the Shuberts and went into rehearsal. The box office was opened and in a week he had a twenty-thousand-dollar advance sale.

On a hunch, he invited the Boston drama critics, who were in New York for the opening of *Up in Central Park,* to the final dress rehearsal of *Bella's Got a Fella.* After the performance he called Kober and Rice to his office.

"We're not opening," he said.

"For how long?" Rice asked. He was accustomed to postponements.

"Never," said Mike.

They were shocked and incredulous.

"Why, Mike?" Kober recovered first. "It got laughs!"

Mike nodded. The show had gotten laughs but not the kind his sensitive ear had expected.

"I wanted to do your story, Arthur," he told Kober, "because it reminded me of my father. My father was a good man, a good Jew and a good American. When we moved to Bloomington, outside Minneapolis, we were freaks. Few people in Bloomington had ever *seen* a Jew before." Mike's face softened in remembrance. "My father won them over, by what he was. He was the greatest American citizen I've ever known."

Mike paused. "I intended this as a valentine. It came out a caricature. An anti-Semitic one at that. I watched their faces tonight. They were laughing and snickering *at* the play. And at the image of my father. It would not cost me a cent to open the show, and it is going to cost me a lot of money *not* to open it but I have to do it. If I didn't, it would defeat the cause for which I set out to do the play. It would be a betrayal of my father and a betrayal of my people."

Kober wept unashamedly. Rice threatened a lawsuit.

Mike, unmoved by either, asked Lee Shubert to cancel his contract for the Wilbur Theater.

"Lee Shubert may be a miserable s.o.b. to everyone else on the Street," Mike reported at Lindy's that night, "but he tore up the contract immediately, even without asking J.J. That's why he's a Shubert. The phony and the blowhard are afraid of sentimental gestures, afraid of getting a reputation as a nicer or softer guy."

Mike Todd proposed but, more often than not, Avrom Goldbogen disposed.

He strolled along the Street and the marquees passed in memory . . .

Music Box—Sam Harris Presents OF MICE AND MEN

He had made those same lights spell: *Michael Todd* Presents STAR AND GARTER, with Gypsy Rose Lee

Alvin Theater—Sam Harris Presents I'D RATHER BE RIGHT, with George M. Cohan

He had made those lights spell: *Michael Todd* Presents SOMETHING FOR THE BOYS, with Ethel Merman, Music by Cole Porter

Winter Garden—The Shuberts Present HOORAY FOR WHAT?, with Ed Wynn

He had made those lights spell: *Michael Todd* Presents MEXICAN HAYRIDE, with Bobby Clark

Century Theater—Michael Todd Presents UP IN CENTRAL PARK

Never before had this theater housed such a hit.

He had produced four shows in less than a year, and three of them were running.

He had been flattened his first two times on Broadway but he had scored the next seven times, at the box office or in the critics' columns, or both. He had won every big one. And he had done it all in less than seven years from the night he walked under those marquees after the lights had gone out on his *Man from Cairo*.

He had taken 'em all on. Sam Harris, Max Gordon, the Shuberts, Brock Pemberton, Vinton Freedley, Jed Harris, Billy Rose and Ziegfeld . . .

Mike Todd was the *Wunderkind* of the theater by their lights.

THE
SIXTH
LIFE

"When you know what you can do,

do something else."

THE
SIXTH
LIFE

⁂

"When you know what you can do,

do something else."

* 23 *

The General

It was May 1, 1945. The Third Reich was crumbling. Total surrender was a matter of days, possibly hours.

The U.S. Army jeep burrowed deeper into the heart of Germany. No other American equipment or personnel was in sight. Suddenly, over a rise, the jeep was stopped by a roadblock. Two Nazi sentries came up with drawn bayonets.

The American officer seated next to the G.I. driver presented his credentials, an order with an official stamp, somewhat smeared, on the bottom.

It satisfied the Nazis, so much so they threw down their arms. Every Kraut in the country was looking for a deal.

"I'm not the give-up guy," the American officer said. "They'll be coming along soon, maybe a day or two. All we want are some supplies."

They were given all the supplies they requested and went on, into the no-man's land between American and German lines. The driver, named Bosco, wanted to stop now and then to accept one of the villages offered in surrender, at least to spend an evening with a beautiful *fräulein,* but the officer, Mike Todd, would not have it.

"We don't stop until we get to Berlin," he said. It was a command.

Todd was nearly killed in Nordhausen, a village in the center of Germany.

An ancient chain in a men's room almost ended his career. He pulled it. It was stuck. He pulled it again, harder. It was still stuck. He gave it a third jerk and looked up, fortunately. He had pulled the water tank loose. He ducked instinctively and that saved his life. Otherwise he would have been decapitated.

He shuddered. He could see the snide cracks in the gossip columns and he could hear the derisive laughter echoing along Broadway. "Mike Todd killed heroically under fire . . . in the line of duty." It had been a close call, his name had almost become a synonym for gents' room accidents.

They continued eastward, racing against the inevitable surrender.

Twelve miles outside Berlin they were stopped by another roadblock. Mike flashed his orders. The sentries did not throw down their arms and surrender. They were Russian soldiers.

Todd and Bosco were taken into custody.

"Who are you and why are you going to Berlin?" a Russian officer demanded.

He was Mike Todd. That answered both questions. He was going for the sake of *going.* He never missed a first night, and V-E Day in Berlin would be the season's top opening.

The Russians ordered him kept under guard until his story was checked, but he talked them into taking him toward the city. Germany's capitulation came on May 7, and on that same day Avrom Goldbogen celebrated war's end in Berlin, the first American in the city *unofficially.*

He remembered Hitler's triumphant jig over the corpse of France, and he did his own dance in front of the Adlon Hotel.

But he wasn't kidding himself. He wasn't a fighter, he was a tourist.

This was his third trip to Europe for the Army and this time he was determined to accomplish something.

He had not gone in for glory but, as in everything else he did, out of compulsion. He had not taken any bows. He had ducked cameras as if he were a criminal, not that it was necessary if a senior officer was around. The uniform was sacred to him and it did not come from Abercrombie and Fitch, as the creeps at Lindy's claimed. He had not had *time* to get tailor-mades. It was trivial, but what wasn't on Broadway? Like the professionals, most of them 4-F gossip columnists, who went around slobbering, "How can you sit there and drink Scotch when men are out there dying?"

Now he was out here dying, of boredom. The war had been the most quixotic and frustrating experience of his life. His undisciplined mind could not function in a disciplined organization. He was born a rebel, an enemy of conformity and standardization. He had to express *himself* in order to exist. Assembly-line thought and action was, to him, hideous bondage. He could not be middle link in a chain of command, he had to command. He was too impatient to wait for red tape to unravel, he lived by one word: *now*. The endless, senseless waits and waste were, in his book, the greatest crimes man could commit. He had hoped it would be different.

He had done so little. He did not consider entertaining the G.I.'s with condensed versions of *Star and Garter* and *Up in Central Park* serious contributions to the war effort. He could have put on better shows if they had let him have his way.

Nürnberg Stadium impressed him. "I got a great finish," he told U.S. Army officials after he cased the amphitheater, but they rejected it with horror.

"This is the heart of Bavaria," he was told. "Hitler's National Socialist party held its annual conventions in the stadium. We are liberators and must make *friends* with these people."

"Who won the war?" Mike asked.

"You don't understand, Todd. Diplomatically . . ."

He did not wait, but went to the Commanding General.

"Sir," he said, "I got a great finish for the show tonight. During the big fireworks finale, let's shoot down the swastika from the center pole of the stadium." Avrom Goldbogen was talking.

The Commanding General considered the request. "Go as far as you like," said General George S. Patton, and handed him one of his silver revolvers to make certain it was done right.

He liked Patton but soon became, to his astonishment, one of his press agents. Mike was not used to getting second billing. Neither was General Patton.

He was almost tempted to pull his white card. He was a general too. His identification card read: GENERAL GRADE. He was self-conscious about flashing it and did so only in emergencies. The first time he showed it, a colonel saluted him and introduced him to fellow officers as "General Grade." Mike never found out whether he was kidding or not. On second thought, momentarily blinded by Patton's silver pistol, he decided not to match rank with the original Blood and Guts.

He had used rank to make a special short-wave broadcast to the United States, with a personal message to "J. B." Joan was making a film with Clark Gable but stopped the shooting to listen. Mike was certain she was flattered. She was.

Broadway seemed far away. Its news neither cheered nor depressed him, not even when Rodgers and Hammerstein brought in another smash hit on April 19, *Carousel,* based on *Liliom.*

Molnár had been shocked six years before, aboard the *Rex,* when Mike had asked for the rights to make a musical out of the play. The Hungarian playwright had dismissed it as a Toddian pipe dream.

Mike sighed and thought of Liliom's dying speech to Julie. "*Nobody's right . . . but they all think they are right . . . A lot they know.*"

It was V-E Day plus ten, but the Battle of Red Tape continued at the Paris Headquarters of Special Services on the Rue de Rivoli.

"The boys will need more entertainment now, not less," Mike stated at the daily conference. "While the war was on, there was no need for morale. There was excitement, the excitement of survival."

His first idea was to bring the annual All-Star Major League baseball game to Europe.

A. B. (Happy) Chandler, the commissioner of baseball, was appalled at the thought. "What if the plane crashes?" he asked. "No more baseball."

"No moxie," Mike snapped. "I've located one of the best circuses in Europe," he reported at the conference the following day. "The Knei Brothers, a Swiss show. It's in Bern. I'll fly over today and make 'em an offer."

"Not so fast, Todd," said General Beatty, the Purchasing Officer. "Permission to begin negotiations must come from Washington. Make your request for transportation to Captain Clayton."

"But, General, that will take . . ." Mike protested.

"Protocol," General Beatty cut him off. "Captain Clayton will expedite it. Your travel orders will come through in ten days."

An hour later Mike was in the office of the head of the Swiss Legation.

"I got to have a visa to Switzerland," he said.

"That must come through the U.S. Army," the Consul told him. "You *are* in the services?"

"I'm a Consultant to Special Services," he said, "and I'm by-passing the military. I got to have a visa *now*, not ten days from now. You Swiss are practical, realistic people. Here's an opportunity to get a deal for one of your own circuses. The Swiss will make a buck and G.I. morale will be lifted. That's what you and I are here for."

Mike pulled out his wallet and flashed his white card.

The Consul's eyes widened. "Yes, *General*," he said with deference and reached for a visa form.

"While you're at it," Mike said, "back-date that visa ten days."

The Consul looked up questioningly, shrugged and antedated the visa ten days. "I'm doing this for one reason, General," he said. "When I was in New York in 1939 I went to your *Hot Mikado*. Best musical I ever saw."

"Thanks," Mike said. "It's the best musical I ever produced. The purest."

A few minutes later, at Headquarters, Captain Clayton inspected the visa with a quizzical smile. "You'd think the ink would dry in ten days, wouldn't you?" he asked in a lazy southern drawl.

"You would have done the same thing, Clayt," Mike said. "I've been watching you, pal. You're the best promoter in Paris."

"The *second* best." Captain Clayton smiled.

Mike shook his head. "Nobody can *appropriate* stuff like you can. Trucks, gasoline . . . even that warehouse of harmonicas in Germany. I don't know *what* you traded them for, but I can imagine. You're sharp, Clayt. Where did you come from?"

"I'm a hillbilly from Morgan, West Virginia. My daddy was a pretty good trader, but I took a postgraduate course with General Patton. The first day he told me that all I had to learn were two words: 'liberated merchandise.' He said they covered a multitude of goods."

"Liberate me travel orders, pal," Mike said.

The phone rang. Captain Clayton answered it. "A dozen golf balls?" he repeated the request. "What brand?"

Mike regarded him with genuine admiration. General Patton would have been proud of him.

It was difficult to get to the border that turbulent May after surrender. They could not get into the airport.

"If I was you," said Bosco, his chauffeur, "I'd go back to Dijon. There's no Army there yet, at least very little."

They went to Dijon and found a small plane, a one-motor L-5, on the deserted airfield.

"I need your plane," Mike told the pilot and flashed his identification card.

The pilot was unimpressed. *This joker is no General,* he surmised. *He probably stole that card, like I stole the plane.* Everything was liberated merchandise now.

"No gas," he said.

"Get him gas, Bosco," Mike ordered.

Bosco jumped in their jeep and, a few minutes later, returned with a load of fuel.

They took off. They were in the air two or three minutes when Mike noticed that something was missing from the instrument panel.

"Where's your radio?" he asked.

The pilot shrugged and continued to climb.

Mike did not like the way he was handling the ship. "Get me down," he said.

"Too late," the pilot said.

"Get me down!" Mike repeated. "That's an *order.*"

The pilot reluctantly landed and, after Mike left, took off alone. Mike watched him lift the ship, unsteadily, to one hundred fifty feet. Suddenly a wing sheared off and the plane plummeted to earth. Mike had to run to escape being hit by it.

He pulled the pilot out of the wreckage and, with Bosco, whom he caught as he was leaving the field, took him to the Catholic Hospital. The pilot had suffered a broken pelvis and back injuries.

"In this world it pays to speak up," Mike told Bosco as they headed for Switzerland. "If I hadn't, I might have been killed."

"Yes, General," Bosco said.

"Forget rank," Mike said. "We're entering a neutral country. Break out the civilian clothes."

A boy about seventeen years old was thumbing for a ride on the outskirts of Bern. Mike picked him up.

The boy took inventory of Mike in his civvies. "You are an American on a diplomatic mission," he said.

"And what about you?" Mike asked.

"I'm looking for life," the boy said casually. "I think I can find it with you. You *are* life."

This kid ain't for real, Mike thought. "What's your name?" he asked.

"Urs. U-r-s. And I might say that, no matter what your mission is, you cannot complete it without me."

"How come?" Mike went along.

"In the first place, everything in life is six to five against . . ."

"That isn't original, son," Mike said sternly.

"Nothing is original," the boy said.

"Damon Runyon happens to be one of my best friends," Mike said. "I don't like to see people stealing his lines without giving him credit."

"You *know* Damon Runyon?" Urs asked in disbelief.

"I told you, he's one of my best friends."

The boy embraced him emotionally. "We're blood brothers. I *worship* Damon Runyon. I've read everything he has ever written, several times. I can quote him all day or, as the master would say, 'more than somewhat.' "

"Where did you load up on Runyon?" Mike asked.

"The same place I read the New York *Times* every day and the *New Yorker*—everything American—at the U.S. Legation library. I grab all the U.S. reading matter first."

"I'll bet you're the biggest pest in town," Mike said.

"That, as the master would say, 'is a very nice price indeed,' " the boy responded.

Urs spoke half a dozen languages fluently. Within an hour after their arrival in Bern he had promoted the best quarters in the city, a car, food and drink.

There were approximately two hundred American fliers interned in and around Bern. In addition, the Swiss government and travel bureaus were encouraging G.I.'s to visit their country for vacations and honeymoons, legal and informal. It was the loveliest country in the world for touring, but something was wrong.

"The exchange is all screwed up," Mike said.

"It was established at fifty francs to a dollar," General Beebe, the U.S. Army Purchasing Officer in Bern, told him.

"Some jerk in Washington pegged the franc at fifty to a buck," Mike said, "but no one told the bartenders and broads over here. Another thing, if we're supposed to help the economy of these countries, let's *really* help."

"On whose authority?"

Mike flashed his General Grade card.

Post Exchange cards were issued to civilians in the government employ, and the Swiss government was persuaded to place a nominal cost for a tour of its famous resorts for G.I.'s. This done, Mike was ready to deal with the Knei Brothers Circus.

After reaching an agreement with the circus owners on specific dates, the transportation of rolling stock and other general details, Mike went to General Beebe to arrange passports for the three hundred performers and crew.

A few days later Mike collected the applications from the Knei Brothers Circus and, to his consternation, sixty had answered after the question of nationality, "Unknown."

"That means they're Nazis!" Mike shrilled.

"They're good circus performers," the negotiator for the Kneis parried.

Mike stiffened. He had just come from a German concentration camp, one of the first Americans to inspect it after the Nazi surrender. Avrom Goldbogen still smelled gas.

He told General Beebe he was dropping negotiations. The General did not understand Mike's mission and, becoming suspicious, sent a rocket to Paris asking some questions about him.

"PERSON CLAIMING TO BE MICHAEL TODD MUST BE IMPOSTER," came a reply from HDQ in Paris. "TODD CANNOT BE IN SWITZERLAND BECAUSE HE IS IN PARIS. HIS VISA TO SWITZERLAND HAS NOT YET BEEN ISSUED. HOLD IMPOSTER FOR QUESTIONING."

General Beebe sent the Military Police to haul in Todd for questioning.

He was gone.

In Paris, on the Rue de Rivoli this Monday in June, the Executive Secretary-General, an Englishman, shuffled his papers to begin the regular staff meeting.

Mike stood up. "I want to make a report on my trip to Switzerland," he said.

The Secretary-General glared at him. "No sarcasm, old boy, please. Only five days have passed since you applied for your visa. You will get it five days from now, not one hour sooner."

"I went to Bern," Mike said, "and I negotiated with the Knei Brothers Circus but . . ."

The Secretary-General's hackles rose. "I told you," he interrupted, "your visa to Switzerland will not be issued for five days."

"Okay," Mike sighed, sitting down. "Let's pretend I'm going *back*."

In a sudden flash, everything was crystal-clear to him, all the inane parroting about him. He did not have to listen to another word, nor remain another minute. He had learned more about men in the E.T.O. this last minute than he had in all his previous experience. The pros made the decisions. They had only one thing in common with the dilettantes: *They didn't want the war to end.* They didn't want to go back to civilian responsibility and morality. If they weren't killed, and that wasn't much of a risk if they played it smart, this was the softest touch in the world. They didn't have to dig up eating and rent money every week. These were the best years of their lives and they knew it.

"Too bad it's over," Bosco had sighed honestly.

It made him sick. He thought of the famous crooner who came over with his press agent, got a million dollars' worth of publicity and would not even put on a show. He thought of the Hollywood "he-man" who had to be shipped home because he was afraid to leave Headquarters and go out where the *men* were. He thought of the Hollywood tough guy who proved how tough he was by getting drunk every night and shooting the locks off officers' doors. That was why he liked Marlene Dietrich. She might be ninety-nine percent hokum, he admitted, but the *one percent* left was so much greater than everyone else he had seen in show business out here, it was no contest.

He had not thought he could be disillusioned, but he was. In some things he was still naïve. He had taken his job seriously.

Abe Lastfogel, head of the U.S.O., stopped him at Lindy's on his first night back. "You've gone too far, Mike," Lastfogel said gravely. "I hear you've been impersonating a General. You can get in a lot of trouble for that. This is *war*, fella!"

Mike did not bother to reply. Nobody would believe he was a *bona-fide* General. He had asked for the rank only because he had wanted to *do* something; he had found out on his first two trips that he could not get anything done as long as he was a mere one-star General. He would have gone as an office boy if it would have done any good. Unfortunately, a man's authority was weighed by the stars on his shoulders.

At least he was one of the most unusual generals in the history of the United States Army. He had not turned in an expense voucher or used his Post Exchange card or cashed a pay check. He kept returning the checks.

It was over and Mike had no complaints. He had done his best.

It could have been worse. He might have been killed in the crash of the little L-5 at Dijon, not to mention in the john at Nordhausen.

* 24 *

To Be or Not To Be

He skimmed through the clippings that had piled up while he was overseas.

Collier's magazine had published another article on him. "Mike Todd has the soul of a pitchman and the ambition of a Napoleon," John Chapman wrote in the May twelfth issue. "He's a reticent enemy and an industrious friend. He never lets his dislikes become public brawls. Joe E. Lewis, the comedian, succinctly characterized him by remarking, 'He definitely belongs on a runaway horse.'"

"The only things that really matter to Mike Todd are Mike Todd, the theater and Michael Junior," John K. Hutchens wrote in the *New York Times Magazine* of May 13. "He's a born gambler, on Broadway the stuff of heroes, with a flair for showmanship and the gift of good judgment. He has the indefinable old-fashioned quality called 'color' and is almost certainly going to be a legend."

Louie Sobol had done a character study of him for *King*

Features. "Todd is about the shrewdest showman in America," he wrote. "He is also a free-spending, reckless wizard who made so much money on *Star and Garter* that he was able to lose thirty thousand dollars on one day's wagering on the horses. He considers himself a rough and tumble mug, points with pride to the fact that he didn't graduate from public school and just had enough schooling to read box-office grosses and distinguish an ace of spades from a king of hearts. He is right out of a movie of the old-time Bowery. Slant a derby on his head, dress him in a Lou Levy, let him lip one of his cigars, set him to jiggy and you have a picture of the type chap he seems to be."

He was mildly amused. He was still good copy because *Up in Central Park* was still playing to standing room only. Now they were analyzing him. "Don't get analytical," he kept saying, "you'll overdrive the green." They were judging him on what he had done, as if he intended to go on repeating himself. He was changed. Every thinking man came home from the war changed.

He picked up the book he had been reading.

"When you know what you can do, do something else."

He reread the line in astonishment. He had lived by the philosophy all of his life without knowing that Kipling had put it into words. Few people had read it, he surmised, and even fewer practiced it. It would never replace the Horatio Alger law.

Start as a chimney sweep. If you cannot find a sooty chimney become an office boy and, as soon as you get off work, sell newspapers, especially in hail, storm and flood. Work hard. Find your groove. *Keep plugging, nose to the grindstone, shoulder to the wheel and ear to the ground. Stay neat, keep your fingernails clean and never drink out of someone else's beer can. Better yet, never drink.*

Never miss a day. Let them set their watches by you. Be

ever steady and true. Save your money. Help old ladies cross the street, especially the boss's wife and mother. Tote that barge, lift that bale and stay in the groove. *Marry a wholesome girl for True Love, remembering always that the boss's daughter has as much right to be loved as anyone else.*

Sire a son within a year and name him after your father-in-law. In another thirty years, with luck and pluck and perseverance, you'll become president of the firm. For there is always room at the top of the groove. *For you, that is.* Now stay *there, fighting off all ambitious contenders by* any *means until you retire at seventy with a pension, or your son is ready to take over, or you are stricken with some fatal but fashionable disease and can live, or die, happily ever after.*

That was the formula in all business, including show business. Never change a good act. If you're Jolson, keep singing, "Mammy." If you're Todd, produce a *Star and Garter* every two years. Bankroll guys were begging him to let them back him in another *Star and Garter*, high girls and low comedy. It was money in the bank, a sure format, like the *Follies*, the *Vanities* and the *Scandals*. All you had to do, as they did, was to change the year on the marquee. Why monkey with anything else? Why throw away a sure thing?

Because it was a sure thing, he threw it away. Keeping a good thing was the biggest delusion, to his way of thinking. And Kipling's. If you lived by it you won all the battles and lost the war: you were a "success" all your life and died a failure. The big question, of course, was: What is success *or* failure and according to whose standards? The second-guessers said he was a genius for putting on *Mexican Hayride* and a chump for producing *Pick-Up Girl*. They were wrong on both counts. He had contempt for their criticism because he had no respect for their praise. Their judgment was worthless, good or bad. How, then, could he worship their gods, especially Success?

He could not and did not. His first rule of life was that there were no rules. He could not run with the pack. He had no interest in cycles. He foresaw the future by studying the past: he could prophesy what would happen the next ten years by examining the past ten years. He did not deny that each man had a definite rhythm and lived by a pattern. In his case there was no pattern, which *was* a pattern. The fact that he ran off the form *was* a form.

One of his favorite authors, since his discovery of *A Message to Garcia*, Elbert Hubbard, had said that a retentive memory was a good thing but the ability to forget is the true token of genius. He was going to forget everything he had ever done, especially his successes. He was interested solely in setting precedent, not in conforming or copying, least of all himself.

The war had sobered him. He wanted to become many Todds before he was forty. He knew what he could do, and he was going to do something else.

He had to change his personal life too. Joan would receive her final decree on July 28, and would be free to remarry. But he would not be free to marry her. Although Bertha, at last, seemed reconciled to a divorce, she refused to be hurried into discussing a settlement, let alone setting a date. More important, he had not yet broken the news to Junior.

Junior was slight physically but he was the biggest man on the campus at Lawrenceville Prep School. He was certainly the most successful prom chairman in Lawrenceville history. With a limited budget of a few hundred dollars, he had brought one of the most popular and expensive orchestras in the country, Les Brown "and his Band of Renown," to play at the annual dance.

The name of Mike Todd, *père ou fils*, was an Open Sesame! in show business. When Junior was running the soda pop concession at the World's Fair on Flushing Meadows, Brown, a struggling young band leader, was given his first big opportunity by Mike in the *Dancing Campus*. He welcomed the opportunity to reciprocate in Junior's behalf on *his* first experience as a producer.

Junior, unfortunately, was unable to take bows at the prom for getting Brown at a union minimum fee. He was kicked in the head at football practice the day before and was confined to the school infirmary.

"How are things, son?" Mike asked when he arrived at Lawrenceville for the annual Father's Day program.

Junior, a sensitive, humble and self-effacing boy, did not like Lawrenceville because, he felt, it was a snob school, but he did not complain. It was probably no worse than most leading prep schools.

The fathers sat with their sons through an average day of classes. Mike was particularly intrigued by modern European history.

The head of the History Department, Professor Shea, a fabulous figure—a learned and devoted teacher, one of the most formidable authorities in the United States and an immensely wealthy man who had built a $200,000 house on the campus—was lecturing on the historic parallels of purges and asked for a contemporary event that compared in status with the activities of the French Revolutionary Tribunal in the 1790's.

"The Moscow Purge Trials!" came the instantaneous answer in Mike's confident ringing voice.

Junior cringed. "Don't embarrass me, Dad," he begged.

"You are right, sir," Professor Shea beamed.

"You were lucky," Junior whispered.

"Now you hate my guts," Mike said. For Junior's sake, he answered no further questions, but, when the class broke for lunch, he made his way to Professor Shea's desk.

"Professor," he said, "I think you made a mistake a few minutes ago."

Junior, a step behind him, was aghast. "Please, Dad," he pleaded. "You're in front, stop!"

Junior was only fifteen and did not know his father yet. Mike never quit when he was ahead.

"You referred to the House of Savoy in 1800," Mike went on. "There was no House of Savoy in 1800."

"Stop it, Dad," Junior entreated. "Professor Shea hasn't made a mistake in his twenty-two years here."

"Charles Emmanuel the Fourth abdicated in 1798," Mike continued. "He tried to regain his kingdom a couple years later but blew the duke to Napoleon at Marengo and abdicated again. So there couldn't have been a House of Savoy in 1800."

Junior was ashen.

"Come with me, Mr. Todd," Professor Shea said and led him to the library. He speared a book from the shelf and leafed through it, confidently. In an instant he had the place he wanted. His eyes traveled down the page.

Junior was dying.

Professor Shea's face suddenly tightened into a scowl of disbelief. "You are right, Mr. Todd," said the man who had not made a mistake in twenty-two years, "and I was wrong."

Mike's bootleg reading had paid off again.

Junior, his mouth unhinged, stared at his father. "Dad," he said in awe, "this is your greatest moment. You'll never top it."

Mike was happy, not for showing up Professor Shea but for making Junior more proud of him than he had been the Christmas Day he and Kute Kris Kringle had given him three thousand bucks' worth of toys. He hoped he would always be able to top himself with Junior.

"Michael Junior should be very proud of you," Professor Shea said.

"Professor," Mike said, offering him a cigar, "a father has to go to the post every twenty-four hours."

Things were drawing to conclusions.

The first atom bomb was dropped on August 6, and Mike cabled General MacArthur: IF HIROHITO PROVES INTRACTABLE, PUT BILL ROBINSON ON THE THRONE OF JAPAN AND CALL HIM THE HOT MIKADO.

His friend Runyon was playing out his third act too, as a courageous mute. Some time previously his larynx had been removed: he had been given the death sentence of cancer.

They were leaving the Empire race track. Mike had bet big. He could do nothing in moderation. More than a hundred and fifty thousand dollars had changed hands. Runyon was curious. He wanted to know the details, but Mike did not tumble.

"You're supposed to be the greatest reporter in the world," Mike needled him affectionately. "You pride yourself on being able to read a man's face. Read!"

Runyon studied Mike's face for several minutes and then wrote on the pad that was always with him: "I hear the stakes were between 150 and 200 G's."

Mike nodded.

Runyon's gimlet eyes were fixed on Mike for several minutes longer. Then, with great reluctance, he wrote on his pad: "Win or lose?"

Mike stared at the pad in disbelief. "That's the unforgivable, Damon," he said.

Runyon pointed to his question. He *had* to know whether Mike had won or lost a hundred and fifty thousand.

"I can't remember," Mike said impassively.

Runyon's pique turned to pride. Mike had vindicated his judgment, printed in his column years ago: "He is the greatest natural gambler I've ever known."

Mike did not know why he had become a reckless gambler and he was leery of analyzing the cause. He couldn't help it, as far as he wanted to know, and let it go at that. It made no difference whether *he* was gratified by the excitement, the important thing was that Mike Todd was becoming a legend because of it—and that was worth every dollar he lost.

Columbus Circle Theater, opening December 13—Michael Todd Presents HAMLET, Starring Maurice Evans.

"You can't sell Shakespeare," his friends kept telling him. Mike chewed on his cigar. They meant no one *else* had ever been able to sell Shakespeare. He had studied the form sheets. John Barrymore, the greatest of Hamlets, held the Broadway record, only twelve weeks. But Barrymore, for all his virtuosity, had played a conventional Prince. Shakespeare was not sacrosanct to Mike or Evans. They cut boldly across whole scenes. There were no grave diggers in their version, no "Alas poor Yoricks" and no obsequies for Ophelia. Their Prince was not a self-pitying, self-mocking, sixteenth-century psychopath but a nineteenth-century man of energy, action and authority.

Mike was producing a tough-guy's *Hamlet* and, for a lark, he costumed his strolling players to look like a pack of playing cards. He would show Broadway how to sell Shakespeare.

Evans was unhappy, so unhappy he consulted his attorneys and also went to Actors' Equity.

"I like Todd personally," he stated. "He is a competent man and most charming *but* . . ." His face darkened. "He owes me four thousand dollars and has not given me any hint when he intends to pay it. *To be or not to be, that is the question.*"

"Walk out of rehearsal until he comes up with it," Actors' Equity advised.

"Let's discuss it with him first," Evans countered.

Evans, flanked by his attorneys and a representative of Actors' Equity, went to Mike's office. Mike began talking from the moment they sat down, on a variety of subjects, all amusing and none remotely related to Evans' four thousand dollars. Each time one of them started to speak, Mike was reminded of another anecdote or the telephone rang. It was impossible to get the floor.

The soliloquy was interrupted at last by a secretary who entered and handed Todd an envelope.

"Oh, Maurice," Mike said offhandedly, giving Evans the envelope, "as long as you're here, you might as well take this."

Mike continued the anecdote where he had left off. Evans

opened the envelope. Inside was four thousand dollars cash.

Mike arranged for Toots Shor, the restaurateur, to review the opening in a Broadway column.

"How's it going, Toots?" he asked Shor during the second-act intermission.

Shor was groggy but game. "I'm the only bum in the audience," he said, "that's going back to see how it comes out."

"Mike Todd is an aesthetic and impartial impresario," Rascoe wrote in the *World-Telegram,* "and to amend an ancient motto, nothing concerning the theater is alien to his generous purse. He has lavished just as much care and money on his production of *Hamlet* as if it were a drama like *Naked Genius* or a musical like *Something for the Boys.* It is a production to see, perhaps to see twice in order to be sure you saw right the first time, in all a bizarre theatrical experience."

"Mike Todd is a zealous connoisseur of the arts," Waldorf wrote in the *Post.* "His *Hamlet* is stirring, moving, impressive and beautifully done."

"Mike Todd has produced *Hamlet* in his usual handsome style," Kronenberger echoed in *PM.* "It is swift, moving, cleanly blocked out . . . and went over with a bang."

"The undernourished theatrical season gains mightily by the production that Evans and the dauntless Todd have brought," Morehouse added in the *Sun.* "It is a *Hamlet* that has rhythm, beauty and vitality."

"TO BE—A HIT!" was the headline on Barnes' notice in the *Herald Tribune* that hailed it as "an ingenious piece of showmanship that matched eloquence with theatrical excitement."

"The event was momentous," Garland reported in the *Journal-American.* "Evans voiced his and the audience's thanks that his playwright, a chap named Bill, and his producer, a chap called Mike, had joined forces and put on a show which, believe me, they had done."

"A fine show!" Nichols shouted in the *Times.*

"Todd's *Hamlet* is clean, alive and exciting," Chapman wrote in the *News.* "It is novel in its speed, its untraditional costumes, its belief that *Hamlet* was neither melancholy nor a nut."

"A grand, fast moving, brilliantly played show!" wrote John Mason Brown.

Nathan hailed it an unqualified triumph and praised Todd and Evans "for revealing Hamlet not as a half-desperate psychopathic case and half-ancestor of Robert Mantell but as a rational figure driven to acts rationalized not by the mind but by sound emotions."

Bill Doll, returned from the war and back on his tom-toms, read the papers with genuine astonishment. "What quotes!" he exclaimed.

"I don't want any of them used, not one line," Mike said, to Bill's consternation. They had raved about Barrymore's Hamlet. And Gielgud's. And Leslie Howard's. And others. And they had lasted twelve weeks or less.

His first advertisement featured a quotation by Bill Corum, sports columnist of the *Journal-American*: "Mike Todd's *Hamlet* will remain the champ for a long time to come and will retire undefeated like his old pal, Gene Tunney."

The following day's ad had a quotation from Runyon: "Mike Todd's *Hamlet* is the most exciting show I ever saw. Real cops and robbers stuff."

"It's twice as exciting as a prize fight!" Jimmy Powers, sports columnist of the *Daily News,* stated in the third advertisement.

He let Earl Wilson, the columnist, play the barnyard scarecrow for one performance and one column.

As a result of his campaign, guys who would not have been caught dead near a Shakespearian drama dropped in to see what it was all about. He would make a hundred thousand dollars out of the show, considerably more than Shakespeare had.

Evans gratefully inscribed on a published book of the play,

"For Mike," quoting Shakespeare, " 'He's for a jig or a tale of bawdry'—fortunately for us."

The old excitement returned. He had two hits. A third, by Molière, was ready to open. A fourth, by William Roos, was going into rehearsal. A fifth, with Orson Welles, was in preparation. A sixth, by Edna Ferber, would be his first motion picture. A seventh . . .

The ring of his semiprivate phone interrupted him. Bertha was on the line, highly agitated.

"A thief broke into the apartment last night!" she exclaimed.

"What did he take?" Mike asked.

"Quite a few things—and some of my fur coats."

"How many?"

"Eleven of them."

"Did they get the one that cost fifteen G's?"

"Yes."

The robbery was dismissed with a paragraph in the back pages of the newspapers. What was unusual about Mike Todd's wife being robbed of eleven fur coats?

* 25 *

Retreat from Broadway

1946, destined to be the most tumultuous year of his life, began.

On January 9, less than four weeks after he opened *Hamlet*, he presented *The Would-Be Gentleman* at the Booth Theater, with Bobby Clark starring in his own adaptation of the comedy Molière had written and also played in two hundred and seventy-five years previously.

"I'm producing this play for Toots Shor," Mike solemnly announced to the press. "It is only fitting that I do this, because Molière and Shakespeare knocked out their plays for the Toots Shors of *their* day. Clark and I have taken some liberties with the original. For instance, there wasn't a dame in the whole first act of Molière, and you can't get away with that."

Le Bourgeois Gentilhomme was originally a satiric comedy about an upstart boob, M. Jourdain, who ached to shine in high society. Everyone swindled and snickered at him: the dancing masters and fencing masters he hired to teach him the graces, the Count who was to present him in Court, the Marquise with whom he craved a modish liaison, and even his tailor.

"At this point," Clark scrawled a typical notation in the script, "I toss a snuffbox into the pocket of a lackey across the stage. I can do this, Mike, I've practiced all summer."

Clark romped across the stage as the outrageous dolt, his voice now gargling in his throat, now baying like a hound's at the moon. Sascha Guitry and the cast of the French Repertoire Theater, who were making an American tour, hailed Clark's performance as greater than any portrayal of the role at the *Comédie Française*, and the New York Drama Critics would give him their annual award for acting; but half of that jury felt that his gifts as a buffoon failed to conceal his inadequacies as an adapter.

"There isn't a line of genuine humor in the script," Gibbs knelled in the *New Yorker*.

"A wonderfully funny show," Barnes disputed in the *Herald Tribune*.

"It does not make for a full evening's happiness," Nichols disagreed in the *Times*.

"It looks as though Todd has another hit," Vernon Rice raved in the *Post*. "Clark is a riot, a scream, a howl."

"It's more horseplay than play," Morehouse groaned in the *Sun*.

"How odd of God to choose Mike Todd," Irving Hoffman, Broadway sentinel of the *Hollywood Reporter*, began his devastating report.

"It is frequently a belly-buster," Nathan recorded. "Todd should ignore his critics. Molière had plenty of deriders in his own day."

"It never was much of a play," *Time* concluded.

Mike could not afford to give the play another thought even if he had wanted to. He was opening another show in Newark and negotiating to buy an office building, a transaction that would introduce him to the greatest bankroller he would ever know.

"Why should I meet this Todd?" the slender, patrician-faced man, a Legion of Merit in his boutonniere, asked Colonel John Gottlieb.

"If Mike Todd can be channeled," his chunky, leonine-faced companion answered, "he's a genius."

"But I'm not interested in show business," said Colonel Henry Crown, multimillionaire Chicago industrialist and capitalist, a widower with three sons.

Gottlieb shrugged.

Colonel Crown met with Mike at the Plaza Hotel. When Mike mentioned that he had an option to buy an office building on which his lease was expiring, Crown agreed to the financing.

"If you are satisfied it is a good buy," he said, "I'll lend you a hundred thousand dollars to purchase the equity. How long will you need it for?"

"One year," Mike said.

"Okay," said Crown.

It was not an important investment for Crown. He had recently bought the United Artists Theater in Chicago from William Zeckendorf, and was now negotiating with Zeckendorf to buy the land on which the United Nations ultimately would be erected, a transaction involving twenty million dollars. Crown later became a director of Hilton Hotels Corporation, Columbia Pictures and Rock Island Railroad, among other companies.

January Thaw, adapted by William Roos from a Bellamy Partridge novel, was a featherweight comedy about rural life in Connecticut. A New York writer and his family are coerced, by lease, to share a farmhouse with the original occupants: a crusty, self-reliant farmer, his old-fashioned wife and their wolfish, shiftless son. The two clans squabble over everything from politics to plumbing, from who owns what to who sleeps where. The city slickers get the worst of everything, freezing and starving while the country folks are warm and well fed. Eventually one family moves into the barn.

Mike was worried about it, and with cause. He was standing in the lobby of the Newark theater, trying to decide whether he should close it there, when a gale of laughter echoed from inside.

"That's the first time I ever got laughs during intermission," he said and went inside to investigate. The audience was roaring at the antics of two members of the cast, a pair of pigs that were loose and running up the aisles. He still had faith in animals, their failure to save *The Naked Genius* notwithstanding.

He took it to New York and opened at the Golden Theater on February 4.

During the first-act intermission a critic was discussing the direction of Ezra Stone, who had recently returned from the armed services. "Ezra is clearly not yet adjusted to civilian life," the critic sighed.

Someone came on stage in the second act with a chamber pot and put it under a sofa that had been converted into a bed. Three critics simultaneously reached for their hats.

The notices were bad enough, but what hurt Mike most was that they had come from the second-string critics. For the first time since he had come to Broadway, most of the first-string critics had passed up a show that bore his name.

"Showmen, even the best of them, sometimes lose their balance when they try to occupy the two stools of Barnum and Frohman," George Jean Nathan pronounced. "Perhaps the Barnums are wiser to stick to their elephants."

It was the worst chastisement Mike had ever received from the dean of critics, and Broadway wondered how he would react to it.

Mike said nothing. It was Nathan's prerogative, as an arbitrary maker of wonder boys, to unmake them as capriciously. And it was Todd's right, as a producer, to stage anything he could finance. He did not want to be Barnum the rest of his life. Nathan could not understand that, because Nathan wanted to be Nathan the rest of *his* life. Almost everyone who had become a "success" wanted to remain that way without change. Mike did not. Change was the essence of life. He could change directions in the middle of a stride. He was not afraid to switch barrels going over Niagara. It was better to have produced a type of play he had never attempted before—even a foolish comedy about cretins, chamber pots and outhouses—and flop with it than to rehash a *Star and Garter* or a *Mexican Hayride* and have a hit.

He wanted the critics' affection and wooed them assiduously, but chiefly for economic reasons. He did not take them seriously. Some were more clever than others, some more honest than others, and one or two were occasionally intelligent. They knew that if you didn't throw your hat in the air as fast as to the ground, you ought to quit. But they were kibitzers. They lacked the stuff to be players. He had little regard for second-guessers *per se*. They talked glibly of artistry and lamented the lack of originality in the theater, but when he answered their pleas with experimental plays like *Pick-Up Girl* and *The Would-Be Gentleman*, their most eloquent spokesman told him to stick to his elephants. Who were they kidding, outside of their publishers and themselves? What *was* the Theater they held so sacred?

Oscar Serlin had defined it. "Don't call it theater when you're parked in Sardi's. If you're talking about Broadway, don't call it theater. Call it show business, entertainment, medicine show, fabrication, hippodrome, carny con, midway or grab-bag distraction, but don't call it theater." One of their own guys, Percy Hammond, called the theater "the shell game of the arts." It was a popular medium, and as long as it existed by the slight formality at the box office, it would never shun hokum, even in its most noble flights. Let them call things by their proper terms. It was the Age of Gullibility and he was one of its high priests, along with Roosevelt, George Bernard Shaw, L. B. Mayer, Stalin, Huey Long, Hearst, Billy Sunday, Tex Rickard, Hitler, Winchell, Aimee Semple MacPherson, Mussolini, Dr. Coué, Dr. Townsend and Dr. Gallup.

They were all in the same business. Like Doc, the pitchman, each poked a tip with the best spiel and break-away potato peeler he could find or fashion. Their own idol, George Bernard Shaw, had no illusions. "G. B. S. is about as real as a pantomime ostrich," he had written of himself. "I have never pretended that G. B. S. was real: I have over and over again taken him to pieces before the audience to show the trick of him. The whole point of the creature is that he is unique, fantastic, unrepresentative, inimitable, impossible, undesirable on any large scale, utterly unlike anybody that ever existed before, hopelessly unnatural and void of real passion."

Mike took stock. He had four plays running simultaneously. *Up in Central Park*, the magic operetta, had grossed almost four million dollars and was still going strong. His *Hamlet* would run one hundred and thirty-one performances, the longest of any *Hamlet* in Broadway history. And he had made a bold experiment of modernizing Molière. By anyone else this would have been hailed as a stupendous feat. For him it was failure. He had spoiled Broadway. It would no longer be satisfied with ordinary miracles from him.

Yet he had to try to bring in one more big show before leaving for Hollywood. The one he was preparing with Orson Welles could be, he was certain, the biggest anyone had ever produced.

* 26 *

Almost Around the World in Eighty Days

Orson Welles had been fascinated by Jules Verne's *Around the World in Eighty Days* since he was a boy in Kenosha, Wisconsin. He had dramatized it on his Mercury Theater of the Air in 1938, the radio series in which he scared the United States out of its wits with his memorable "report" of a Martian invasion.

Mike was no less intrigued by the man who raced a clock around the world.

Welles' conception of Verne's classic, as daring and more extravagant than anything he had ever attempted, included a circus with a complete assembly of trapeze artists, tightrope walkers, jugglers and acrobats; a magic show that was an outgrowth of his old enthusiasm for sawing a former wife, Rita Hayworth, in two; a saga of the Old West with an Indian massacre; a miniature train speeding across a canyon just before the bridge collapses; and primitive motion pictures, heavy on bank robberies, storms at sea with the heroine firmly lashed to the mast, runaway trains with the hero helplessly bound to the tracks, and debauchery in Chinese opium hells—the characters frequently stepping out of the flickering films to take part in equally frenetic action on the stage.

His Phileas Fogg, who wagered he could girdle the globe in eighty days, was the finest flower of the British upper classes: gallant, intrepid, ever urbane.

Confronted on the Western plains by an Indian warrior in a mask of hideous design, bent on separating him from his scalp, Fogg maintained his poise. "Ah, how do you do, sir?" he asked.

In Egypt, when sordid purveyors of vice offered him a lovely dancing girl, Fogg's manner was a credit to the Empire. "No, *thenk* you," he refused with the precise mixture of formality and repugnance.

On another occasion, he was carried off in the talons of a gigantic papier-mâché eagle. Suddenly, Aouda, a native princess, flanked by a detachment of the United States Marines, appeared from the back of the theater. She came down the aisle, grabbed a rifle from one of the Marines and fired at the eagle to the tunes of the "Marine Hymn" by Cole Porter, with overtones of "Rule Britannia" sung by the leathernecks and a group of young women on the stage dressed in Union Jacks.

Five seconds later a dozen feathers fluttered down from the main chandelier at the top of the theater. The gag necessitated the services of one stagehand whose sole duty was to drop twelve eagle feathers at each performance.

Suddenly two geniuses were reduced to one.

TODD'S VERSION

One day Orson came up with an idea for our Out West scene: someone struck an oil well.

"How do you do that on the stage?" I asked.

"You have no imagination, Todd," Orson replied.

I never had a musical that played less than a year. I suppose I've been lucky, and part of my luck is a pet superstition: I have to have a script, even a bad one. Here it was two weeks before rehearsal and Orson was still ad-libbing the script.

I complained to Orson and he said something to the effect that he had heard I didn't need a script in some of my cultural achievements, like *Star and Garter.*

"I don't mind if the script is in my head," I said, "but I do if it's in *your* head."

I had put $40,000 cash into the show and I walked away from it. *Around the World* would be a bigger and better show than Billy Rose's *Jumbo,* I was sure, and it would lose even more money.

WELLES' VERSION

I originally offered *Around the World in Eighty Days* to Mr. Mike Todd, but after some time, when it became apparent that, among other things, he was in no position to provide finances, I was forced to take over the responsibility of this myself.

Welles and his new production partner, Richard Wilson, interested Sir Alexander Korda, the head of London Films, Inc., in financing the show. Korda, who held the European rights to the title, visualized its possibilities as a motion picture. Welles did not wish to commit himself for a film and, in return for Korda's interest, signed over his rights as author.

Around the World cost two hundred fifty thousand dollars when it opened its tryout at Boston, and Welles was drawing only an actor's minimum salary. Alan Reed, miscast in the essential role of Inspector Fix, left at New Haven, and Welles took over his part. After six weeks of tryout, it opened at the Adelphi Theater in New York.

"It is a perfect musical extravaganza," John Chapman raved.

"It is a damn good show and certainly like nothing you've ever seen before," Wolcott Gibbs concurred. "It's a spectacular roughhouse, a fine musical cheese dream and I was delighted."

The other critics seemed to have watched a different show. Lewis Nichols said it was "only fitfully amusing." Vernon Rice said, "It is always on the move but it doesn't seem to get anywhere." John Garland wrote, "It is fun for Welles but not too easy on the outsider. By outsider I mean me." William Hawkins said, "It must have seemed hilarious on paper but it is just not very funny." Louis Kronenberger groaned, "There's something too hollow and half-cocked about it and its hot-foot technique leaves you cold."

The calamity lost more than three hundred thousand dollars, a new record for the course.

He had gone to bat four times since coming home from war and had struck out three times. He had gotten to first base with *Hamlet* on an assist from Maurice Evans, who, as a U.S. Army Major, had pre-tested the version with G.I.'s in the South Pacific. It would run an additional two years on the road and, stripped of Toddian extravagance, would make money.

The Would-Be Gentleman closed after seventy-seven performances. It took in $9,000 its last week, and could have run longer. Clark offered to cut his salary but Mike would not permit it. This was an old story. He had made a profit of $4,000 the week he closed *Star and Garter*. This was his pride and his code: he would not cut a scene or fire a chorus girl, he would make no compromise with quality, *whatever* that quality was. "It's the ham in me," he said.

January Thaw died after forty-four performances, and he had not even gotten to Boston with *Around the World in Eighty Days.*

He was pressing. If he had not lost his touch, he had misplaced it. "It's impossible to control people's minds in a theater," he rationalized. It was an excuse, not a reason. He was losing too much energy in friction. He was spreading himself too thin. He was torn between his Broadway and Joan's Hollywood. She was becoming impatient and he was anxious to be with her. But he could not leave until Bertha agreed to a settlement.

"The Mike Todd divorce is held in abeyance," Louella Parsons reported in her syndicated column, "because Mike can't afford the half million dollars the lady requests for his freedom. However, Todd and his estranged wife apparently are on better terms than they were. She is allowing their son to visit him in California during his summer vacation."

The story was relatively accurate. Bertha had given permission for Junior to spend his vacation with Mike on the Coast. And she had consented to a divorce. Mike's old friend, Jack Dietz, made the arrangements. It would be an uncontested suit. Bertha would receive a cash settlement—not the half million dollars quoted, but one hundred thousand dollars in two payments—and she agreed to go to South America during the proceedings.

Dietz guaranteed payment. Mike was in the middle of a losing streak, on stage, at the pari-mutuel windows and at the Friars Club. He played gin rummy at ten dollars a point and lost fifty-three thousand at one sitting. He was making only twenty thousand dollars a week but he was not discouraged. He was confident things would get better.

A position as an executive producer at a fabulous salary, even at Hollywood standards, plus a percentage of the profits of all pictures he made, awaited him at Universal-International Studio on the Coast. He needed a property, and the one he liked, Edna Ferber's *Great Son,* was priced at two hundred thousand dollars.

He was tapped out on Broadway. He thought a moment and called Henry Crown in Chicago. After much negotiation Crown lent him the money to take an option on Miss Ferber's novel.

Michael Todd (left) at the age of five, with his brother and sister, Frank and Edith, and his mother, Sophia Goldbogen

Chaim Goldbogen, Michael Todd's father

Michael Todd (age twelve) and friend

Michael Todd at seventeen

Michael Todd and Michael Todd, Jr. (Los Angeles, 1931)

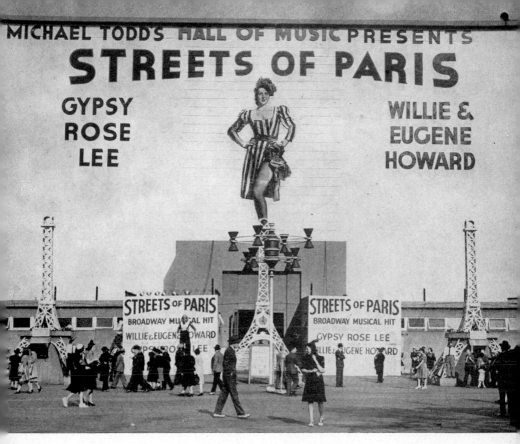

World's Fair, 1940

Left: At Gay New Orleans (World's Fair, 1940)

Mayor Fiorello H. La Guardia and Michael Todd during an intermission of *The Hot Mikado*, at World's Fair Grounds, 1939

Michael Todd with Michael Todd, Jr., during a rehearsal of *Star and Garter*, 1942

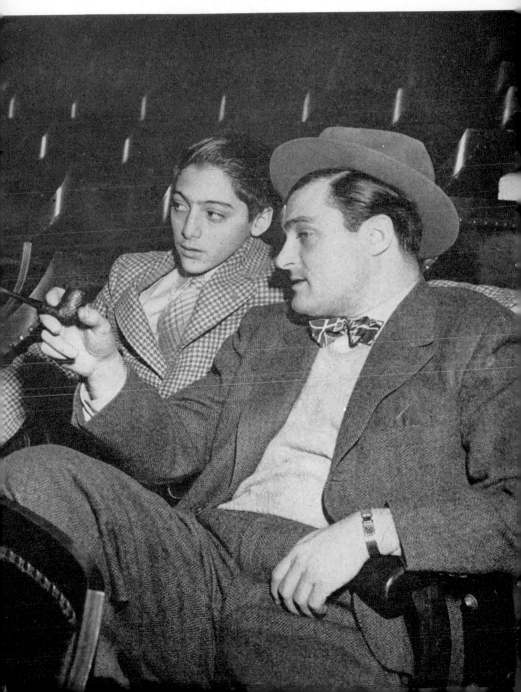

Michael Todd looks over the line of legs of the swimming chorus for his
production of *A Night in Venice* (Jones Beach, New York, 1953)

Michael Todd with Cantinflas and David Niven during production of
Around the World in Eighty Days

Michael Todd, Elizabeth Taylor and Fernandel at party celebrating
opening of *Around the World in Eighty Days*

(photo by Toni Fr

Michael and Elizabeth Todd and daughter Elizabeth Frances

Mike faced one of the most important decisions of his life. He had never promoted anyone for the sake of promotion. He had always had plenty of backers, but almost all of them were in show business. Men like Joe Schenck, Joe Moskowitz, Izzy Rappaport and Arthur Gottlieb of Du-Art Film Laboratories knew what they were doing when they invested in his shows. They had never lost a quarter on him. Henry Crown was different. He owned the Material Service Corporation and the Marblehead Lime Company. He bankrolled million-dollar deals and had a reputation for being impregnable.

Yet he had gotten through twice easily. The temptation was too great. Mike couldn't help himself. A man like Todd, who has contempt for his own money, cannot have much respect for the money of others.

"I have to go to a business meeting in Chicago," he told Arnold Grant a few days later. "I need a lawyer to sit in with me."

Grant accompanied him to Chicago and met Crown for the first time. Harry Wyatt, general counsel for the Crown interests, and John Gottlieb were present at a meeting when Crown agreed to make Mike a further loan—which would make the total indebtedness half a million dollars—so he could liquidate his debts. Mike offered to put up all his assets as collateral, including securities, interests in stage properties and the contract just given him by Universal-International Studio.

He'll get his money's worth, one way or another, Mike said to himself.

He threw a farewell Sunday breakfast for a few dozen friends at the Sherry-Netherland and served a typical Toddian Sunday breakfast of caviar, smoked sturgeon and salmon, kosher pickles, cream cheese, sliced Bermuda onions, scrambled eggs, coffee and bagels.

One of the guests, Al Jolson, shook his head. "People are starving all over the world and Todd lays on caviar for breakfast."

Up in Central Park was Broadway's top money-maker for
the season when he closed it on April 13 after five hundred and
four performances, yet he was apprehensive about taking it to
Chicago.

Mike Todd was not a success in Chicago. Around town he
was the fresh young punk who had grown up on Randolph
Street, the gabby hustler who had gone broke in the construction business, the barker for a strip act on the Midway during
the Exposition, the promoter who had been run out of town by
Pete Fusco when he got too big for his breeches at the old
Rainbow Gardens on North Clark Street.

Chicago was filled with unhappy memories for him: walking
the streets in the early thirties looking for work, living on the
buck a day Bertha doled out to him, the hand-to-mouth existence as a gag writer, the scrambling for tab shows, the beating
he had been given outside the Oriental Theater, the desolation
of his father's grave.

He defied the odds and opened the show at the Shubert
Theater.

"Thank you, Mr. Todd, for one hundred and thirty joyous
minutes," Ashton Stevens began his review. "*Up in Central
Park* is more than the best you have ever given this city, it is
one of the most original musical shows I have ever seen."

"Someone once said, 'You can never go home. Better live
with the memories where you were raised than go home,'"
Nate Gross wrote in the *Herald-American*. "Todd didn't believe it. He wanted to impress his home town and he did. He
is the most important theatrical figure of our generation—and
still a Randolph Street guy at heart."

It was a day of rejoicing for the Goldbogens.

Dave, who had lost his hair in inverse ratio to his weight,
proudly pasted the newspaper clippings on the bulletin board
of Beret, Inc., his loft on 323 South Franklin Street, where he
manufactured fabrics, ribbons and other trimmings for mil-
linery.

"When the mark of greatness is on a man," he said with deep pride and innate eloquence as his workers gathered around the board, "when the mark is on the brow, it is discernible as a child. If Pop, *olav hasholem,* had been rich and Mike could have had an education, he would have become a doctor or a lawyer, and he would have been the *greatest*. Because the mark was there."

The workers nodded. Mike had gone far. They were happy for him and envious.

"How old is he now?" one of them asked, noting Mike's youthful face in the clipping.

"I'm thirty-five, I was born September 10, 1910," Dave said. "Mike is two years older. By my figures he was born June 20, 1908."

A few blocks away, in the small office of his Chief Envelope Company, Frank Goldbogen, a virile man with a heavy shock of iron-gray hair, was showing the same newspaper to a customer.

"Great courage," he said proudly. "Guts ordinary guys don't have. It was his nature to be an undaunted guy, whether he'd become a king or a common laborer. You should've seen him as a kid, so skinny, he didn't get much to eat, mostly soup bones when we lived in a rat-infested joint on Lyndale. Now he smokes buck cigars . . ."

"How old is he?" the customer asked. Mike's age intrigued people. He had done so many things so many years, they refused to believe he was as young as he claimed, let alone as young as he *looked*.

"I don't know when in hell *I* was born!" Frank replied. "None of us had birth certificates. But let me see . . ." He thought a long moment. "Mike is about thirty-six now, he was born in 1909 or 1910."

Down at Democratic Headquarters, the Twenty-fourth Ward, Artie X. Elrod had the floor as usual. "Mike's got it coming," he said. "When twenty bucks was like two thousand around here, he treated it like twenty cents. Mike would give you half of anything he had."

In a dark, cheerless cubicle on the eighth floor of the Studebaker Building, a pale, retiring theatrical agent read the raves.

"Lucky stiff," the office boy, who had stopped to read over his shoulder, said enviously.

"Luck has nothing to do with it," the agent said. "Mike is the greatest salesman I've ever seen. *Whatever he's doing is the most important thing in the world.* He thinks about it and talks about it twenty-four hours a day, nothing else matters. Total concentration, an ability to *believe,* an ability to make *you* believe, fantastic drive: that, not luck, is Mike Todd."

The office boy walked away, disdainfully. What did a two-bit booker know about Mike Todd and why he was a success?

The booker should have known. He was Danny Goldberg, who had started Mike in show business.

Not far away, in a dentist's office, a middle-aged man looked at the picture in the paper and grinned at the memory of the Avrom Hirsch Goldbogen he knew. Lester (Legs) Kaplin, who had helped Avrom break up Duke's carnival game by winning all the *katchkes* almost thirty years ago, had become one of Chicago's foremost dentists.

In a beautiful home on the lake shore, Mike grinned puckishly from the newspaper at a handsome woman in her thirties. She had married well, the owner of a prosperous ladies dress shop on Michigan Avenue, but Leah Comroe wondered what might have been her lot in life—and Mike's—if she had not had a tiff with him, the night he went on a switch date with Bertha Freshman.

Out at 2034 Lemoyne Avenue, a gentle white-haired woman gazed at the picture of her son.

"Avrumele . . . Avrumele," she sighed lovingly. The rabbi's grandson was doing all right, thank God.

"Too bad Papa couldn't be here to see it," Shirley said.

Sophia Hellerman Goldbogen nodded. Of all her children, Avrumele loved Chaim the most.

Chicago was his. Every night he played to standing room only.

One night Chicago was paralyzed by an electric power shortage. Most stores and many shows were closed at night.

"We'll play if I have to light the joint with candles," Mike said and dispatched Salthouse to buy all the candles, dishpans and reflectors in Chicago to ring the stage and the balcony rail.

"DUE TO THE ELECTRICAL WIZARDY OF GEORGE SALTHOUSE WE'LL PLAY DESPITE THE SHORTAGE," Mike advertised.

Colonel Crown heard of his difficulty and immediately sent him a mobile generator.

The show probably could have run a year, at least, but Mike had other plans. He was impatient to complete his parlay: New York to Chicago to Hollywood. He was going to take over the Hollywood Bowl for *Up in Central Park*. He was going to revolutionize the motion picture industry. And he was going to claim Joan.

Fade me, little world!

He planned carefully and confidently, as if he were the master of his fate. He acted, he thought, by instinct, intuition, experience, logic, common sense and faith. He forgot he was a gambler rolling with loaded dice. Loaded against him.

He would never concede the possibility that freedom of will might be an illusion of human pride and that man's behavior might be dictated by *external* forces which move the universe and its every particle. He could not conceive of blind forces at work in a mindless Darwinian universe, yet his career was a living testament of it. By his ken, man shaped his destiny. He *willed* certain things and he had the energy to turn them into reality. Supernatural power and human intellect had nothing to do with it. You had to go counter to the natural bent of the intellect. He had read that in a book by Henri Bergson, and it sounded reasonable to him. In his jungle there was predictability based on odds. There *had* to be. The strongest survived.

He planned as if he could deny his emotions and govern Bertha's. Because he lived by and for the moment, starting clean at each instant with no past reference, all bygones relegated to the forever bygones, he had forgotten the twenty St. Valentine's Days that had passed since the one on which he had married Bertha. He was unaware of a fuse that had been burning those twenty years.

He was faded.

THE
SEVENTH
LIFE

St. Valentine's Day, 1926

August 12, 1946

One went the distance.

* 27 *

Man on a Runaway Horse

His campaign to make Hollywood Todd-conscious was to be waged on five fronts. It began with a Lucullan party at Joe Schenck's, which had become his home. Joan was the hostess.

"This is better groceries than you can get in New York," Mike said authoritatively after sampling the Cantonese delicacies prepared by the caterer, Don (the Beachcomber) Beach. In New York, Todd had cultivated a reputation as a gourmet and indulged in the Lucius Beebe habit of sending a twenty-dollar bill to the chef of the Colony Restaurant or "21" with his compliments. This was Hollywood; it called for a different gambit.

"I'm going to back you," he told Beach, and commissioned him to go to the South Pacific for genuine fittings, from the hull of a ship and fishing nets to oriental furniture. He had a location in mind, a building at 115 East 54th Street, New York.

Beach was inured to Hollywood enthusiasms that vanished in the broad daylight of reason and sobriety. He smiled indulgently. The next morning, to his astonishment, one of Todd's secretaries delivered his tickets and generous expenses for the trip.

Beach went to the South Pacific and the Orient, Todd leased the building on East Fifty-fourth Street—but the restaurant was never opened. That was of little consequence. For a few days Mike had enjoyed the illusion that he was a boniface. The transitory fervor was all that mattered.

He opened negotiations to take over the Greek Theater and bring plays to benighted Los Angeles, but nothing came of it.

He cased Hollywood. It was a village of tasteless producers and scentless flowers, controlled by frightened little men armed with buckets of sand to extinguish any fires of creative originality that might break out. Here people ate well *or* slept well. Most of its stories had a basis of cruelty. Like the framed cablegram on Buster Collier's wall, sent to the actor and his wife Stevie, while they were in London, by his then employer: "MERRY CHRISTMAS, HAPPY NEW YEAR TO YOU STEVIE AND THE BABY. WE ARE NOT TAKING UP YOUR OPTION. WARM REGARDS."

Brynie Foy, a Kohinoor in the rough, was an exception. He took neither himself nor movie-making seriously. "When I decided to come out here," he said, "I asked my father what I should be: a writer, director, producer or actor. 'Be a producer, Brynie,' my father told me. 'It'll take 'em longer to find you out.'"

Fugitives from Broadway, Mike discovered, those who had *made it* on Hollywood terms, were the most pathetic. They had found what the less "fortunate" still searched for: nothingness. The more sensitive writhed on the crucifix of success, the others blissfully drowned in heavy cream. Everyone hungered for what everyone else had, and consequently enjoyed nothing. Their only real joy was in spoiling, in watching someone fail, in seeing a big talent made small.

He was a guest at a party where a famous producer remarked gleefully, "I hear there's all kinds of trouble on Goldwyn's picture . . ." Everyone within hearing pressed closer, eager to hear the lurid details.

"You're a bunch of hypocritical bums," Mike spoke up. "Every one of you pretends to be a good friend of Sam Goldwyn. You genuflect when you see him but, because he happens to be in the other room right now, you can't wait to hear of some disaster that has come to him. How can you bastards live with your-selves?"

The wife of a director invited him to a party after exacting from him a promise that he would not indulge in five or six of his worst habits—like talking continuously, insulting the guest of honor and making phone calls throughout dinner. He ac-cepted her conditions because he was genuinely fond of her hus-band, and said he would sincerely try to behave himself.

All went well until he picked up a book, a current best seller. "I hear this is pretty good," he remarked.

"You don't know what you're talking about," a tweedy fellow with a pipe chirped.

"That's possible," Mike conceded. He was on his best be-havior.

"You're like all producers," the fellow went on. "If it's a suc-cess it has to be good. As a matter of fact, the best things don't sell."

"You must have written a book that didn't sell," Mike said.

"I did. It was a good book. My wife is a tough judge and she liked it."

"You ought to write books for your wife, not the public," Mike said without animus. "I got nothing against the art form. I've been dealing in it all my life. I respect and worship artistic in-tegrity, but if you choose to enter a medium for *public accept-ance,* you must seek its approval. Unfortunately, the worst and dirtiest thing about it is that money is involved. That happens to be the scale on which it is weighed. The alternative is *not* to seek public acceptance."

The hostess passed. "You *promised,* Mike!" she said with a withering look.

The conversation throughout dinner never digressed from movies, naturally. Mental incest, Mike called it. A producer whose latest dud had just had a disastrous preview in Long Beach was boasting that he had another smash.

"How was the preview?" purred a rival producer who had had a report on it before the cards were counted.

"What do those idiots in Long Beach know?" the first producer exploded.

"The whole world is full of 'idiots from Long Beach,' " Mike said tartly.

He wondered if a recent movie preview at a local theater was typical. Following the film the lobby was crowded with teen-agers in sweaters and jeans sucking Cokes and filling out the printed ballots handed them at the door. Most of them put a check mark after the top grade, EXCELLENT, others marked a more restrained VERY GOOD. The most astringent criticism permitted was FAIR. No motion picture was bad, lousy or stank unless you made a write-in comment, in which case the ballot was thrown out. No tampering was permitted. A card with the comment "This was a damn good picture" was counted, but one with an angry "This picture was a damn outrage" was canceled because of profanity.

At this particular preview, the executives were slapping each other on the backs and embracing the boss. "You done it again, L. B.!"

Everyone was happy, especially the audience. As each teen-ager had come out, an assistant manager handed him five cards. "Fill out three Excellents and two Very Goods," he whispered, "and you get a free Coke."

"Nobody in this town ever makes a mistake," Mike said, deadpan. "Admission of a mistake is not a sign of humility but of ego, and I'm the most egotistical man in the world. There isn't enough ego in Hollywood."

The habits of the natives he found amusing, when they did not sicken him. Darryl Zanuck of Twentieth Century-Fox carried a croquet mallet around the lot, even taking it to lunch. Harry Cohn of Columbia Pictures had a riding crop always within reach on his desk. Dore Schary of R.K.O. made his points at story conferences with a totem-pole cane. Each was the head of a studio and each had his scepter. It was their privilege, they were America's last royalty.

There was a Gemara of stories devoted exclusively to Cohn, a fearsome dragon. The current favorite, possibly true, concerned an infrequent visit he had recently made to the studio back lot. Employees scattered in dismay as he approached. One man stood his ground.

"How come you didn't run?" Cohn was said to have asked.

"I'm not afraid of you," the man replied quietly.

"That's the kind of courage I like to see. You're fired."

Cohn, who had given Mike his first job in Hollywood seventeen years before, to soundproof two stages at Columbia, now wanted him to produce pictures on those stages. Mike had a contract with Universal-International but there was no law against talking to other studios.

"Now is the time to make pictures that *say* something," Mike said. "I want to do *Pick-Up Girl,* the play on juvenile delinquency I did on Broadway, and *Brick Foxhole,* a gutsy novel that shows what war does to men."

The president of Columbia Pictures nodded.

"But they must be done honestly and simply," Mike added. "I'd bring in *Pick-Up Girl* for three hundred fifty thousand and *Brick Foxhole* for four hundred."

Cohn shook his head. "Those are B-picture budgets. Make *Pick-Up Girl* for seven hundred fifty and *Brick Foxhole* for a million."

Broadway's most profligate spender argued for the lower costs, but Cohn was firm.

"You can't improve the pictures and can only ruin them by

spending the extra million," Mike said, "but it's your dough. All I ask is that we get something for it."

Cohn was puzzled.

"Invite the press to the back lot," Mike continued. "Then we'll back up a couple of Brink's trucks and dump a million bucks, real dough, in one-dollar bills on the street. It'll make a pretty big pile. Then you set fire to it."

Mike was serious. The projects did not need or justify the additional million dollars, he believed, because of the ceiling they had in public interest, but a million-dollar bonfire would make every front page in the country. That it was illegal to destroy currency was of minor concern; in the next year he would burn up a million dollars on his own.

A studio head who could not visualize the possibilities of such a publicity stunt obviously was not his man. Another producer subsequently made *Brick Foxhole* at R.K.O. under the title *Crossfire,* the first film tract dealing with anti-Semitism; it was an outstanding success and won a wallful of plaques.

He learned, on a celestial level, that Twentieth Century-Fox would pay him ten thousand dollars a week to move his humidor to the Pico Boulevard studios.

"What's the catch?" he asked.

"There's no catch. You'll be your own boss, nobody over you except Zanuck . . ."

"*Assistant* to Darryl? *Never!*" He had filed Zanuck's philosophy in his fabulous memory. It was too close to his own. "I definitely believe in luck," the head of Twentieth Century-Fox production had admitted. "That is the only way I can justify another's success."

Mike figured there wasn't enough luck at one studio for both of them, and continued studying the town.

Peter Rathvon, the head of R.K.O. Pictures, was positive that a film biography of Sister Elizabeth Kenny produced by his studio would make millions.

"How do you know?" Mike asked.

Rathvon reached for a portfolio on his desk, took out a thick packet of oversize graphs and spread them on the floor of his office. Mike stared at the collection of multicolored diagrams and symbols.

"The best audience research survey in the business," Rathvon said. "This poll *proves* that *Sister Kenny* is a public want-to-see picture."

"I don't want to see it," Mike said.

"You're not the average moviegoer," Rathvon snapped. "Taking it by social and economic groups, the survey shows that eighty-nine percent of the people in Class A here *know* of Sister Kenny and her Foundation, and of those who go to the movies at least once a week, fifty-seven percent . . ."

"Suppose a seat in a theater breaks," Mike interrupted, staring at one graph on anticipated capacities and grosses. "It'll throw off all the figures."

Rathvon glared at him. Hollywood empires rose and fell on audience-research surveys, with an occasional assist from Louella Parsons, Hedda Hopper and the daily astrology forecasts published in all Los Angeles newspapers.

"What's that for?" Mike asked, pointing to a painting of Rosalind Russell in a nurse's uniform as Sister Kenny.

Rathvon was furious. "That's our main poster, you idiot! By James Montgomery Flagg! It will be sensational—cost us eleven thousand dollars."

"I'd give a hundred and eleven thousand dollars *not* to use it," Mike said. "You put that out in front of a theater and people won't walk by, they'll *run* by. They'll think you're taking up a collection for Sister Kenny's Polio Foundation."

"Thanks, Genius," Rathvon said.

"There are no geniuses around," Mike said. "If there were I'd be self-conscious." He waded through the graphs toward the door. "On second thought, there's an unconscious genius: the public."

Universal-International Studio was changing its policy from horror pictures to "class" productions, and had attracted Nunnally Johnson, Mark Hellinger and other leading producers. Mike moved into the biggest bungalow on the lot, with a kitchen, dining room and bar. He hired a writer to adapt *Great Son* for his first picture. His second project was to be *Rhubarb*, H. Allen Smith's droll novel about a cat. He talked about making *Galileo*, by Bertolt Brecht, with Charles Laughton; the life of Stephen Foster with Al Jolson; a revival of *The Merry Widow* with Rise Stevens; *Song without Words*, based on Tschaikovsky's life, with the Don Cossack Chorus; the life of Arturo Toscanini *and* Jules Verne's *Around the World in Eighty Days*.

He was rattling off his hourly press communiqué to Doll, then suddenly stopped. "How are you coming along with that talking horse in Virginia?" he asked, as if he had last mentioned it within the hour instead of three and a half years ago.

"We're negotiating," Doll said and changed the subject.

He inspected Hollywood Bowl, and shook his head.

"It isn't big enough," he said.

The manager of the Bowl was astonished. "There are more than twenty thousand seats, Mr. Todd!"

"Not enough," Mike said.

"You can gross more than one hundred twenty-five thousand dollars a *week* here! No musical in the history of show business has ever made that much money."

"I'll have to enlarge the stage," Mike said.

"But it is already one of the largest stages in the world!"

"It isn't large enough for *me*. I'm increasing my chorus to three hundred singers. I'll have my contractor out here from New York in the morning."

"Contractor?" The manager of the Bowl was apprehensive. "What do you intend to do?"

"I need a scenic drop of sixty feet," Mike said.

"But, Mr. Todd, you produced *Up in Central Park* on the

Broadway stage, and the average theater drop is only seventeen
feet."

Mike regarded him with icy scorn. "I am aware of the dimensions of the proscenium," he said and turned to the vast stage of
the Bowl. "From the floor to the top of the Bowl shell measures
approximately forty feet," he said.

The manager nodded in amazement. It was exactly forty feet.

"I want it twenty feet higher," Mike said. "We'll remove the
shell of the bowl. That will increase the illusion there is no
proscenium, just sky."

He did not think in terms of theater but of circus, his ultimate
goal to eliminate the proscenium arch and make a show an extension of the senses.

"You can't remove the shell!" The manager was frantic. "There
are no supports."

"We'll construct steel towers sixty feet high. I'll also build a
tunnel so that the orchestra—we'll have a big one—can reach
their places conveniently. Oh yes, no curtain."

"No curtain?"

"I'll use an album of Currier and Ives prints, sixty feet high
of course. As the big pages are turned, the scenes will be
quietly changed. That'll do it. Seventeen pages."

The manager stared at Mike as countless men had before him
and would after him. "Mr. Todd," he asked, "have you any idea
how much this is going to cost?"

"At least two hundred thousand dollars," Mike said and
walked away.

There wasn't enough action for him. Californians, even the
transplanted New Yorkers, walked too slowly, talked too slowly,
ate too slowly and acted too slowly. He agreed with Fred Allen
that Los Angeles was all right if you were an orange, and he
seconded Joe E. Lewis' summary that although Hollywood was
hot in the daytime there was nothing to do at night.

Joan was a source of frustration; they had been advised by

his local lawyer, the well-known Jerry Giesler, not to be seen together until Bertha was on her way to South America and the divorce suit was filed. They met clandestinely. With the assistance of the wardrobe and make-up departments at Warner Brothers, Joan rendezvoused with him in a variety of disguises, her favorite a white-haired old lady.

Infrequently, on impulse or defiance, she would neglect the disguise. On one occasion they strolled leisurely through Farmer's Market, a tourist Mecca, a shopping basket on Mike's arm. They were so absorbed with each other, they were oblivious of a mob of fans trailing behind them.

The script on *Great Son* was crawling at the rate of a page a week. Hollywood Bowl was booked until September. Bertha had not yet left for South America. He was crazed with boredom.

He was not a drinker, he had no taste for the stuff, and he had no talent for promiscuity. That left gambling. He had played for top stakes at gin rummy in Hollywood three years previously, and he had lost almost two hundred thousand dollars on horses, cards and dice in 1945, but they were only a prelude. He would get more action than even he could handle.

Everything in Hollywood must be superlative, from the vital measurements of its sexpots to the fortunes owed the Internal Revenue Department. Its games, naturally, assume astronomical proportions.

A singularly ungifted director, with an unbroken string of flops, was kept on the payroll of a major studio at five thousand dollars a week for several years because he owed studio executives three hundred thousand dollars in gambling debts and there was no other way they could hope to be recompensed.

Harry F. Sinclair, the oil operator, and Joe Schenck played stud-poker games in which a hundred-thousand-dollar pot was not unusual. Half a million dollars changed hands many nights.

Mike heard all the legends, some apocryphal, and he set out to top them. He moved into the fastest games with Schenck,

Jay Paley, Irving Berlin, Darryl Zanuck, Sam Goldwyn, Eddie
Mannix, Benny Thau, Al Lichtman, Bert Friedlob and Jack
Warner.

The stakes became so big that the carry-over point reached
fifteen thousand dollars. That is, if one player did not owe another player more than fifteen thousand dollars, he did not even
bother to settle. It was small change that would be carried over
until the next night.

For many of the players, gambling was a form of exhibition-
ism and they did not plunge unless they had an audience. Not
Mike. He gambled for higher stakes than any other man had
before in Hollywood and he would shoot the works with no one
present except the other players.

There was no limit for him. A player rarely tackled him alone
in gin rummy. Syndicates played him. One producer won
enough money from him at a single sitting, two hundred thousand dollars, to start his own motion picture company. Grad-
well L. Sears, one of the heads of United Artists, filled an inside
straight one night, lost the pot and suffered a heart attack at
the table.

One day, after he had been clipped badly by a syndicate,
Dietz brought Mike evidence that he had been in a crooked
game.

"Stop the check," Dietz said.

Mike shook his head. "Then I couldn't play tonight," he said
seriously.

Winning *or* losing was unimportant. The only thing that
counted was *playing*.

Schenck felt sorry for him and decided to make one last bet.
"I'll put up fifty thousand dollars you can't stop gambling for a
year. What's more, I'll give you fifty thousand *every* year you
don't gamble."

"I'll take it," Mike said.

The next night he went to Schenck and begged to be released
of his vow.

His friends gave him a gold plaque on June 22, his thirty-seventh birthday. On one side was engraved the story of his life that spring and early summer of 1946:

I was even till the last half-hour. . . . Boys, I'm quitting at twelve sharp. . . . Is four good? . . . Zei nicht ein yold (Don't be a calflike idiot). *. . . Give him as many stacks as he wants. . . . Raise you, they're only chips. . . . Tell 'em where you got it. . . . Tell 'em how easy it was. . . . Say a good word for the joint.*

Engraved on the other side were the identities of his well-wishers: "Joe, Ben, Bert, Eddie, Jay, Pasquale, Charlie, Billy, Harry, Doc and the little lady who waited and waited for him to get even."

Joan was learning to wait.

Mike did not gamble to win, only to gamble. He was a psychopathic loser. He had no card sense.

"Why is it," Thau asked one night, "that three of the shrewdest gamblers in show business—Sam Goldwyn, Jack Warner and Mike Todd—are probably the three poorest card players in town?"

There was no answer.

Man gambles, according to the currently fashionable theory of psychiatrists, "to deny his weakness, his anxiety and his fear of death." Gambling, for Mike, was a form of action, another manifestation of his incessant high voltage. He was a compulsive talker and cigar smoker, physically incapable of sitting still or standing still. The story of his life was written in a series of interrupted sentences. He had no continuity, no predicate, only razzle-dazzle and the resolution of survival. He would seldom sustain a conversation on any subject more than a few minutes at a time. His conception of cohesion was a lack of cohesion. If there wasn't turbulence he created it. Action, the more tempestuous the better, must be ceaseless. Peace of mind was for the dead. He could not stop moving. He had to have total communication. A telephone was as vital to him as a pair of lungs

to the average person. Orson Welles insisted that Mike came
out of his mother's womb with a phone in one hand. He was
awakened by its ring and it never stopped, nor did he stop
calling, throughout the day and night. No subject was too
trifling at the moment to discuss. He gathered people around
him from the moment he arose. They did not stop coming and
going, nor did he stop keeping them from coming and going, as
if he were driven by demons, talking, scheming, talking, scheming, until he fell asleep, usually at dawn, invariably so exhausted
he did not hang up his clothes but left them on the floor where
they had fallen from his body. One or two faithful friends always remained until he dropped off. He could not be alone.
Even in sleep he was not in repose. A few hours of respite and
the phone would ring again; a new day was born and he began
gathering his flock.

Gambling was a part of the compulsion that governed every
minute of his day. It did not have deep psychological roots.
To say that he was fulfilling a need to show that he could play
with fate, just as fate played with him, would be a quick answer and an oversimplified one. Part of it had to do with boredom. Boredom was a dragon he fought unceasingly with every
breath. His Excalibur was action: activity of his brain, his body,
his voice and his money.

Too, there was a shrewd, practical reason. Gambling was the
quickest and cheapest way to gain entry to high places.
Through ordinary channels it would take a lifetime to reach the
Schencks, Zanucks, Goldwyns and Warners. You could wait
years for an appointment. With a deck of cards he figured he
had saved twenty years.

He checked in occasionally at Universal-International Studio,
where his *Great Son* was still an embryo, mainly to have lunch
with the executives. The food was good. One day he was invited to a symposium to be conducted for Universal producers
by a lecturer representing an audience-research organization.

The speaker, a young Princeton graduate, delivered an erudite discourse on "What Is Showmanship?" punctuated with a plethora of statistics from his company's surveys. After an hour he recognized the impassive face behind the cigar in the third row. He blanched.

"And now," he said, changing gears with enviable dexterity, "I would like to hear from a top showman: Mr. Michael Todd!"

Mike got to his feet slowly. "Being called a top showman by the top showman of all time," he began, each syllable dripping with sarcasm, "is the greatest tribute I have ever received."

The lecturer stiffened.

"I wonder what Barnum did," Mike went on. "He was a *pre*-audience research showman, son." He pointed to the charts behind the poll man. "*This* takes all the gamble out of show business."

The other executives became restive.

Mike took off his gloves. "The fact that you can perpetuate this fraud," he lashed, leveling his steely eyes on the lecturer, "that you can pull this on us showmen, is proof that you are the daddy of all showmen!"

There were gasps and "sh-h-h-hs" from the other executives.

"Don't worry," Mike went on. "As a carny I was taught never to blow a whistle on another carny. However, since you have asked to hear me, I will oblige."

He paused to light a fresh cigar.

"To repeat," he continued, "you are perpetuating an unconscionable fraud by telling anyone what kind of a picture to make. Some time ago I was in Peter Rathvon's office over at R.K.O., and he showed me a floorful of surveys by one of you audience-research outfits *proving* that *Sister Kenny* would make so many million dollars figured out right to the number of cents. I believed the cents figure. Mister Showman, you and all your statistics couldn't persuade me to make *Sister Kenny*. I consider the Sister Kenny Foundation one of the worthiest charities in the world and, because I do, I hope that it receives as much money this year as the *Sister Kenny* picture will lose. That is, unless your outfit will reimburse R.K.O. for one or two *mills* it is certain to go in the red."

Mike paused. "I feel a little guilty," he went on, "because I'm responsible for you guys getting in show business. Back at the World's Fair in New York. There was a show called *American Jubilee*, with music by Kern and Hammerstein, and it did no business, even at two bits a rattle.

" 'I can't understand it,' Harvey Gibson, the president of the Fair, said.

" 'I can,' I told him. 'The name is wrong. People won't go to see a show called *American Jubilee*.'

"Gibson said I was nuts. 'I asked a hundred people,' he said, 'and they all liked it.'

" 'You didn't ask the right people,' I told him—and conducted a poll of my own. Everyone is a great authority. I never opened a show in Boston that someone didn't walk up to me after the first performance and start a half-hour spiel with 'I don't know anything about show business *but* . . .'

"One time I did a play called *Naked Genius*. A studio bought it and Hunt Stromberg, the producer, inherited it.

" 'The title is wrong,' he told me. 'The title on Gypsy Rose Lee's book, *The G-String Murders*, is much better.'

" 'You sound like a Hollywood producer,' I told him. 'Ask anyone at Sardi's what a G-string is and he'll tell you. Like asking anyone at Lindy's what cheese cake is. But there ain't no Sardi's in Muncie, Indiana. Ask a thousand people there what a G-string is.' First thing you know everybody out here was subscribing to a survey, trying to find out from all the shoe salesmen, plumbers and truck drivers how to make movies.

"All I know about polls is this. Last week I came out on a plane and the fellow sitting next to me was absorbed in a copy of *Fortune* magazine that was open on his lap. I suppose if you were taking a poll you would say he was a *Fortune* reader. I wouldn't. Because in between the covers he was reading a copy of *True Detective*."

Mike paused. "The subject of your lecture, I believe," he concluded, "was, 'What Is Showmanship?' In other words, you came here to teach us showmanship. It can't be done, son. Because there *ain't* no rules. If there were rules it wouldn't be showmanship. You're confusing a showman with a producer. A producer is a guy who puts on a show he likes. A showman is a guy who puts on shows he thinks the public likes. Civilians—that's anyone who isn't in show business, like the Madison Avenue boys with the double vents in their coats—civilians picture showmen as quaint people and coin words like pitchmen and hucksters. Being a showman is a hard way to make an easy living. End of survey."

A few months later, in a poll conducted by George Gallup's audience-research organization, moviegoers from Coast to Coast were given a long list of celebrated producers and directors to identify. Mark Hellinger led the entire list with correct identification by forty-two percent of all those interviewed, George S. Kaufman was second, and Mike, who had never made a picture, was third. Far behind him, among the also-rans, were L. B. Mayer, Darryl Zanuck, John Ford, Cecil B. DeMille, Joe Schenck, David O. Selznick, Adolph Zukor, Arthur Loew and the Brothers Warner.

If this vindicated Mike's judgment of research outfits, he did not mention it.

Bing Crosby wanted to buy into the Pittsburgh Pirates, but, because of a sanctimonious law in organized baseball prohibiting its votaries from having a financial interest in horse racing, he first had to sell his holdings in Del Mar, a picturesque race track "Where the Turf Meets the Surf" near San Diego.

Crosby offered to sell the track to Arnold Grant. Convinced that the track would be an excellent investment, at least in the first postwar year, with gasoline rationing off and the public starved for entertainment, Grant contracted to purchase Crosby's majority stock, thirty-eight percent of the plant, at five hundred dollars a share, on the condition that the additional stock necessary for fifty-one percent control, would be available. Pat O'Brien's seven percent was up for sale and the remaining of the thirteen points were available.

Three months later, when news of the sale broke in the L.A. papers, Todd called Grant in New York and said, "Racing is a showman's business, Arnie. I'll buy the track from you."

Grant was surprised. "Haven't you got enough problems?" he asked.

"I'm unhappy out here, Arnie, a fish out of water," Mike admitted candidly. "You know Hollywood. You're only as big as people *think* you are. If I take over the track it'll give me prestige and they'll treat me with more respect. All I want to do is run it and make a little bet now and then."

"Mike, why should I cut you in?" Grant retorted. "There's no reason for us to be partners. You've got no part of this deal."

Several days later Mike called again and said, "Would you be interested if Crown wants to buy into Del Mar?"

Grant said that Crown would be a welcome partner.

Mike's next call was to the Colonel.

"I don't want a race track," Crown told him.

"You won't own it," Mike assured him. "You're only *loaning* the money—at four percent. You'll get fifty-one percent of the stock in the track as collateral. At the end of one year you will have the right to purchase two thirds of that stock for six hundred and forty-eight thousand dollars. Those are Grant's terms, not mine; he has the deal. Oh yes, if you don't exercise the option the loan will continue for five years." Crown agreed.

The first order of business at the track was a general housecleaning. To counteract persistent rumors of "boat races" being run at Del Mar, Spencer Drayton's Thoroughbred Racing Bureau, the industry's best police force, was retained and the purchase of the latest cameras and other detective devices was authorized. Charles Carr, former United States Attorney, was named president of the track, and racing's most feared crusader, Jerry Giesler, former chairman of the California Racing Commission, was put on the board of directors.

Grant, as chairman of the board, laid down the law before the opening: *not a nickel was to be bet by any member of the board of directors.*

Mike, who was a member of the board and called himself Managing Director, suggested that a souvenir gift be given to each customer on opening day.

A grizzled member of the track staff stared at him in amazement and pity. "Tracks don't give anything *to* horse players, but vice versa, Mr. Todd," he said. "It has never been done."

"That's why we'll do it," Mike snapped. "Habit is a horrible thing."

He collected all the horse-player stories written by Runyon, had them published in a book titled *All Horse Players Die Broke,* and arranged to have them presented to each customer as he entered the track.

His associates were nonplused. "You're going to remind them they'll die broke *before* they go to the windows?" one of them asked. "It's suicide."

"You must have flunked Psychology 1-A," Mike retorted. "Horse players are bred to suffer and live to be insulted. They are the worst cynics in the world. They are positive life is a ghastly joke, so they reduce it to its greatest absurdity. They risk their jobs, their rent money, their families, their happiness —everything essential to life—on the most ludicrous procedure they know of: predicting, seven times an afternoon, which one of ten or twelve neurotic horses can run past a finish line first." He smiled bitterly. "When they get together they don't talk about the long shots they brought in but about the times they lost by a photo. Runyon's book will *encourage* 'em to bet. They'll lay odds he's wrong! And it will make every sports column in the country."

His name predominated in the theatrical, sports and gossip

columns, every part of the newspaper except page one. That was to come.

Junior had no objections to the divorce and his subsequent marriage to Joan. He loved his mother but he got along well with Joan.

Mike had made the first payment to Bertha as per agreement, fifty thousand dollars, and was waiting impatiently for confirmation from New York that she had sailed for South America. She had agreed to go early in July but, at the last minute, postponed the voyage.

Bertha left New York late in July, not for South America but for California.

* 28 *

Exit Bertha

Mike was frantic.

He was pulling *Up in Central Park* out of Chicago even though it was playing to packed houses (the Shuberts were enraged because their theater would be left without an attraction). The cost of rebuilding Hollywood Bowl in time for his opening in September had soared far beyond his expectations. The second-draft screenplay of *Great Son* was as deplorable as the first, and William Goetz, the new head of production at Universal-International, was demanding a script that *could* be shot. He had lost close to two hundred thousand dollars on hot tips and cold dice; he was borrowing heavily from friends. Joan was becoming impatient.

And Bertha was in Beverly Hills, staying at the home of friends.

She reminded him of her presence almost daily. One day she found the station wagon he used for commuting to Del Mar and appropriated it without asking permission.

"What does she want?" he asked Dietz, who was acting as an intermediary.

"Friends are steaming her up to hold out for more money." Dietz shook his head sadly. "But it's not that. Bertha doesn't want anything except what she has always wanted: you. This is just an excuse. She can't go through with it."

"But she made a deal!"

Dietz sighed. "You know Bertha. She still feels you made a deal twenty years ago."

Desolate, Mike absently shuffled through the papers on his desk, including the guest list of Hollywood's elite that had been invited to the formal opening of the Jockey Club the following day.

"Oh, yes," Dietz was reminded. "Bertha wants to go to the opening."

Mike paled. "She can't! It will be embarrassing for everyone."

Bertha obtained an invitation without his knowledge, and when the horses paraded on the track for the first race, she was mingling with Hollywood's *haute monde* in the exclusive Jockey Club.

She made her move toward Mike immediately after the second race, but before she could reach him mutual friends separated them.

"Blow," Dietz and other friends advised him.

Mike was aghast. "I'm a director of this track. I *have* to be here!"

"Blow," they ordered.

He left.

Outside he saw a familiar car, his station wagon that Bertha had taken. He drove off in it as Bertha ran out of the club-house in pursuit.

She cruised in a taxi for several hours until she found his home, a ranch house at nearby Rancho Santa Fe. Bertha stormed in and took possession.

Mike and Junior spent the night at the Del Mar Hotel.

"How do *you* feel about things, son?" he asked.

"Mother is a fine person, Dad," the boy said gently, "but she's very emotional."

"I don't know *what* she wants," Mike said desperately.

"I guess Mother can't admit that the marriage was a mistake . . . and she doesn't want a divorce." He paused and added, "I know you've held off a long time only for my sake."

Mike hesitated. "Do *you* think she should have come here?"

Junior was thoughtful a moment. "Mother promised to go to South America," he said. "She went back on her word." He had always tried to be scrupulously just with both of his parents. His father had not won him over. His mother had lost him. "I'm on your side, Dad," he said.

Junior was Mike's conscience, inflexible and incorruptible. He respected his son's character too highly, and loved him too much, to attempt to buy him or delude him. He had concealed none of his frailties from Junior and had never asked for tolerance or grace. If Junior was on his side, he was free to act.

He called Crown and said he had to borrow fifty thousand dollars to make the final payment to Bertha. Crown sent it immediately.

Mike then instructed Giesler to begin a divorce action. It was filed in Superior Court, on grounds of mental cruelty, Wednesday, August 7.

Its aftermath made front-page news the following day.

MRS. MIKE TODD HURLS KNIFE, SON SAVES HIM! screamed the headline in the New York *Daily News* over a story by Florabel Muir, its Hollywood correspondent, that read:

The divorce action filed by Mike Todd against Bertha Freshman Todd came within inches of a bloody out-of-court settlement early today when Bertha heaved a sharp, heavy knife at Mike as the Broadway stage impresario entered his home at Rancho Santa Fe to collect a few of his effects.

Sixteen-year-old Michael, Jr., held his enraged mother, after the blade buried itself in a wall, until Mike, Sr., could escape. Today Mike was accompanied by a police guard as he combed Hollywood for new living quarters.

Hollywood now awaits the gong for the next round!

Four days later, one o'clock in the afternoon of Monday, August 12, Mike was summoned to St. John's Hospital in Santa Monica. He sped to the beach city and arrived twenty minutes later.

A surgeon, his face ashen, his eyes glazed, came out of the operating room. At last he saw the black-haired man waiting in the corridor.

"Are you Mr. Todd?" he asked.

Mike nodded.

"They are still trying to revive her . . . but I'm afraid your wife is dead."

Mike was stunned insensible.

"What happened?" he asked at last.

Dr. Stanley Immerman, one of the most competent surgeons in Southern California, did not know for sure what had happened. It had been minor surgery for a slightly severed tendon, but the woman was dead.

They waited vainly. The pulmotor stopped.

Mike's first thought was of Junior.

He went to the phone and, in a matter of minutes, Dietz was at his side with Lou Epstein, another close friend. Harry Brand, head of Twentieth Century-Fox's public relations department, rushed Casey Shawhan, one of his best men, to handle the press.

"You got to keep this out of the papers . . ." Mike begged, stammering as he always did under emotional stress.

"You can't bottle *this* story, Mike," Shawhan said. "It's too big, it'll backfire."

"I meant *only* until I can tell my son," Mike said. "He's at Del Mar."

Shawhan was noncommittal.

"What if he heard it on the radio first?" Mike's face contorted with pain. "I got to tell him myself!" He turned to Dietz. "Get Junior. Charter a plane . . ."

He collapsed.

Epstein left for Del Mar. Dietz remained with Mike. This was going to be a rough one and he was not leaving Mike until it was over.

The ordeal began.

An autopsy was performed by the Los Angeles County coroner's office the day after Bertha's fatal surgery, and the general belief that she had died of a heart attack was ruled out. Her heart was found to have been in good condition.

That was a headline.

Dr. Victor Cefalu, the autopsy surgeon, issued a "pending" release permitting burial but refused to sign a death certificate because the specific cause of death had not been determined.

That made a bigger headline.

Coroner Ben Brown ordered an investigation and laboratory tests, including a chemical analysis of body fluids and microscopic examinations of cell sections. The district attorney's office stood by for developments.

Hollywood had a new mystery, the makings of the year's biggest scandal, and it made the most of it. The strange death of an estranged wife four days after she hurled a knife at her husband's handsome head would sell more newspapers than any story since the murder of William Desmond Taylor.

If they could hang it on Mike.

Some newspapers could not wait until the test tubes and microscopes decided his fate. Indictments were quicker. He had already been tried in the bars, boudoirs and studio commissaries, Hollywood's courts of justice.

Bertha's remains were sent to Chicago, the only real home she had ever had.

"Don't go, Mike," Dietz pleaded.

Mike had heard the threats supposed to have been made by members of Bertha's family, vows of vengeance to kill him if he came back to Chicago for her funeral. He would not be intimidated.

"I *got* to go," he said. He was Bertha's husband. She had died Mrs. Michael Todd and she was going to be buried as his wife. It was his last duty to the mother of his son, and he was going to perform it, regardless of the consequences.

Again Death had beckoned him from Los Angeles to Chicago, this time to West Lawn Cemetery on Foster Avenue.

He looked at Bertha's face, serene at last, and his eyes were filled with regret, for her.

Why didn't you let go and give yourself a chance long ago when I begged you? Why, Bertha? Why aren't you in South America instead of here?

Because, dear Avrom, love has no foundation in reason, therefore it cannot be thought out or talked out. It has to wear out. Hers did not wear out.

The casket was lowered. Bertha had kept her word. She had been his wife "until death do us part."

His lips moved. He thanked her for giving him a son. And he prayed for her eternal rest.

Her family stood in silence broken only by sobs. They could not find hate for the man their Bertha had loved so fiercely for twenty years.

Junior stood up like a man. He had become a man August

12. He was sixteen years old, the same age his father was when he married his mother.

He stood at his father's side and sweated out the wait for the coroner's findings, ten seemingly endless days.

It had begun that doomed Thursday of August 8 after the divorce suit had been filed. His father should not have gone back to the ranch house, no matter how much he needed his clothes and papers. His mother could not conceive of a world in which she was *not* Mrs. Michael Todd. His father should have known.

But they had gone. And the terrible thing had happened.

There had been words. Bitter words. They could not pacify her. Bertha could not be reconciled to giving up her name to Joan Blondell. It was all she had.

The truth came out slowly.

Dr. John E. Novak of Del Mar stated that he had been summoned by Todd, who escorted him to the house, but because Todd felt that his presence would upset Mrs. Todd, he had remained in the caretaker's house a short distance away while he, Dr. Novak, went inside.

Michael Todd, Jr., was with his mother, Dr. Novak stated. She told him that she had been slicing an orange and had cut her hand. He examined the gash, about an inch in length on the left hand, and treated it.

Bertha calmed down, and four days later, on Monday morning, August 12, Mike persuaded her to consult a leading physician in Los Angeles and make certain there was no infection. All of his life he had been terrified by the possible consequence of any neglected accident or disease, no matter how trivial.

Bertha chose Dr. Immerman.

Dr. Immerman examined the cut and said that a tendon had been severed between the little finger and ring finger. There was no infection. To be on the safe side, he suggested suturing the tendon and offered to drive her to the hospital. It would be extremely minor surgery.

They stopped for a cup of coffee at the Armstrong-Schroder Café in Beverly Hills and then proceeded to St. John's Hospital in Santa Monica.

Bertha was given cyclopropane gas. It had no effect. Sodium pentathol was then administered, intravenously. Still she did not lose consciousness. She was then given ether. The third anesthetic was the last. She died almost immediately.

On August 22 the coroner's office announced the findings of its ten days of chemical and microscopic examinations.

"Bertha Freshman Todd's death," the official report stated, "was caused by the collapse of the left lung and circulatory failure while under anesthesia."

It made no headlines. The story did not even get on page one.

Ambrose Bierce defined an accident as "an inevitable occurrence due to the action of immutable laws," but even the most cynical of lexicographers is too naïve for Hollywood. It has its own Devil's Dictionary. Blameless accidents cannot happen to its celebrities. An "accident" must be a cover-up for a crime. The testimony of physicians and surgeons of highest repute, the incontrovertible evidence of chemical analyses and microscopic tests? In the world of make-believe *nothing* is to be believed. A patient's lung might collapse during surgery in Newark, Little Rock, Milwaukee or even Los Angeles, *if* he or she is not a celebrity or married to a celebrity.

It would have been a better story if the mystery had not been solved and the cloud of guilt had remained over Mike, so that was the one those who envied or resented him believed. In Hollywood the *story* is the thing. Whether it is factual or fictional is immaterial.

He paid Dr. Immerman a minimum fee. There had been rumors he had bribed the well-known surgeon. Mike had never met him until the moment he told him Bertha was dead.

One person alive knew the whole truth. Junior was the first to reach her. He had wrapped a bandage around her hand. He knew how it happened. There had been drinking. There had been an accident. He knew his father was innocent.

There *was* a bona-fide mystery, but it was not made public. Bertha's jewelry, a precious collection of which one necklace was worth at least a hundred thousand dollars, was not found. The jewelry obviously had been stolen. Mike suspected it was an inside job executed by a platonic friend Bertha had been assisting. He did not care about the estate for himself, but it belonged to Junior: he would have inherited it.

His lawyers and friends urged him to go to the police, but Mike overruled them. There had been too much tempest over Bertha's death. She had been an unobtrusive girl who disliked publicity. She deserved to rest in peace.

The jewelry Bertha had treasured disappeared forever.

Up in Central Park opened at Hollywood Bowl with a Toddian parade led by Leo Carillo, the perennial grand marshal, on his favorite palomino, followed by every available band in California, from the Monterey Drum and Bugle Corps, one hundred and eighty-four strong, to the Clan McLean Bagpipers and twenty drum majorettes.

The extravaganza drew $127,310.50 its first week, a world record never approached by any musical in the annals of the theater. He would produce an annual festival at the Bowl, Mike announced; attractions too big for a theater would be staged for a whole month.

Fog and cold set in the second week. Acres of seats, even the ten thousand offered at one dollar each, went begging the last three weeks of the month for which he had rented the Bowl. There were more people on the stage than in front of it. Not even Bill Doll's $40,000 publicity campaign could pull Southern Californians from behind their smudge pots.

The engagement ended in disaster, a deficit of approximately a quarter million dollars.

He had the most successful show in the country and did not

know what to do with it. No theater in San Francisco was available to him. The Shuberts, still boiling over his cancellation in Chicago, saw to that. He had to rent a wrestling arena and build a proscenium, and attempt to make a musical come through microphones tuned for the foghorn voice of a wrestling announcer. The Shuberts gave him only a two-day booking in Portland and Seattle, and then made him make a $30,000 jump to his next date in Minneapolis. Vengeance was theirs.

Mike had a monster on his hands and could not let go. His only chance of recouping was to keep the show going until he could revive it in New York.

His position at Universal-International became untenable. The studio bought the film rights to *Up in Central Park* and gave it to Deanna Durbin's husband, Felix Jackson, to produce. He could not even get *Great Son* off the ground. He bought the motion picture rights to John Roy Carlson's *The Plotters*, an exposé of fascism in the United States, but was unable to get a script on it either. Bill Goetz, the head of production, was demanding *something* on paper, a screenplay or his resignation.

The tragedy at El Rancho Santa Fe hung like an albatross around his neck.

Del Mar had the most prosperous meeting in its history. Million-dollar days became commonplace where $600,000 had been the highest daily handle previously. Mike plunged into fathomless debt. He often went for two thousand dollars a race and lost consistently.

"You could bet, Dad," Michael Junior said cogently, "if you could find the two-dollar window."

A breach between Grant and Todd developed.

Conversely, the relationship between Grant and Crown solidified.

Crown exercised his option to purchase two thirds of Grant's stock at the stipulated price of six hundred and forty-eight thousand dollars. Del Mar had made a fat profit its first meeting.

At the end of the year Grant told Mike that he would not be re-elected to the board of directors.

"Because of the pressure of other activities, as a producer at Universal-International Studio," the *Hollywood Reporter* stated, "Mike Todd has resigned from the board of directors at Del Mar Race Track."

The story was given out by Arnold Grant.

Observe how the Sport of Kings is played by kings.

A multimillionaire crooner wants a baseball team, but is told he cannot have the new toy until he had gotten rid of his merry-go-round. A wealthy lawyer offers to take the merry-go-round off his hands, and, in turn, a bored showman seeks to take it off *his* hands. In the end, a multimillionaire capitalist puts up almost three quarters of a million dollars for an option on one.

The crooner takes a handsome profit from his merry-go-ground. The lawyer also gets a large profit by retaining seventeen percent of the stock in the track at no cost. The capitalist adds to his holdings a controlling interest in a race track worth a million dollars. *And the man who brought the capitalist and the lawyer together on the deal goes deeper in debt.*

"I'm sorry, Carl," Mike told his brother as he sat in his little house on Dillon Street. He had promised to secure a concession for Carl at Del Mar's next meeting. He wouldn't even have a pass to the next meeting.

"Don't worry about it, Toddy," Carl assured him. "Esther and I are doing fine now. We're in the *movies!*"

"That's right, Toddy," Esther said. "Carl got a job as an extra —at Metro-Goldwyn-Mayer no less!—and got me in for one of the big crowd scenes."

"There's a lovely child in it, only fourteen years old, but she steals the picture. My, what a face! What's her name, Esther, the little English girl?"

"Taylor . . . Elizabeth Taylor."

Mike was not listening.

He never went to the post at Universal-International, and Goetz took over his bungalow. It was the best one on the lot.

"Son, it's tough to be a rebel in Hollywood," he told the office boy as he cleaned out his desk.

He left behind, under the glass top of his desk, his favorite quotation from Runyon:

> *"My measure of success is money. I have no interest in artistic triumphs that are financial failures."*

He had no immediate use for the dictum. Neither did Runyon. Damon, whose measure of success was money, had died a relatively poor man on December 10.

It was a year of havoc.

He shed another skin.

The scenery changed and he imagined that he changed with it. "This is the new Mike Todd," he said with each fancied transformation. Was he a new Mike Todd? Was he Mike Todd at all?

Of course he was, he assured himself. He had created Mike Todd.

Mike Todd was everything he ever wanted to be. Mike Todd had an unfettered imagination. Mike Todd acted out his dreams, on the stage, with beautiful women and powerful men. Others were halted by the fear of consequences. To the majority, money was the most important consideration: they had to have it before they could act. That, to Mike Todd, was illogical. Money to him was the least important consideration. Its proper priority was after the act. Otherwise it was more essential than man himself and deserved to be his master. That, of course, was ridiculous.

He was Mike Todd. Who, then, was the observer?

There was an observer. He wept with Mike Todd in his despairs and exulted with him in his triumphs. He was his own best audience. He shared every success with his alter ego: admiring, applauding and fulfilling.

In the beginning, Mike Todd had been a shadow that he projected. In time, it seemed, the shadow had come to life and had traded places with the man. He had become *Mike Todd. He believed he was Mike Todd. Everyone believed he was Mike Todd. Wait . . . there was one who did not. He had never convinced Bertha he was Mike Todd. To her he had always been Avrom Goldbogen.*

Who was he? It took the average man sixty years to find out, he had observed, and then he wasn't sure.

Mike Todd, he could not deny, was a wish fulfillment made possible by his incredible energy and ego drive. Yet, with his ceaseless trumpeting in his own behalf to make himself one of the most publicized persons in the world, he had succeeded, within himself, in maintaining his privacy. He had permitted no one to know him. He was acting every minute.

"One man in his time plays many parts," Shakespeare *wrote. Everyone acted but few performed well. Most had the good sense not to attempt difficult or varied roles and were content to be strolling players in the "noble farce." Not Mike Todd. He had a thousand masks to conceal his true self. Change of face, change of pace, that was the trick: keep 'em off balance. Now, for the first time in his life, he was off balance. But it would not be for long. He was certain of that. He could be flattened but nothing could* keep *him down.*

He knew what he could do because he knew what he had done. Not the accomplishments others knew about but the victories only he knew. He knew what he might have been. A man of his instincts, intelligence and ambition was more likely to become a Charles Ponzi, an Ivar Kreuger or an Al Capone.

He was a shrewd businessman, he knew how to get money

and use money: he could sell almost anyone almost anything. It was a power few men could resist using. Instead, he had set out to entertain the world without a specific talent to entertain. That is the most difficult feat of all: creating that which you do not possess.

Aside from his successes and failures as a showman, which more or less balanced each other, what had he achieved within himself?

If, as he liked to believe, he had become Mike Todd, a fearless, uninhibited fellow with a Scotch name, why did he spice his conversation with Yiddish phrases, often needlessly? Did he say repeatedly in discussion, "I've never been so sure of anything since I've been Jewish," because he was self-conscious about being a Jew? If he was Mike Todd, a bold man, totally secure, why was he a compulsive talker? Was it because he lived from the outside in instead of from the inside out? Why was he easily unpoised? Why was he incapable of controlling childish fears and petulant rages? If Mike Todd was the con man and freebooter his enemies said he was, with the hide of a rhinoceros and the morals of a mink, why did he bleed from the slightest criticism? Why was he so deeply concerned about everyone's reaction to his every word and deed? Why did he require constant approval? Why did he care? Most people were deceived by the veneer, one way or another—those who liked him and those who hated him. Why couldn't he remember that great line from Proust: "Three quarters of all efforts to impress and the vainglorious lies that men have indulged in, to their detriment, since the beginning of time, have been lavished upon inferiors."

Was he schizophrenic? It was possible.

It was also possible that Avrom Goldbogen was not dead. It was possible that with the shedding of each skin a new Mike Todd was not emerging, but rather an old Avrom Goldbogen. It was possible that, try as he might, for all of the world's pottage, he could not sell his birthright.

It could be that Avrom Goldbogen would reclaim himself. There was time. He was thirty-seven years old.

"Fade me, little world!" he would continue to shout with brave defiance.

He thought he was rolling the dice.

He was the dice.

THE
EIGHTH
LIFE

"I've been broke many a time

but I've never been poor."

* 29 *

The Bill

"The long, long romance of Joan Blondell and Mike Todd is over," Louella Parsons announced on January 18, 1947. "I won't say it's final, lovers have battled from time immemorial, but this battle looks final. Joan's bitterness when I talked with her seemed to be uncalled for. Mike gave up all of his business interests in the East and rented Joe E. Brown's house in Malibu Beach to be near her."

Miss Parsons issued a sequent manifesto on June 2.

"Mike and Joan have definitely separated," she stated. "This is not a rumor. I verified it with the gentleman myself. He said he was sorry to report that it was all over and this time it was final. 'When you're too much in love,' he said, 'you can't work.' However, there is no truth to the report that Joan asked him to take his cars out of the garage. They're still there."

Apparently another Hollywood marriage was sundered. Not so. Mike and Joan were not married.

All final separations notwithstanding, they were reconciled and, in the presence of her thirteen-year-old son and eight-year-old daughter, were married shortly before midnight on July 5 at El Rancho Vegas in Las Vegas, Reverend R. V. Carpenter officiating. Joan wore a flowered afternoon dress and orchids.

It was her third marriage.

Joan set out to reform Mike, and he was a willing, indeed an eager, subject.

"She remodeled him completely," Warren Hull reported in the *American Weekly*. "The new Todd won't even play gin rummy for a tenth of a cent a point. He is seriously considering starting an organization to be named Gamblers Anonymous. He even resigned as Abbot of the Friars Club because his duties might tend to keep him out evenings.

"The pre-Blondell Todd used to think of home as a place to receive mail, but Joan insisted on a clause in the marriage contract in which he promised to be home at seven-thirty each evening and stay there. He's buying a place in the country so he can keep his pledge."

The place in the country was a magnificent estate extending more than thirty acres along the Hudson River at Irvington. It adjoined the estates of multimillionaires, including Averell Harriman's. In addition to the main house, there was a six-room guest house and a six-room apartment over the stables. He had to furnish the bedrooms one at a time, on credit.

Joan's mother, brother and both children came to live with them. Private detectives were kept on duty twenty-four hours a day: Joan had an oppressive fear of kidnappers.

Mike became a squire. It was the first fine home he had ever had and he was certain it was what he had always wanted. It was his refuge from New York, Friday to Monday. He enlisted in the Irvington Volunteer Fire Department and Joan joined the Parent-Teachers Association. They became solid citizens.

Michael Junior was with them during the summer vacation.

He had his own Cadillac convertible and an allowance of a hundred fifty dollars a month. He got along well with Joan and her children. And a wonderful girl named Sarah Jane Weaver lived next door. Junior had no complaints. He was almost eighteen, he was entering Amherst College in the fall, and he was accepted as an adult, even at the cocktail hour. It was a family joke that he and Joan taught Mike to drink that summer. Mike was not an apt scholar; he did not get beyond the second martini.

He had the sets but no script.

The Todd bubble had burst. He had not produced a hit since *Up in Central Park*. That was January, 1945, for him centuries ago. This was 1947. *Streetcar Named Desire*, *Brigadoon*, *Allegro*, *Finian's Rainbow* and *High Button Shoes* were playing to standing room only, and he could not even find a property, let alone a backer.

He read a story in a newspaper about a bus driver who stole a bus and went to Florida. He was intrigued by the premise, bought the rights to produce it as a motion picture with Frank Alperson, to be called *Busman's Holiday*, and hired Ben Hecht and Paul Jarrico to work on the script. Jarrico attempted to convert the project into a social document. Mike was solely interested in making a film, with humor, of average people trying to escape the humdrum of daily routine.

The project was shelved and Mike was twenty thousand dollars deeper in debt.

People tried to talk *down* to him, that was the worst about being broke. A whoremonger who tried to pass as a respectable guy, always resentful when Mike was going good, could not conceal his satisfaction that he was out of the chips, 'way out.

"What would you do, Todd," he said condescendingly, "if you had fifty thousand bucks?"

Mike looked at him with contempt. "I'd give twenty-five thousand girls two dollars apiece," he snapped.

He picked up a newspaper. After two successful meetings,

the Crown-Grant combine had sold Del Mar Race Track to Joe Schenck and Jay Paley. They had made a substantial profit.

The bucolic atmosphere of Washington Irving country palled quickly. And there were not enough alarms for the Volunteer Fire Department to alleviate Mike's pastoral boredom.

It was a more virulent form of ennui. He was out of action. A static hero is a public liability. He had not lost confidence in himself, but everyone else had since the disastrous summer in California.

His organization had disintegrated.

Harry Bloomfield, an assistant since the New York World's Fair, long had had ambitions of following in his footsteps. The opportunity had come in 1946, during Mike's absence, and Harry had seized it. He emulated the master too faithfully, alas, without his Houdinian gift of extrication. He produced three shows in one year: *Many Happy Returns*, with Mary Astor and Neil Hamilton; *Foxhole in the Parlor*, with Montgomery Clift; and *Polonaise*, with Jan Kiepura and Marta Eggerth—the last from Mike's old office in the Alvin Theater.

The shows lost half a million dollars, *Polonaise* accounting for a three-hundred-thousand-dollar debit.

Another loyal associate, Sammy Lambert, general stage manager of practically every Todd production from *Hot Mikado* through *Mexican Hayride* and *Up in Central Park* to the last one, *January Thaw*, often had been credited by that phantom cognoscenti, "those in the know," with being the brains behind Mike.

Lambert and a backer, Anthony Brady Farrell, multimillionaire chain-and-cable manufacturer, produced a show, *Hold It!*, starring Red Buttons, at a cost of $300,000.

Hold It! was a sarcophagus and lost $300,000.

Convinced that the critics and public were wrong, not they, Farrell and Lambert then produced *All for Love*, with Grace and Paul Hartman and Bert Wheeler. The show lost upwards of half a million dollars.

Jimmy Colligan, another Todd associate, was trying to raise money to produce *Cry the Peacock*, by Anouilh, and, unfortunately, he did.

Bill Doll had opened his own public relations office and he too was looking for a play to produce. Mike had made it seem so easy.

A year passed, even more miserable than the calamitous year before. He could not even lose himself in the madness of gambling. He felt constrained to maintain a front, and he could not afford it. He didn't have the price of oats for the two horses he maintained.

Mike had been broke when he was making twenty thousand dollars a week. Now nothing was coming in. His credit was entirely gone. He was tapped out.

"Don't go to strangers"—Joan forced a brave smile—"I got a few bucks in the grouch bag."

It was 1932 again and Bertha was doling out a dollar a day. Only this time it was thousands, money Joan had worked for since she was a child.

Irvington-on-the-Nut was bleeding him to death.

He and his current lawyer, Sam Becker, went to Chicago to see his old friend Gottlieb.

"I want your advice, John," Mike said.

"Advice or confirmation?" Gottlieb responded skeptically. He knew why Mike had come.

"I can't breathe; they won't get off my neck." Mike was desperate. "I got nothing to eat. I got to feed my family . . ."

"You're *not* going into bankruptcy," Gottlieb said sternly.

"It's not what I owe, John, it's the *interest*! It keeps piling up every day. Compound interest *has* to kill you. I can't *ever* get out!"

"You're *not* going into bankruptcy," Gottlieb repeated. He looked from Mike to Becker. "You have to promise me, both of you, not to go into bankruptcy under any circumstance."

Mike and Becker promised, a promise they could not keep.

Shortly after, on September 19, three creditors filed an involuntary bankruptcy proceeding against Todd: A. Sheldon Jaffe, 630 Fifth Avenue, $11,150 for unpaid promissory notes on real estate commissions; Kaj Velden Studios, Inc., $2,152.20 for painting and decorating offices; and Alan H. Bonito and Company, Inc., $600.23 for fire insurance.

Mike's liabilities were *one million, one hundred five thousand, six hundred and sixteen dollars and seventy-eight cents,* including $636,500 in so-called secured claims and $288,516.78 in unsecured claims.

His assets were listed as $275,360.70, including personal property valued at $225,000, securities worth $25,000 and insurance with an aggregate worth of $16,360.

The press wanted a statement.

"Looks like I ran a million dollars into a shoestring," he said. He had to remain in character, for them.

On September 23, Michael Todd was adjudged bankrupt in New York Federal Court, Judge Vincent L. Leibell presiding.

He and Joan had been married ten weeks.

It is not a pleasure to go into bankruptcy, voluntary or involuntary, but if it is bona fide, it should not cause shame. Bankruptcy is a statute of repose, conceived so that a man should not be forever harassed by his debtors: when debts overpower a man, he is incapable of functioning. The law provides that a man can take a bath and start clean.

For most it is a routine process rarely protested. For Mike it would be an ordeal that would last more than three years.

His name was no longer in lights. He had no name or the price of a fifty-watt bulb. The spender was spent. He was dead in Hollywood and buried on Broadway. An operator in stocks and real estate who shot for millions could recoup, but a show-man peddling tickets at $6.60 tops could not beat a rap for a million one, everyone was certain, not even Mike Todd.

Maybe not, but a man named Avrom Goldbogen might.

Arnold Grant read the item in the legal notices. He had been interested in bankruptcies since 1929, when he was a member of the bar association committee which investigated fraudulent bankruptcies in New York, but none had aroused him as much as this one.

He felt it was his *obligation* to make certain that Mike Todd, the man and the legend, would never again be capable of victimizing anyone.

* 30 *

Cliff Hanger

"Try it out in New Haven first," Harry Bloomfield, who had returned to Mike, pleaded.

"Harry is right," Bill Doll, back on the bellows, agreed.

Mike shook his head. "We'll open in Boston," he said. "I'm not afraid."

"Boston has *critics!*" Doll argued. "Good men like Elliott Norton."

Mike smiled. "Norton is a friend of mine," he said. "Don't worry about a thing. I can do no wrong with my pal Elliott."

As the Girls Go, a musical comedy starring Bobby Clark and

Irene Rich, opened in Boston. It was a catastrophe. The critics, without exception, bombed it from overture to final curtain, and the most devastating notice was written by Elliott Norton in the Boston *Advertiser*.

Mike crumpled Norton's column in his fist and hurled it across the room.

"You and your pal Norton!" he lashed at Doll. "The newspaper guys just don't like you, Bill!"

Doll said nothing. Mike was a changed man. For the first time in the years he had known him, Mike was unfair and unkind. It was not solely because of the bankruptcy proceedings, now going into their second year. He had been with Todd all the way from *The Hot Mikado;* Mike had been broke many times but never mean. It was because of Joan, and it was not her fault. Mike felt compelled to play the big man in front of her. He showed off when she was around; he insulted and blamed his employees, regardless of their innocence, for all errors including his own. Doll was not angry with Mike, he felt sorry for him.

Mike was in a vise. This was his first show since he married Joan. He had to prove himself to her. He had to prove that his disaster in California, at Universal-International and Hollywood Bowl, was a fluke. He had to prove *The Naked Genius* was a fluke. He had to prove he was not bankrupt of ability. He had to prove he could produce a hit. And he had to do it *now* with a flop that had just had the worst opening he had ever suffered, probably the worst tryout *anyone* ever had. Hopeless as it appeared to be, he could not let go. He had no place to go. He had beaten odds of a million to one to put this show together, but if it died he could not do it again. This was his last chance. He was using borrowed money, most of it Joan's. He was C.O.D.

Joan was kinder and more affectionate than he had ever known her to be. She massaged his feet and back, which were aching from the physical and emotional strain.

"You're a pro," he said with admiration. It was the highest tribute he could give.

"After all"—she smiled wanly—"I was the star of *Model Wife*."

Mike looked at her and thought how lucky he was, at a time when the going was rough, to have a wife like Joan.

She was a comfort but the show was a debacle. No amount of massaging could relieve the affliction.

How had he been so wrong? It had seemed a solid idea on paper: a political satire on the first woman President of the United States, played by Irene Rich. Why hadn't the critics liked it?

"Dear Mike: Close it and forget it," the *Variety* critic had begun his review.

"Miss Rich has as much chance of getting to Broadway with this turkey," one of the Boston critics prophesied, "as she has of going to the White House. Or, for that matter, as much as Harry S. Truman has of remaining in the White House after next Tuesday's election."

Mike called a conference of his principals, as well as William Roos, who had written the book, and Jimmy McHugh and Harold Adamson, who had composed the music and lyrics.

Bobby Clark, the funniest man in the theater, now was the most disconsolate. He had made a terrible mistake, he realized, in taking the insipid role of Waldo Wellington, husband of the first woman President. He and Todd had gone down the drain together with *The Would-Be Gentleman*. He should have called it quits then but he had been unable to say no to Mike.

"I'm calling from the police station," Mike had admitted when he telephoned him in California, begging him to take the part.

Clark had been playing *Sweethearts* for twenty-two months and probably could have gone on for another year, but he had to bail Mike out, at least try. Mike had brought him back from oblivion in *Mexican Hayride*. He owed him a debt of

gratitude that he considered he had repaid only partly by doing *The Would-Be Gentleman*. Clark did not believe in waiting
for benefits or funerals.

It was a kind of benefit nonetheless, put on by friends who
felt sorry for Todd. Like Bill Roos, author of *January Thaw*.
He *had* to write the book for him. He knew Mike had no money
to hire a Kaufman and he still owed the Fieldses royalties on
Up in Central Park.

After receiving part of the music and one act, Clark called
Mike and told him it wouldn't work.

"I know damn well it won't," Mike replied, "but it's the best
I have. Start writing."

Obviously, Clark reflected as he waited for Todd's Don't
Give Up the Ship speech, he had not written enough.

"Miss Rich and gentlemen," Mike began. "One critic has
staked his reputation that our show has no more chance of getting to Broadway than Mr. Truman has of getting elected next
Tuesday. That is strictly an overlay. I just called my *ex*-bookie
in New York. The price on Governor Dewey over Truman is
twenty to one. And the odds we *don't* open on Broadway are
a thousand to one and no takers"—he chewed his cigar and
glared at his desolate associates—"except *me*."

His listeners looked at him with indulgence and pity. It was
too late for locker-room orations. The game was over. They
figured that Mike, by some miraculous persuasion, had cuffed
their expenses thus far from an addled long-shot gambler
wagering on the wild possibility that Mike had one hit left in
him. (They did not suspect it was Joan.) Now, with the knell
of the Boston notices, they could not conceive of a single backer
putting up eating money for an additional day of a tryout.
They would be lucky, they thought, if they weren't stuck with
their hotel bills and stranded with no fares back to New York.

"We ain't here to sit *shiva* [in mourning]!" Mike shrilled. "My
father used to say that if ten men said you're drunk you better
go home and lie down even if you haven't had a drink. Ten

men say we're drunk. We got *one week* to sober up." He paused. "The first thing I'm doing is *throwing out the whole book.*"

It was not an impulsive decision. He had been apprehensive about the book since an understudy fell asleep during a rehearsal. He had suspected the plot was leaden. Too, he was haunted by the cataclysmic notices he had received for doing irony à la Molière with Clark and sex à la mode with Mae West. The memory of those casualties shook his faith in the box-office value of satire. He had been trying to sell satire since the beginning. *Call Me Ziggy* and *Man from Cairo* had not discouraged him. Neither had the receptions to *The Naked Genius, Pick-Up Girl* and *January Thaw.* Aside from *Hamlet,* he had not had one hit in the seven straight plays he had produced. Yet here he was back again, gambling his last borrowed dollar on a political satire.

He had forgotten his own maxim: A producer is a man who puts on shows he likes; a showman is a man who puts on shows the public likes. He had forgotten that he had never pulled up lame in six musicals.

He remembered now.

He remembered the Bobby Clark of the painted-on spectacles, lascivious leer, goatish hop-and-skip, cigar butt and cane capering after gorgeous, slightly clad girls. *That was the combination.* High girls and low comedy had made *Mexican Hayride* the most raucous hit ever to play the Winter Garden. Mike sighed. Five years had passed since *Hayride.* It was his last rowdy girl revue.

George Jean Nathan could have been right. I should have stuck to my elephants. What are two mugs like Clark and I doing with satire, Molière's or Bill Roos's?

He had one week to work on the show only because he *said* he had. Actually, it should have folded already. There was just enough money in the till to get the cast out of Boston and back to New York. Not a cent more. He had to gamble that money.

It was not logical, but show business was not logical. He was in the middle of a losing streak and he could not wait for the dice to get hot. He used their case dough to go to New Haven and create, if possible, a new show.

This was the true test. Only a man with real class, Runyon used to say, could make the clutch pitch without choking up. *Grace under pressure,* Hemingway called it. Did he still have it? A million one in hock, everything he could hope to be riding on a turkey: could he play the hand as if he had Cole Porter, Ethel Merman and George Kaufman in his corner?

For most men it would have been a week of agony. Mike exulted in it. He junked all vestiges of satire and subtlety and converted it into a lusty one-man show for Clark, with new sets, new skits and new songs. If a line got a laugh it stayed in. If it didn't get a laugh it went out, regardless of how essential anyone else thought it was to the plot. When in doubt he put in another girl number. He was back to meat and potatoes. He had to eat.

It was November 2, Election Day. Three of his friends, like himself, were short-enders who had been given little chance of survival. Truman was still one to twenty against Dewey. A closer friend from Minneapolis, Hubert Humphrey, was one to two in the race for United States Senator from Wisconsin. And another good friend, Adlai Stevenson, was five to six to be elected Governor of Illinois. How much muscle did his old pals, Jake Arvey and Artie X. Elrod, have?

"I've quit gambling, as you know," he told his ex-bookie in New York, "but this isn't a bet, it's an investment. A four-way parlay: two hundred bucks on Truman, a hundred each on Humphrey and Stevenson, and let it ride that I open my show in New York."

The odds-maker shook his head. Mike was worse than he thought. The bankruptcy proceedings *had* unhinged his mind. No one who had half his marbles would bet on Truman. Didn't Mike read the Gallup Poll? It was borrowed money, he knew, and he hated to take it from Mike. Poor Todd. He had never wagered as little as a hundred before. He used C-notes only for tips. Mike was insistent, so, for old time's sake, with a heavy heart, the bookie took the bet.

Mike crowed loudly that night as Truman, Humphrey and Stevenson swept to astonishing victories. Now it was up to him.

There was one critic out front when the show opened in New Haven, Robert Coleman of the New York *Daily Mirror*, who had come up ostensibly to do an interview on Mike.

"How would *you* fix it, Bob?" Mike asked.

Coleman was astounded. Critics told producers what was wrong with their shows *after* the opening, not before. It was irregular, but Mike was an irregular man, Coleman told him.

The first advertisements appeared in the New York newspapers.

"Anyway, Todd's going out *big*," was the sad consensus. The opening was scheduled for November 13 at Broadway's biggest theater, the Winter Garden, and he was charging the highest tariff any producer had ever levied, $7.20 per ticket, every night of the week.

There was still money open he would never bring the show to New York.

Forty ticket brokers, the toughest hustlers on the Street, listened impassively as Mike pleaded for his life, proudly.

"You guys made a lot of money with me in the past," he said, his eyes darting from one to the other and to the glistening rocks on their fingers. "I never cut you a nickel, no ice. I'm not bringing it up because I want anything. I don't want *any* favors." He paused. "I got a *winner*! As big as *Star and Garter*, *Something for the Boys* and *Mexican Hayride*—maybe bigger! I know everyone of you by your first name and you know me —for eleven years. I've never tried to sell you guys a bill of goods and I'm not going to start now. I need cash and you need a hit. *I got a winner*. Is it a broker's buy?"

A broker's buy, in Broadway parlance, is an advance purchase of tickets to a show by brokers who are confident it will be a hit *before* the opening-night critics have brought in a verdict.

You have to be flinty and a shrewd judge of character as well as of the public's taste (which, more times than not, it doesn't know itself) to make a living as a ticket broker in New York. Many of the forty hustlers liked Mike, and a few hated him, but none could afford the luxury of backing their emotions. There was no sentiment on their side of show business. They had to handicap Mike as they would a horse: on past performances and present condition, weight for age.

He had a great record but not lately. He had not won a big one since *Up in Central Park*. That was almost *four years* back. He had run out of the money in his last two starts with *Would-Be Gentleman* and *January Thaw*. And he was going down in a million bucks' worth of red ink, twenty fathoms deep. By any yardstick Mike Todd was a bum risk.

No bank or businessman would lend him a dime. But when Mike Todd said he had a winner, they *had* to back him because they believed in his judgment and his integrity more than in their own: he had more at stake.

As the Girls Go became a broker's buy. The hustlers guaranteed the money that enabled him to open in New York.

He was not afraid of the public, only the New York critics. They could close the show before the public had a chance to see it. He had to brief them. He invited the critics individually to lunch or dinner the week before the opening. Two or three rejected. This was a Todd production without social significance, he warned the others, and after outlining the show, asked for their reactions. Some were shocked and others flattered, but all gave opinions.

"The show is so bad," word got around, "Mike is copping a plea with the critics."

His few friends stayed away. It would be too painful. His enemies awaited the last gasp.

He sweated out the early-morning editions. They were the money. The afternoon papers never changed a verdict. He grabbed the New York *Times* first. Brooks Atkinson always gave a fair shake, often brutal, but never unfair.

"*As the Girls Go* is the peace offering of Mike Todd, the free-wheeling showman who has recently been recuperating from prosperity," Atkinson began. "It is a beautiful and uproarious show, gay and rowdy entertainment with a full cornucopia of music hall pretties."

Mike exhaled and picked up the *Daily Mirror*.

"Mike Todd has a smash hit," Coleman wrote. "You will have to be as stolid as the Sphinx and as grouchy as Scrooge not to have the time of your life at Mahatma Todd's irrepressible new gloom chaser. Bobby Clark is the funniest man in the world."

The afternoon papers were equally ecstatic.

"Here are the greetings of this corner to a new *hit!*" Ward Morehouse cheered. "It is a strident and opulent extravaganza."

"The great, magnificent and incomparable Clark met in a head-on collision with a musical comedy book," Dick Watts, Jr., wrote, "and I am happy to report that the First Comic emerged victorious."

"Todd has given us a voluptuous show in which Clark, our foremost catalytic agent in the matter of youth and age, ogles forty-two girls with cannibal relish," commented Nathan, who admitted enjoying it with cannibal relish.

"This is Todd's outstanding production," Garland added in the *Journal-American*.

The magazines added their kudos.

Before the week was over, New York was singing, whistling, dancing and making love to "Lucky in the Rain" and "You Say the Nicest Things, Baby." The town was clamoring for tickets if only to see Clark and five fierce children equipped with cornets dedicated to blowing the roof off the Winter Garden.

Todd was the liveliest corpse on Broadway.

He commissioned Arthur Szyk, the fine Czechoslovakian artist, to paint a huge outdoor sign over the theater, showing Clark chasing girls, and behind, ardent critics chasing Clark.

When the canvas was completed, a majority of the critics insisted that Szyk's profiles had not done them justice. Mike ordered them redone.

One of the two or three critics who had no complaint was Ward Morehouse, a short man. He liked his caricature very much.

"I'm as tall as Dick Watts!" he chortled.

A slightly built young man stood in front of the theater, gazing enviously at the marquee. He had applied for a job as a singer and Todd had auditioned him six different times. The sixth was the last: he was rejected.

"I can sing, Mr. Todd," he had pleaded.

"This is no George Abbott musical, you're too young," Mike had said and a moment later grabbed the boy by the shoulders. "I'm sorry to be so cruel but this is a different type of show. Older, know what I mean? It's a shame to hire singers and dancers this way, but what are you gonna do? If you've got it, son, you'll get there."

The boy, Eddie Fisher, would get there.

"How does Todd do it?" friend and foe were asking once more.

"Mike is happiest when the going is toughest," Dorothy Fields commented. "If he has a flop in Boston he's in!"

The question remained unanswered: How did a man in hock for more than one million one, and all credit shut off, come up with a quarter-of-a-million-dollar show that would run for 420 performances?

It was simple with the Todd Formula: Think of money *after* the act. As he had always contended, a man who thinks with his wallet will never get off his back, because he wonders what he can't do instead of what he can. The brokers would have bailed out no other kind of man.

How did he maintain his privileged standard of living, including his thirty-acre estate at Irvington, his penthouse apartment, his Broadway offices and a large staff of employees, his caviar and champagne at the Colony, "21" and the night clubs?

"I owe over a million," he answered. "What am I supposed to do—cut down on my cigars?"

All that mattered was that his name was back in lights. He had started another parlay.

He received a gold invitation to sit at the President's table at the exclusive Electoral College banquet to be held at the Mayflower Hotel in Washington.

He bought three dresses for Joan so she would have the right one, and she wore a southern crinoline that attracted envious attention.

The band played "Hail the Chief," and Harry S. Truman, beaming, entered the ballroom. It was the most triumphant moment of his life. He moved through the crowd joyfully greeting friends by their first names, shaking hands and affectionately embracing old cronies.

Mike was self-conscious. His embarrassment mounted as the minutes passed. Truman was ducking him. He was certain of it. Panic hit him. He kept turning so that his back was to the President as he circulated around the room. It went on for twenty minutes.

It was nearly time to sit down for dinner. Someone tapped him on the shoulder. Mike, rigidly tense, turned around. It was Truman.

"What's the matter, Mike?" the President asked. "You got a big hit and you don't know anybody?"

Mike and Joan sat close to the President at dinner. Mike and the President had many things in common. They spoke plainly and acted fearlessly. They were fighters, superb counter-punchers, unbeatable in the clinches when the chips were down.

"I told Tom Dewey he might have been President," Mike

recounted, "if he had thrown away his black homburg and shown his suspenders and sweated.

" 'Perspired?' Dewey asked me.

" 'No, sweated,' I said. 'More people sweat than perspire.' "

Truman chuckled.

"I've been broke many a time," Mike commented on his financial straits, "but I've never been poor."

The President understood. He had gone through bankruptcy too.

* 31 *

Exit Joan Blondell

Arnold Grant studied the schedule of 116 creditors.

Todd owed $165,000 to the Department of Internal Revenue and $12,000 in New York State income taxes. He owed the American Broadcasting Company $69,177 on a theater sale. He owed Herbert and Dorothy Fields $30,000 in royalties. He owed Sigmund Romberg $18,000. He owed Bill Goetz $25,000. He owed Jack Dietz $20,000. He owed Alfred Strelsin $36,000. He owed Frank Alperson $20,000. He owed Emanuel Cohen of Paramount Pictures. He owed Irving Florsheim. He owed Bert Friedlob, Al Rogers, Jack Lennon, Samuel Adams, Dave Dietz and Jack Morse. He owed the Dictograph Company $202.48. He owed a tab of $58.10 at Toots Shor's restaurant. He owed the Book of the Month Club $52.23. He owed Womrath's Rental Library. He owed the Royal Window Cleaners.

He listed Arnold Grant for services rendered and Henry Crown for $600,000.

Broadway gossip, its source attributed to Grant, was that Mike had a half million stashed away. Grant made no secret of his conviction that there was fraud behind the bankruptcy, and he was determined that Todd should not receive a discharge of his debts.

It was spring, 1949, and another tryout in New Haven—not his, but he was deeply affected. He walked out of the theater shaking his head. Josh Logan, co-producer, co-author of the book and the director, collared him.

"Was it that bad, Mike?" Logan asked.

"I'm shaking my head," Mike said, "because after this, nobody should ever produce a show again, it's that good."

Around three in the morning he got a yen for some delicatessen and went to Max Asnas' in New York. Winchell was there looking for delicatessen and other tidbits.

"Walter," he said while his pastrami was being bageled, "I've just seen *South Pacific* in New Haven. It's the greatest show ever staged."

"You sound like you have a piece of it," Winchell remarked.

"I wish I was an usher in it," Mike said.

Two days later, Billie Pyser, Mike's wardrobe mistress for many years, came to his office. Billie was greatly agitated.

"I've worked for only three producers," she said with a heavy sigh. "First the great Mr. Ziegfeld, may he rest in peace. Then wonderful Sam Harris, may he rest in peace. And now you, Mr. Todd."

"Get to the chorus, Billie," Mike said, "before I'm resting in peace too."

"I can't believe it," she said. "I just can't believe it."

"What?"

"I heard Walter Winchell's program last night. And do you know what?"

Mike dummied up. He would not admit, even to Billie, that he had not caught the program. As Gerald L. K. Smith had learned, you never can tell who is doing undercover work for Winchell.

"He said," Billie went on, "that you called *South Pacific* the best show you had ever seen. Say it isn't so, Mr. Todd."

"I'd like to help you out," Mike said, "but Winchell never misquotes anyone. Not this time anyway."

"Oh, no!" Billie shuddered. "You didn't . . . you couldn't!"

"*South Pacific* is everything I said it was," Mike told her. "Wait until you see it."

"I saw the dress rehearsal," she said defiantly and looked at him with a kind of charity. "You like *that* show?" She held up the thumb and forefinger of her right hand about half an inch apart, contemptuously. "The seams in the dresses are *this* thick."

Billie was serious.

Mike was impressed. It became his favorite story to illustrate the importance of details. Everyone in every department of a show or any organization, he now realized, saw only his own work. To him, no matter how minute the detail, it was the most important.

A producer had to see all the seams *and* everything else.

Joan was miserable. Marriage had ruined a wonderful courtship and her career. She had almost lost hope, after three tries, of finding happiness as a wife. In the summer of 1949 she returned to the stage.

She starred in *Happy Birthday* in summer stock and enjoyed the experience until it moved into the McCarter Theater at Princeton for the annual Princeton Drama Festival. Mike was along as adviser and Michael Junior was assistant stage manager.

On July 9, Harold J. Kennedy, producer of *Happy Birthday*, called the police to stop a brawl at the theater, asked Actors Equity to suspend Joan from playing in summer stock and announced his intention of filing assault and battery charges against Mike.

"Miss Blondell used foul and abusive language on my cast and hurled a mirror at me," Kennedy charged. "Todd hit Miss Blondell twice and choked me. I managed to get away but Todd chased me up the aisles of the theater and hit me over the head with a chair."

Mike's version differed slightly from Kennedy's.

"That pipsqueak is trying to make a mountain out of a mousehill," he told the press.

"You mean a molehill," a newspaperman corrected him.

"Not a molehill, a mousehill," Mike snapped. "He's a mouse."

"Did you strike Joan?" a newspaperman asked.

Mike stared at his questioner. "*I* hit Joan? I'd be afraid."

"What did happen?"

"A girl in the cast was canned. Joan didn't want her to leave until the end of the run because she didn't want to rehearse a new actress. Kennedy came to me and changed the whole thing around. I jumped down his throat. He locked himself in his office and called the riot squad. Then he hired a six-foot-six bodyguard."

"Did Joan curse the cast and throw a mirror at Kennedy?"

"Positively not!" Mike shouted. "She might have said 'gosh' or 'darn it,' but that's all. She started to throw a wadded paper at him but I told her not to. If she threw it when my back was turned, I'm sorry. She positively did not hit him with a mirror. That would have been bad luck."

It was bad luck anyway. Their marriage was on the rocks.

Mike did not want to give up Joan. He had waited so many years for a wife he could love, and now, after two years, it was done for. He tried desperately to hold Joan and even consulted a psychiatrist chosen by her. She did not trust him to select his own.

He was disdainful of psychiatrists and did not think he needed therapy. Neither did the psychiatrist.

Mike's frenetic habits, his compulsive talking and smoking, did not deceive the doctor. Certainly they were neuroses, but Mike made them work for him. They were a part of his success, the web of illusion he wove about himself. Every moment of living for him was free association. He did not require the listening ear of a psychiatrist because he would bend the ear of anyone within reach of a telephone.

Joan smiled wryly when she recalled the complaint she had signed in her divorce from Powell: "He kept his office in our home. The phones kept ringing and we had no privacy."

The bankruptcy proceedings lagged into 1949.

"How did you get into financial difficulties necessitating your going into bankruptcy?" Referee Peter B. Olney asked Todd.

"Most of the shows that I produced that were successful I had partners," he replied, "and the ones that were unsuccessful I financed myself. It was just bad business judgment, I guess."

QUESTION: Were you accustomed to gambling, Mr. Todd?

ANSWER: Yes, sir.

Q: What kind of gambling did you participate in?

A: Most every kind that was devised, I think.

Q: How much do you estimate you gambled?

A: I couldn't be sure. I kept no records of my bets.

Q: You must have some approximate idea.

A: I would say I bet over a hundred thousand in forty-five and in forty-six maybe a quarter million dollars.

Q: What about 1947?

A: I believe that was the year I stopped gambling; so much so that I was going to start Gamblers Anonymous.

The financial records of his shows were complete but his personal accounts were in chaos. All he could furnish were canceled checks, notations on some deposit slips and his bank statements. There were no check stubs, ledger or cash book.

His failure to keep any check stubs staggered his skeptical questioners.

"It was, I admit, a very lax procedure," he said, "but there were no stubs, if that is what you mean, no stubs."

Irving J. Galpeer, attorney for a group of creditors, was firing the questions now.

Q: Did you have any transactions with Lew Brice, the actor?

A: Yes. I played gin rummy with him from time to time.

Q: Did you disburse any money to him?

A: Yes. Quite a lot.

Shown a check for $3,750, made out to cash and endorsed by Joseph M. Schenck, Todd said that he was quite sure the money went to pay a gambling debt but not to Schenck.

Q: Can you tell us to whom you paid the $3,750?

A: No, sir. I couldn't tell you to save my soul.

Q: And there is no record you have that would tell us?

A: That is right.

Shown canceled checks totaling $126,385 in 1946, Todd said that eighty percent had gone to pay gambling debts.

Could he estimate how much money had passed through his hands during the years under question?

"In and out, maybe a half million dollars in 1945," he said, "in 1946 maybe $200,000, in 1947 maybe $100,000 or less."

Having established the amount of money involved, his interrogators insinuated the element of doubt that the proceeds of canceled checks which he claimed had been devoted to gambling had in fact been used for that purpose.

"Suppose I were to say to you, being a very skeptical person," the question was fired, "how do I know you gambled this money this way? How do I know that you did not take $100,000 of this money for which you cashed checks and put it away somewhere, and that you have got it today? Suppose I were to take that attitude. Have you any books and records except those check vouchers that could convince me that I was wrong, except your statement?"

Todd looked his interrogator squarely in the eyes. "I cannot answer for what goes on in another man's mind. I have no books or records."

In the midst of the hearings Referee Olney was retired and Herbert Loewenthal succeeded him as Referee. A new Trustee, Elihu D. Sarasohn, was appointed and there was another adjournment.

The heavy artillery was coming up.

He turned a page in *Life* magazine, and all other thoughts fled. "Bill Doll!" he shouted.

Doll hustled into Mike's office.

"Remember that talking horse in Richmond, Virginia, I asked you to investigate?" Mike asked.

Doll remembered. He had hoped Mike had forgotten, although he knew better. "Nothin' to him, Mike, he's a fake."

"His name is *Lady* Wonder, Bill," Mike said evenly, "and *she's* such a fake it took her almost five minutes to solve the kidnapping of Danny Matson up in Quincy, Massachusetts, that has been stumping the police for days. I always had confidence in that horse." He tossed the magazine with the imposing layout on Lady Wonder across the desk.

Doll started to explain but Mike cut him off.

"There's still time!" He picked up the phone and put in a person-to-person call to Lady Wonder, then turned to Doll. "Grab the first plane to Richmond. Sign her up for the best price you can get."

Bill was rarely puzzled by anything Mike proposed, but this was an exception. "What are you going to do with her?" he asked.

"I'm going to put her in Madison Square Garden for one night, what else? Out of nine million people there must be twelve thousand who will pay to hear a horse talk. *I would*. Get goin', Bill!"

En route to the airport, Doll stopped at the apartment of his friend, Maurice Zolotow, a magazine writer who studied psychic phenomena as a hobby.

"I got a problem," Doll told Zolotow. "You know what a sucker Mike is for animals. Now he wants to put that talking horse in the Garden, and frankly I'm scared. All I can see is those twelve thousand people sitting there and waiting for the nag to talk. What if she gets laryngitis or something?"

"It's possible," Zolotow admitted.

"How can I get off the hook?" Doll begged.

"Go to Richmond," Zolotow advised, "ask the horse where you can get another horse to do the same work she does, and see what she says."

Doll thanked him and went to a press party he suddenly remembered. After two drinks, he forgot all about the talking horse again. Mike did not, but, fortunately for Doll, some twenty other projects had higher priorities.

The new Trustee, Elihu Sarasohn, charged Todd with concealing assets in the name of Michael Junior and petitioned the Referee to direct the boy's guardian to turn over the money to the bankrupt estate.

What were these assets he allegedly concealed out of the millions that had passed through his hands? The proceeds from the sale of some furniture in his apartment back in 1946 amounting to $6,500.

"I purchased the furniture for my son shortly after the death of my wife in August, 1946," Mike explained. "He had a sentimental attachment for the furniture and the apartment, where he spent his week ends from Lawrenceville School. He wanted to buy the furniture on his own, so I loaned him the money and told him he could repay me out of his mother's estate. The transaction was based on love and affection, emotion and sentiment."

Michael Junior was subpoenaed.

The boy was incorruptible, incapable of shading the truth

for anyone, even his father, but under skillful cross-examination he gave the impression of being a perjurer. He was a pathetically confused witness; his testimony was at variance with his father's on several points.

There was no denial that in December, 1947, two and a half months after Mike went into bankruptcy, the furniture was resold to Orrin Lehman, nephew of United States Senator Herbert H. Lehman, for $6,500 and the money was held by Junior's guardian.

"The Todds' testimony was hopelessly false and unworthy of credibility," Referee Loewenthal stated in his decision. "The bankrupt purchased the furniture and exercised dominion over it and sold it when it was advantageous for himself so to do. He was insolvent at the time. His son was used as a dummy. This is obvious to the Referee, having observed all the witnesses and heard the testimony and the manner in which it was given."

The Referee directed that the disputed sum (all that was on hand was $4,577) be delivered to the Trustee.

Why a Dreyfus Case was made out of a few pieces of furniture when there was more than a million dollars in liabilities involved was not clear to Mike unless there was nothing else to hang on him.

He was wrong.

Sarasohn, speaking for the creditors, formally opposed granting Todd's application for a discharge from his debts, specifying a long list of objections.

"The bankrupt committed offenses punishable by imprisonment," Sarasohn charged. "Among these alleged offenses was the concealment of property unlawfully, willfully, knowingly, fraudulently and feloniously."

In addition to the sale of Junior's furniture, Sarasohn continued, Todd's concealed assets included a matter of $200,000 which, the Trustee contended, the bankrupt had received from loans, gambling and other transactions and whose whereabouts he had failed to reveal in his schedules of testimony.

Sarasohn further contended that Todd concealed, destroyed, mutilated, falsified and made false entries in documents affecting or relating to his affairs after the petition in bankruptcy was filed against him or in contemplation thereof, and was believed to have drawn checks which purportedly repaid alleged loans whereas they did no such thing but were a cover to siphon off the moneys involved.

In closing, the Trustee stated that Todd had failed to explain satisfactorily the total deficiency between his receipts and expenditures, a gap that came to $830,256.08.

That was the case against Mike.

He did not bat an eye. If they could prove it, he might go to prison. Even that possibility did not bother him as much as the fact that they had tried to prove Junior was a liar.

It was the end of the line. For them.

Their house at Irvington had been put up for auction. She was going to Las Vegas. He was sweating out the bankruptcy and trying to put another musical together. He was down to his last hundred dollars and he owed Joan $80,000, her total savings.

Her bags were packed. There was an awkward silence before they said good-bye to seven years. Her attention was diverted to the cocker spaniel puppy he had given her.

"What has he got in his mouth?" she asked.

Mike picked up the puppy. It had chewed to bits the bill he had left in his trousers on the bed, his last hundred bucks.

The door closed and he was alone. His thoughts turned to Michael Junior, somewhere in the Middle East.

"I want to find myself, Dad," he had said after mid-term examinations and, halfway through his junior year at Amherst, had signed on as an ordinary seaman aboard a Standard Oil tanker to go around the world. His last letter was from Port Saïd, with tales of derring-do which included a mutiny, a drunken battle on deck with axes and the smuggling of women aboard ship.

Junior was finding himself.

Mike reread his cable in response to the news that Joan had decided to get a divorce: WE'LL BUILD A NEW SAN FRANCISCO, DAD.

Mike's face softened.

He was not alone.

✷ 32 ✷

They're Wise to Us, the Jig Is Up

He had Lilly Christine, a New Orleans stripper whose lithe torso imitated the writhings of a cat, ergo her title, the Cat Girl.

He had seven famed burlesque comedians—Bozo Snyder, Peanuts Mann, Hi Wilberforce Conley, Red Marshall, Loony Lewis, Spike Hamilton and Dick (Gabby) Dana—under the direction of the master, Bobby Clark.

He had a take-off on Nobel Prize Winner T. S. Eliot's *The Cocktail Party*.

He had five songs composed by Rama IX, Phumiphon Aduldet, the King of Thailand.

He had forty-eight of the loveliest girls in the world.

But he didn't have a finish, and the opening was seven days away. He cudgeled his brain. A Todd show without a spectacular stage effect was unthinkable. Fire came to mind first. It had fascinated him since his Flame Dance. Animals were an old stand-by. And water . . . he had never created a better effect than his forty-foot waterfall of bubbles in *The Hot Mikado*.

Good old soap bubbles! His forty-eight beauties would take a bath on stage. He picked up the phone and, within an hour, a consultant from the Procter and Gamble soap company in Cincinnati was flying to New York. His first mixture of suds made the girls itch. He altered the formula until he had perfected a gigantic bubble bath that passed inspection. It cost $36,000.

The last $36,000 came hard. He had put the show together by a miracle of hocus-pocus. Facing a possible prison sentence for alleged fraud, he had gone to the ticket brokers and borrowed $150,000 on a security of four words: "I got a winner." Other chunks came from the scenery builder and the suppliers of costumes and property, who agreed to cuff him until the profits came in. They had read all the charges against him in the newspapers and they still trusted him. They *knew* him. He had never conned or swindled them. In their book Mike Todd was an honest man.

He treated ticket brokers like kings and kings like ticket brokers.

Prince Phumiphon Aduldet of Thailand, formerly Siam, was born in Cambridge, Massachusetts, where his father, a shy little fellow, had been taking public-health courses at Harvard University, hiring himself out as a baby-sitter, at night, at thirty-five cents an hour and scrubbing floors in Boston Hospital. The boy occasionally helped his father wring a mop, and he sang as he toiled.

Mike read a filler item in a newspaper that Prince Phumiphon, now twenty-two, was an accomplished jazz musician and had recently tried his hand at writing songs. He immediately sent him a hundred-dollar cable pointing out that the President of the United States, Harry Truman, was not above displaying his musical gifts publicly and neither should he.

The Prince referred the cable to Prince Chakraband, who had a three-way contract as his cousin, chamberlain and collaborator on lyrics. In a few days Mike received a package of six songs, signed "Bhumibol," Prince Phumiphon's incognito.

" 'Blue Night' is the best of the lot," Clay Warnick, Mike's music conductor, reported after he had played them. "It's a lament, a natural for Billy Eckstine, and should be a hit."

"Use it as the theme for the first-act finale," Mike said and called a press conference.

"Pretty good parlay," he told the reporters. "First, to get a real Crown Prince, and then, get a decent song out of him. What odds!" To intimates he admitted, "If Benny Davis had written them I wouldn't have bought them."

He cabled the Prince that all six songs had been accepted and would be introduced in his *Peep Show* "with regal dignity." A few days later the Prince took a bride, seventeen-year-old Sirikit Kitiayakorn, and on May 5, as a kind of anticlimax, Prince Phumiphon became Rama IX, the King of Thailand.

Mike had taken no chances. He would gamble his own money on long-shot experimental plays but not brokers' dough. He had guaranteed them a winner, and he knew only one sure-thing in the theater: his kind of burlesque revue. He had proved it over and over again, from *Star and Garter* to *As the Girls Go.* Half the critics would hate it, but it would have a run.

A producer is a guy who puts on shows he likes. A showman is a guy who puts on shows he thinks the public likes. He had to remind himself of one of his favorite dictums many times a day. He liked his humor subtle but the customers had a fondness for corn. He winced during rehearsals as his seven comics belabored one another with bladders, squirted one another with siphons and sloshed everyone within range with wallpaper paste. He was not amused to see moths fly out of pocketbooks, hats fly off heads and pants fly loose from their moorings, but he was betting that the customers would enjoy it. They always had. When they stopped laughing at this hoary nonsense he would stop showing it.

His chorus' basic costume consisted of three strategically placed clusters of rhinestones, a wisp of tulle and a navel stone. His choreography revealed scant influence of the Agnes De

Mille school, remaining faithful to the time-honored bump and grind, as primitive as the key lines of the accompanying lyrics:

You've never been loved
Until you've been loved
Below the border.

We've got what they want
And they want what we've got.

Peep Show opened in Philadelphia on June 8, 1950, the day Joan was granted a divorce in Las Vegas.

The censors were appalled by the show and threatened to close it if certain deletions were not made. Todd reluctantly cut the act of Corinne and Tito Valdez: he was no longer permitted to buss her bust or make love to her during their torrid dance number.

The show moved into New York at the Winter Garden on June 28.

"Canasta, baseball and television have been taking the place of women lately," he announced naïvely. "I hope to bring women back."

There was no gainsaying he had made an effort.

"*Peep Show*, presented by Mike Todd, Master of Razz-ma-tazz, is a gawdy, bawdy stag smoker," Chapman wrote in the *News*.

"Todd has another smash hit," Coleman reported in the *Mirror*.

"Being full of solicitude for the tired businessman, Mr. Todd has put together an old-fashioned girlie-girlie carnival," Atkinson pontificated in the *Times*.

"Todd has a hot-weather show in which the girls are not going to suffer from costumes," Barnes sighed in the *Herald Tribune*, "but it is tedious."

Garland summed up the proceedings as "beautiful, bounteous and bawdy."

"*Peep Show* has more standees than *South Pacific* and Helen Hayes' *Wisteria Trees* have patrons," Winchell reported after the first week. "The only one in it who wears clothes is Todd."

Life splashed his bubble-bath finale on its cover and into several inside pages, and referred to the "acres and acres of girls swaying like ripe corn in summer, all with hip bones loose in their sprockets so that they cannot dance or walk or even stand without going into what they call bumps and grinds."

"It is Todd's contention," *Newsweek* commented, "that despite centuries of progress the female figure hasn't changed at all."

The angriest growls came from his old friends, Gibbs and Nathan. "Ziegfeld would have shot Mike on the spot," Nathan concluded.

Peep Show would do a vigorous $52,900 a week, a profit of more than $20,000, and have a respectable run of 278 performances, but that would not assuage the painfulness of Nathan's notice. Mike thought he had outdistanced Ziegfeld long ago. Most of the critics had said he had. Now the *one* critic he had wanted to impress compared him to Ziegfeld and concluded that he did not belong in the same class with him.

This, he knew, was the last musical he would ever produce. He had violated his own commandment: never repeat yourself, not even or especially during a bankruptcy.

He was giving the Winter Garden back to Nathan—and Ziegfeld.

There were no high dames or low comedy, no seltzer bottles or animals, no music or stage effects—not a single trademark of Todd—in his next production.

The Live Wire, written and directed by Garson Kanin, was an earnest little drama about a group of indigent young actors who established headquarters in a Quonset hut on a vacant lot in New York. They pool their resources and work resolutely for the advancement of each and all, until the brother of one slithers in, raids everything from their wallets to their women and thoroughly contaminates their idyllic existence. They are unable to get rid of him until his photograph providentially appears on the cover of *Life*, and the resulting publicity happily removes him from their midst and sends him off to Hollywood.

"How do you get to be a success in television?" one of the characters inquired.

"Take a course in acting," a colleague replied, "through venetian blinds."

Kanin wrote the play in 1947, the year after his *Born Yesterday* hit the jackpot, but, until Mike made an offer out of desperation, no one would produce it except in summer stock. The reason became apparent on opening night, August 17.

"*The Live Wire* blows a fuse," Barnes dismissed it.

"Some place there's a short circuit," O'Connor wrote. "It's a dud."

"It isn't very good," Watts sighed charitably.

"The whole thing seems curiously aimless and trivial," was *Time's* verdict, "not least because it smacks of the very shoddiness it presumably set out to expose."

"Kanin really hasn't a great deal to say," Gibbs commented.

"Kanin's failures have not been proud failures," Nathan thundered, "which, after all, have their share of glory—but cheap failures, since they apparently had no higher aim than to be commercial successes."

It gasped through twenty-eight performances and died.

This, Mike knew, was the last play of any kind he would ever produce. He had had it. For him the theater no longer was what Bob Sherwood said it ought to be, "the dwelling place of wonder." And it was his own fault. He should have quit when he was ahead. If he had said good-bye to Broadway at the peak of *Up in Central Park*'s run he would have retired as undefeated champion of the Street. He had been on too long. They would forget the winners and remember the losers. He had not intended to produce vulgar shows but, out of desperation, he had. *Peep Show* had been a repetition of *Star and Garter* as *Live Wire* was an echo of *January Thaw*. Every carbon copy is less distinct.

"They're wise to us," his friend and fellow producer, Max Gordon, had said. "The jig is up."

He had come to Broadway in the winter of 1937, brave and defiant. *"Call Me Ziggy,"* he had commanded.

After thirteen years and sixteen shows that grossed $18,000,-000, not counting his reign at the World's Fair, they still wouldn't call him Ziggy.

* **33** *

Judgment Day

It was June, 1949.

The semi-bald, conservatively dressed man adjusted his spectacles and looked across his desk.

"Why have you come to me, Mr. Todd?" he asked.

"I hear you're the best bankruptcy man in New York," Mike said.

Charles Seligson, professor of law at New York University Law School, and at Rutgers before that, and a highly respected practicing lawyer for more than twenty years, shook his head gravely. "I am retained by creditors and trustees," he said. "I put people *in* jail."

"You've got a reputation for being honest, Professor. That's good enough for me."

"You had better find someone else to represent you, Mr. Todd," Professor Seligson advised. "I'm leaving for a vacation with my family soon. I can't handle your case."

Mike was desperately insistent.

Professor Seligson recognized the desperation of the man sitting across from him and finally agreed to look into his case. If, after going over the records, he was convinced the case was honorable, he would ask for an adjournment and then take up the matter upon his return.

Satisfied with his findings, Professor Seligson agreed to represent Todd.

"I'm a damn fool but not a criminal," Mike told Seligson. "As God is my judge, I have not lied or done anything wrong knowingly."

Seligson nodded. "That's why I am going to represent you."

Mike's jaw dropped. One of the most respected lawyers in New York was the first human being who believed him.

Seligson took a law book from the shelf and quickly found the page he wanted.

"The Law, under 'Title 18, United States Code Section 3057,'" he read aloud, "requires that 'any Referee, Receiver, or Trustee having reasonable grounds for believing that any violations of the bankruptcy laws or *other* laws of the United States relating to insolvent debtors . . . have been committed, . . . shall report to the appropriate United States Attorney *all* the facts and circumstances of the case.'"

The professor closed the book. "That isn't optional, but a legal requirement," he said. "The fact that they have not gone to the U.S. Attorney, the fact that no civil *or* criminal proceedings for the concealment of assets have been filed against you in all this time, indicates you're innocent."

After hearings and careful consideration a postponement was granted.

When Professor Seligson returned from his vacation he carefully reviewed all the papers Mike had brought him and the proceedings in court, and then participated in hearings. Thereafter he told Mike, "This should have been dismissed within a week after it was filed."

"The question is, when will it end?" Mike wanted to know.

Professor Seligson reflected carefully. "If I were you, I would withdraw the application for discharge."

"Withdraw?" Mike was stunned. "You mean waive all rights to a discharge from my debts?"

Professor Seligson nodded. "As a practical matter, why spend a lot of money fighting for a discharge? Go out and settle."

With what? Mike wondered. "You mean I got no case?" he asked.

"My advice is to withdraw," Seligson repeated.

If I throw in the sponge, Mike realized, *I'll never be out of hock. That's what Grant wants.* If he quit under fire, he felt, it would be an admission of guilt, and Sarasohn's charge in opposing the discharge that he had "committed fraudulent and felonious offenses punishable by imprisonment" would be generally accepted as the truth by default without having been proved. He would be marked lousy on Broadway, a welsher and a crook, and Grant would have his way. But he deferred to Professor Seligson's advice. In July, 1950, Mike withdrew his discharge petition and waived his right to a discharge of his debts.

"Such a waiver shall have the same force and effect of a denial of discharge to said bankrupt," Referee Loewenthal's order read. Meadow and other spokesmen for the creditors requested this specific wording, they claimed; otherwise he would have been able to return to court at some other time and apply for a discharge from the same debts. A denial of discharge precluded this possibility.

Grant had achieved a clean-cut victory.

"I advised my client to waive his right," Seligson rebutted, "inasmuch as he wants to repay his acknowledged debts.

"Moreover, *I* desired the 'same force and effect' wording in order to get the statute of limitations running again in my client's behalf." (There is a six-year limitation in New York State after which creditors no longer can sue debtors, a statute that is held in abeyance during a bankruptcy.) "A denial of discharge," Seligson pointed out, "is necessary to get it operating again."

The story hit the headlines October 8, 1950. The tabloids squeezed every juicy detail from the proceedings, quoting each accusation by Sarasohn of Mike's alleged perjury, falsification and fraud as if they had been substantiated. One fact was undeniable, and that was the headline in the New York *Daily News:*

BROKE FOR A MILLION, MICHAEL TODD BLAMES GAMBLING!

His predicament was received with amazement, scorn and glee but with little compassion.

"Mike's plight has the sympathy of his friends but they are shocked by his appalling gullibility," Winchell wrote in his column, October 18. "Here is a shrewd operator, a man who should know all the angles, yet he was more of a sucker than the most naïve country bumpkin."

Mike said nothing. It was habit by now. He had been hauled in and out of courts, accused of lying, swindling and having convenient lapses of memory to conceal his frauds. Not once, by a syllable or an expression, even with intimates, had he defended his silence. He had a fabulous memory and recalled every detail of every check, every loss, but his lips were sealed. A wealthy owner of a Las Vegas casino had welshed on a $125,000 gambling debt and a well-heeled innkeeper owed him $50,000. His friends in Hollywood had insisted on cash. They were in the top income brackets and had enough trouble with the Internal Revenue Department without accounting for their winnings at cards too. He wasn't concealing his frauds but *theirs.* If he had remembered names and had kept check stubs, many a great name would be facing the prison term he had been threatened with for three years. He had his code, he lived by it and, if need be, he would die by it. If this was Winchell's definition of a sucker, he was a sucker. The biggest talker on Broadway wouldn't talk.

Behind their bagels and scratch sheets, the regulars at Lindy's shook their heads and said, at least Todd went out big.

Mike was oblivious. He considered himself indestructible.

THE NINTH LIFE

"He'll move mountains if necessary.

If it's not necessary, he'll

build a mountain so he can move it."

THE

NINTH

LIFE

* *

* 34 *
Roller Coaster Ride

"There are no more Shangri-Las," Lowell Thomas' familiar voice sighed over the radio. His son, also an adventurer and lecturer, had just returned from an expedition to Lhasa, Tibet, and had found it more realistic than the idyllic utopia depicted in James Hilton's *Lost Horizon.*

Mike wired Thomas that he was interested in his son's lecture. He was interested in anything that might make a buck. The Bobby Clark Show he was producing had just been canceled after seven anemic performances on the Colgate Comedy Hour. Television was not ready for him, or vice versa.

The man whose proud name had been blazoned on the marquees of four Broadway shows simultaneously now was reduced to booking an illustrated lecture by Lowell Thomas, *Junior,* in Madison Square Garden.

The 16-mm. film young Thomas had brought back from Tibet was lost in the huge arena, even the 35-mm. blowup was inadequate. They needed a screen big enough to fill the Garden.

"They're experimenting with a wide one out on Long Island," Frank Smith, Todd's business manager, told him.

Mike grabbed Max Gendel, his press agent, and drove out to look at it.

The indoor tennis court on the Belair estate of William Woodward, Jr., multimillionaire socialite and sportsman, had been converted into a projection room. When Mike saw the spacious screen and what was on it he forgot all about the lecture. He instantly knew that his entire career as a pitchman, promoter and producer had been a prelude to this.

"Potentially this is the most exciting thing in the history of show business!" he exclaimed.

Fred Waller and Hazzard (Buzz) Reeves nodded indulgently. They were inured to enthusiasms that suddenly burst into flames, glowed awhile and then flickered out.

"Tell me all about it," Mike insisted. "Start at the beginning, as Fannie Brice says, from hello to hello."

Waller, associated with the short-subjects department of Paramount Pictures in New York, had experimented with peripheral vision for several years. He perfected the process in 1939 and called it Vitarama. During World War II it was used by the Air Force as a gunnery trainer, battle conditions being simulated with eleven of Waller's projectors covering a circular room, the gunner in a mockup at the hub.

Reeves, a sound engineer, owner of the Reeves Soundcraft Company, joined Waller in 1946. He invested $30,000 and installed a stereophonic sound system. They offered a case of champagne for the best name submitted, and a boy won with Cinerama.

The first Cinerama company was formed by an impressive coterie of investors led by Henry Luce of Life-Time-Fortune and Lawrence Rockefeller of the Rockefeller Foundation. There wasn't a showman among them and nothing was put on the wide screen except Waller's test shots.

"Liquidate the company and write it off as a tax loss," Charles Stillman, representing the Luce interests, advised in 1950.

"That's like flying seventy-five percent across the ocean and turning back," Reeves protested.

Reeves bought the Cinerama company, after an appraisal, for $1,500. This did not affect the original Vitarama company, founded and owned outright by Waller, which had the basic patents and leased the apparatus (cameras, projectors, etc.) exclusively to Cinerama on a percentage arrangement.

"This should be the engineering company for the whole motion picture industry," Reeves said. "Movies were created by science, the invention of Edison's camera. But the industry was unfaithful to the medium that gave it birth. Alongside their office buildings for producers, writers, directors and executives they should have had laboratories. If they had, they would have had television." He paused. "I've shown Cinerama to the top people of every major studio." Reeves shook his head sadly. "What's the matter with 'em?"

"Hollywood is a status quo town; anything with a revolutionary concept can't be sound," Mike said. "The studios are archaic; they're making and selling pictures the way they did thirty years ago. The public is so far ahead of them they can't even *see* 'em. The dam will break one of these days, faster than anyone thinks, and the industry will be done for. But the Big Numbers won't care. They created a *one-generation* business, and they don't care what happens to it after they're gone. They've lived selfishly and they'll die selfishly. Forget Hollywood. Let's talk Cinerama."

Three new groups, one headed by Lowell Thomas, Sr., had expressed interest in reorganizing the company to produce its first feature—famous places and events to be shot all over the world by Robert Flaherty, the father of documentary films—and, Reeves said, he was about to sign a contract with one of the combines, not Thomas'.

"Do nothing until tomorrow morning," Mike said. "I'll make you a better offer."

He did not have the price of a meal; he could not go to his office because it was besieged by creditors. Crown's lawyers were pressing for payment on the $605,000 in notes. He had never made a picture in any process, but there was not a scintilla of doubt in his mind that he would come up with a bankroll the next morning and succeed where Henry Luce and the Rockefellers had failed.

"This is a *big* score, Max," he told Gendel on the way home. He knew it—he visualized on its vast screen what he had always sought: *the strange and the unusual.* The use of *three* cameras, seeing a scene as the human eye does, overwhelmed him. "It'll hit 'em and squeeze 'em," he said.

He was so excited he telephoned Joan, in the middle of the night. "I got big news," he began.

"I heard it on the radio," she said sleepily. "The attempted assassination of President Truman." November 2, 1950, had been a big day in Washington too.

Mike called Joan ten times a day, took her to dinner and first nights, and introduced her as "the former and future Mrs. Todd." Now that they were not married they were friends again.

"Don't let anyone tell you these two haven't reconciled, because they have," Louella Parsons assured her devotees. Actually, Mike was courting more girls than Howard Hughes was credited with having.

He was at Frank Smith's office early in the morning. "I *got* to get in Cinerama," he told his business manager.

Smith represented Thomas, too, and suggested a partnership. They would complement each other, he said. Thomas, with his long experience as a world traveler and commentator, could best supervise the production. Todd would be the front man. Meanwhile, he presented Lowell Thomas, Jr., at Carnegie Hall, and *Variety* reported he made "a boff preem as a gab impresario."

The Thomas-Todd Company was organized with an authorized capitalization of 308,000 shares, Todd and Thomas to own 189,500 shares jointly. Mike did not approve of the company name; it was the first time in his life he had ever taken second billing, but he was not in a bargaining position.

Cinerama, Inc., was reorganized by two financial firms—Gearhart, Kinnard and Otis of New York and White and Company of St. Louis—together with a law firm in which John Wharton was a partner. It started with an authorized capitalization of 3,500,000 shares, par value ten cents, which it registered with the Securities and Exchange Commission and offered to the public at two dollars a share.

Waller became chairman of the board of directors and received 95,000 shares in addition to 170,000 shares paid to his Vitarama. Reeves was elected president of the company and given 110,000 shares plus 5,000 shares for his family and 900,-000 shares for his Soundcraft Company. The underwriters retained the right to put their own representatives on the board and, like all officers, each had options for approximately 110,-000 additional shares at ten cents a share plus the right to buy two additional shares at ten cents if they bought the first.

Translated into Todd English, this meant that the Wall Street boys, loaded with stock that cost them practically nothing, merely had to sit back and wait for the public to hoist it to eight or ten dollars a share. They were riding a gravy train worth twelve million bucks. *And Reeves had offered him twenty-five percent of his chunk.*

Now there were three companies—Vitarama, Cinerama, Inc. and Thomas-Todd—one for each screen. All they needed was a picture.

Toots Shor, an accredited arbiter of Broadway beefs, at Todd's request, arranged a meeting between Grant and Todd at his restaurant, and, as befitted his judicial position, planted his Falstaffian figure between them.

"What do you want?" Grant demanded.

"I have a chance to get on my feet with Cinerama," Mike said, "but they won't issue any stock in my name as long as Crown's claim hangs over me."

Grant faced Mike. "You come to me with a hundred thousand dollars. Get a hundred friends to put up a thousand apiece or ten friends to put up ten thousand apiece. You bring the hundred thousand from your friends, as donations to any Illinois university as a charity gift—which is deductible—and I'll try to get you a complete release from Crown for the entire amount of $605,000. I'll give you ninety days to do it. I want to prove once and for all whether you have any friends. If your friends won't help you, why should Crown?"

Before Todd could raise a dollar, almost on the eve of the start of production, Robert Flaherty died. His work could not be carried on because he had revealed his concept to no one.

Commitments had been made and deadlines had to be met. No two partners could reach an agreement on the subject for the first picture. Weeks of indecision passed.

"To hell with proving anything," Mike interrupted a prolonged discussion on subjects that would display Cinerama to its best advantage, "let's get the show on the road."

He took a camera crew and shot Niagara Falls from a helicopter, the Shriners' annual parade, anything he could get—free. If a sight or subject interested him he knew it would interest the general public: he was, as he always maintained, part hick.

The first rough cut of the film he had shot was unreeled in their projection room on Long Island.

The lights went on and Reeves turned to Todd apprehensively. "What do you think, Mike?" he asked.

Todd winced. "That opening! Whose idea was *that*?"

"Thomas'."

"No showmanship," Mike snapped. "You can't start a *show* with a lecture by Fred Waller! You'll lose 'em before you get 'em. And that girl walking across the screen at the start: that *accentuates* the seams in the screen. You got to sock 'em in the opening scene with something so stunning they won't *see* the jiggle-lines!" He paused and, almost instantly, his eyes glistened. "The roller coaster ride!" he exclaimed. "The test Waller made: *that's* the money shot! I'll reshoot it in color and we'll throw it at 'em quick. Then we *got* 'em!"

Mike did not shoot the scene. Michael Junior, a junior at Amherst, did, on a week end. He went to Rockaway Beach with a cameraman and two technicians, promoted the use of the roller coaster and shot the ride in a couple of hours.

"Saved seventy-two bucks, Dad," he said proudly on his return. "We ran out of film before we finished the sequence, and we needed only sixty feet, so I used short ends of film."

Mike's face turned ashen. "Say that again, son, slowly."

"I told you, we ran out of film so . . ."

"You can't *pick up* a shot like that on a roller coaster!" Mike was incredulous.

"I did," Junior said softly.

"But the action would have to be picked up at the *identical* place on the runway after each strip was run through the camera!"

"I know," Junior said. "That's how we saved seventy-two dollars."

Mike hardly believed what he saw on the screen. It was a million-to-one shot and Junior had brought it in: he had stopped the action on a roller-coaster runway and had matched it, to the *frame*. He looked at his son with wonderment and pride. He wasn't the only Michael Todd who could perform the impossible.

He ran the film over and over again, vamping for an idea. At last it came to him. He went to Thomas Cook and Sons. "What's going on in Europe this summer?" he asked.

He was given a list of tourist attractions. Within a week, he, Junior and Harry Squires, a cameraman, were crossing the Atlantic.

There was no script. Mike was on his own and he gave his imagination full rein. Thomas had told him to shoot castles. Todd didn't dig castles. He went to Austria and shot the Vienna Boys Choir. Before deciding on his next move, he dispatched Junior with the camera crew to Salzburg to pick up a folk-dancing festival.

While Junior was in Salzburg, Mike explored Vienna, not only the three zones governed by the United States, Great Britain and France, but the fourth, under Russian authority.

Michael Junior had not yet finished the Salzburg sequence when he received an urgent call from his father to bring the camera crew to Vienna immediately.

It *was* urgent. The changing of the guard, the monthly transfer of authority among the four major powers, was an event. The following day, Mike had learned, it would be the U.S. Army's turn to take over control from the Russians.

What a picture! Mike grinned. *The Russians hauling down their flag . . . and our guys raising the Stars and Stripes to the top of the flagpole.*

Why hadn't anyone shot it before? he wondered, and he soon had the answer. The Russians would not permit anyone with a camera close enough to take the picture.

Mike went to work. He cultivated the acquaintance of the Russian honor guard, managed to talk to them and drink with them. Making himself understood in pidgin English-Russian, an almost impossible feat, was infinitely easier for him than drinking. He couldn't guzzle in any language. He tried. He had to sell them the idea of letting him shoot the scene he wanted.

Michael found the Todd suite in the Bristol Hotel a shambles. His father was unconscious and the effluvium of kosher salami and pastrami, plus the fumes of stale whiskey, were overpowering. At last Michael reached his father's side.

For a time Junior thought he would need an inhalator. Cold showers, vigorous shaking, shouts and prayers had little effect. At last Mike opened one eye, saw the sun and shuddered.

"Allied Military Headquarters . . ." he gasped.

They arrived as the Russian flag was taken from the flagpole. Mike pleaded with his guests of the previous night to repeat the ceremony for Cinerama. The Russians' bloodshot eyes gazed genially at him but their heads shook no. They could not respect a man who quit before finishing his first bottle of whiskey.

Mike went to Milan and talked the guardians of La Scala into permitting him to take a camera into the famed opera house for the first time. After he had paid for the rights to put an opera on film he had nothing left in his budget for crowd-reaction shots, certainly not enough to pay for a dress crowd.

He hired a piano virtuoso for a concert. The price of admission was an appearance in evening dress. He got his formally attired crowd, a full house, for the cost of one piano player. Mike had some of the world's finest classical music to offer a public that would never get to La Scala.

"I'm going back to mind the store," he told Junior. "Wind 'er up and don't waste film."

Junior took a five-man crew to Edinburgh to get the Scottish bagpipers, then made a sequence of languorous shots of the canals of Venice that would challenge the famed roller-coaster scene he had made for $33—the cost of renting a station wagon and buying bolts to fasten the camera to the careening coaster. He was almost as proud of his accomplishment as he was of his feats at Amherst. Almost. The scenes he had shot gave him some satisfaction, but not as much as his intercollegiate record of eating fifteen hamburgers in thirteen minutes followed by five quarts of ice cream. He doubted if even his old man could do any better. He would not want to challenge his dad to anything, *he* was unbeatable when the chips were down, but his shield of invincibility was slightly tarnished since that day in his suite at the Hotel Bristol. Junior would have liked to defend the family's good name against the Russkys.

It was June, 1952. Crown's lawyers were applying pressure, using Lowell Thomas as a fulcrum. The law permits a creditor, in the pursuance of a judgment, to call a debtor for examination. They decided to subpoena Thomas for questioning on Todd's financial interest in the Thomas-Todd Company and Cinerama, Inc.

Thomas put it straight to his partner. "If I say you have no stock in Cinerama," he said, "you are *not* going to have any stock in Cinerama. I won't perjure myself for you, Todd. Now, how do you want it: have you stock or haven't you?"

Todd was whipsawed. If he did not make a settlement with Crown, he would be dealt out of Cinerama without a share of stock.

With the assistance of Joe Schenck, a friend of Crown's, Todd arranged to settle Crown's $640,000 judgment for $170,000. He paid $120,000 in cash and gave notes for the other $50,000, which were paid several years later. He then received his Cinerama stock.

This Is Cinerama had its première the evening of September 10, 1952, before twelve hundred persons at the Broadway Theater in New York.

It was an unqualified triumph. A gentleman left his seat to phone and, next morning, for the first time in the history of the New York *Times*, a motion picture was reviewed on the front page, by order of its publisher.

Fred Waller's dream had come true. Lowell Thomas took the main bows. The stockholders hugged one another. The Wall Street boys knew they had it made: after tonight the stock would zoom. There was nothing to do but wait for the money to roll in. *This Is Cinerama* would run forever.

A lone dissenter sat glumly in the back row. He was Mike

Todd. The paeans and promises of fabulous profits had no effect upon him. The picture was on the screen: *it was finished.* His partners were interested in what they had; he was preoccupied with what *could* be had. They were overjoyed with the success of the process; he was disturbed by its failure. Mike was a perfectionist. They were not.

He had become aware of an obvious flaw during the shooting: three cameras were so unwieldy it was impossible to achieve intimate scenes.

"We can't stay on that damn roller coaster and the canals of Venice forever," he told his associates. "Sooner or later a boy has to tell a girl, 'I love you.'" They were content to put on Lowell Thomas travelogues forever. He wanted to produce *shows.* If he was boss he would buy *Oklahoma!* from Rodgers and Hammerstein at any cost. The biggest screen deserved no less than the biggest show.

He was as impatient with success as he was with failure, which, in his book, was the same thing. He could not be gratified, let alone content with a winner. That was the Hollywood game: get a formula, steal it if you must, but get it and *keep* it. If Darryl or Jerry comes up with a hit, make a picture exactly like it as quickly as possible and catch the *cycle.* Try anything new when it is old. That wasn't a Goldwynism, it was all ten commandments. Ask De Mille.

Mike had different sights. His norm was swimming upstream with a ton of grief on his back, heading for uncharted waters. *Only the untried is safe. Instincts are man's only protection. It is man's duty, perhaps his most sacred, to keep topping his best. There are no boundaries to imagination; only a coward or a simpleton imagines them. A man should make bigger and bigger circles until he encompasses the world. Wonderment is all. In a life that begins and ends in mystery, how can there be else than wonderment in between? The visionary is the greatest realist. If a man does not know what is impossible, he will do it.*

His acts had not always borne out his philosophy but he always knew what he *should* do.

Cinerama had a bug. The projection of three separate film strips on a screen by three separate projectors precluded the possibility of the three images' being perfectly meshed. There would always be seams, or joining lines, to destroy the illusion. That is, until someone invented a camera that would shoot the three angles out of the same lens and record them on one strip of film.

It could not be done, all his associates told him. Waller had been experimenting for twenty years; he was a genius with lenses, and the triple-camera was his masterwork. Did Todd have a *magna cum laude* from M.I.T.?

There were more serious rumbles from within the corporate machinery of Cinerama. The financiers had discovered, to their chagrin, that they had outsmarted themselves, or, rather, Todd and Thomas had outsmarted them. Of the three companies affiliated with the process, it now appeared that the production company of Thomas and Todd would be the most profitable. The solution was simple: the Thomas-Todd Company would be dissolved and its assets absorbed by Cinerama, Inc.

Lowell Thomas was an asset. He was a good Republican. He had been on the radio twenty-five years, longer than any other man. He had substance.

Todd? He was brash, argumentative and a Stevenson man. He did not belong. Imagine saying they couldn't stay on the roller coaster forever. The hell they couldn't! And his cracks about the flaws in Cinerama: it was treason! Todd was a liability.

Frank Smith was assigned to pull the rug out from under him. Mike threatened a lawsuit that would blow the lid off the stock manipulation: how the public had been misled into believing that stock in Cinerama, Inc., was a bonanza when the truth was that Vitarama and Thomas-Todd were the only companies that could show a substantial profit, and their stock was *not* available to the public.

Smith came back with a deal. If Mike would "sell" his stock, worth approximately $300,000, they would try to arrange a lease on Marine Stadium at Jones Beach, Long Island, for a number of years at a favorable rental. Mike could stage his extravaganzas there, make money and be happy.

The alternative was implicit: if he refused, the Wall Street boys would show him what trouble really was.

Mike was eased out, Thomas-Todd was dissolved and Cinerama Productions took its place. Thomas received approximately 68,000 shares. Dudley Roberts, Jr., a partner in Roberts and Company, New York brokers, got 41,000 shares. And Frank Smith, for services rendered, was given 45,000 shares.

Mike had had his first encounter with Big Business. His next adventure in high finance would be with a dame named Manville.

* 35 *

Enter Evelyn and Todd-AO

Lorraine Manville Gould Aldao Dresselhuys invested $400,000 in a show Mike planned to stage at Jones Beach.

He had to have an extravaganza that would fill the 8,200 seats in the four-million-dollar Marine Stadium. A water show suggested Venice. That meant gondolas. He would have boys and girls singing in gondolas equipped with radio telephones to amplify their voices. And a bevy of mermaids disappearing under water and emerging with fishes in their bosoms. He would bring back his soap-bubble machine from *The Hot Mikado* and *Peep Show:* a carload of Lux and electric fans. He needed music and chose an 1883 operetta by Johann Strauss. It was in public domain, free.

Nobody will hold still for a Strauss operetta, his associates told him.

"They will with fireworks," he said. He was going to have free music if it cost him $50,000.

Michael Todd Presents a Full Moon and A NIGHT IN VENICE, the billboards announced.

Opening night was more of a Nightmare in Venice. A gale that was a precursor of the worst summer weather in forty years blew the scenery away. A coral-bedecked elevator sank unexpectedly and dumped a chorus of nymphs into the lagoon. The audience was half a mile away and did not know what it was all about.

Immediately after the finale he called the cast together and congratulated them. It was a great show, he enthused, the audience loved it and the advance sale assured a run of at least two years. "I had to hypo 'em," he confided to Doll, "or they would have spread the word at Lindy's we have a flop."

It would run two seasons and lose $400,000, Lorraine's.

She would get back every dollar with interest.

"Who is the Einstein of the optical racket?" he asked anyone he thought might know that fall of 1952 after he had been muscled out of Cinerama.

His quest took him to Rochester, New York, where he telephoned a Dr. Brian O'Brien. "My name is Mike Todd," he introduced himself. "I want to see you."

"I'm sorry," the gentle voice replied, "but I'm busy."

"I'm busy too," Mike said, "and I came up here to see you."

"All right," came the reluctant consent, "but only for a brief meeting."

The slender, benevolent-looking man of fifty-six years, with thinning gray locks, peered at his visitor through steel-rimmed spectacles. Dr. Brian O'Brien, director of the Institute of Optics at the University of Rochester, had never heard of Cinerama or Mike Todd.

Todd explained the workings of Cinerama, and concluded, "Doc, I want a Cinerama camera with everything to come out of *one* hole. Can it be done?"

"In science anything is feasible," O'Brien replied. "What you want, however, would require the specialized talents of a large organization. I'm sorry but I cannot help you. Try one of the big commercial optical firms."

Mike could not spell *peripheral* but he knew what he wanted. Dr. O'Brien was his man. He had invented only one camera in his life, but that was the fastest in existence, used for photographing explosions in general, bursting bombs in particular. Todd telephoned O'Brien a minimum of three times a day for five weeks.

Early in November, Dr. O'Brien was granted a leave of absence to become vice-president in charge of research for the American Optical Company, a venerable concern with headquarters at Southbridge, Massachusetts. Todd's urgent calls followed him.

The scientist knew when he had met his match. He dispatched a young colleague to New York to see if Cinerama really did amount to anything. He received a comprehensive analysis, ending with the word "Wow!"

Walter A. Stewart, the elderly, conservative president of American Optical Company, was just another customer to Mike Todd, salesman.

"Your company is fat," Mike told him. "I've cased it. Your net sales last year were more than seventy million bucks and you have a working capital of over fifty million. Now is the time to expand into new fields and search new horizons."

Stewart was sold. He placed all the resources of his company at Dr. O'Brien's disposal.

"I must warn you, Mr. Todd," Dr. O'Brien said before he began the project in November. "It may take three years and cost twenty million dollars."

Mike pulled on his heavy eyebrows. "The twenty million is *no* problem," he said, "but the three years is out of the question. *Doc, you got six months.*"

Dr. O'Brien recruited Professor Robert E. Hopkins and his associates at the Institute of Optics. They organized a team of a hundred and fifty research specialists and engineers. Philips, the Dutch electrical manufacturer, was commissioned to construct the projector.

It was a staggering project. The scientists had to perfect an entirely new geometric process for photographing and projecting film. They had to evolve a series of new-type lenses, ranging from a 37-degree angle to 128 degrees: everything the human eye could see with the sole exception of that peripheral vision which the eye can pick up only by rolling in its socket. They had to produce specially made 65-mm. film for cameras, three and a half times the area of the standard Academy aperture. This meant changing the style of perforation, projecting thirty frames a second instead of the traditional twenty-four, and making provisions for magnetic sound tracks so that full stereophonic sound could be obtained when the master prints were reduced to 35-mm. for subsequent runs in theaters having standard equipment.

Mike was always applying pressure, always prodding, always encouraging.

"The new Todd speaks of aspheric optical elements, aspect ratios and lenticular screens," Winchell reported in consternation. "Quite a switch from the carefree character who used to discuss show biz economics in terms of ducks and deducts, with the deducts usually leading the field."

The game was open. This time he was the dealer. He had

been indoctrinated by the stickmen in Cinerama. From now on *he* picked his boards of directors.

Magna Theater Corporation was organized in March, 1953, to finance the process. Todd owned half of the stock, a percentage that would be whittled down extensively in the months to come. Joe Schenck became chairman of the board of directors. His partner, George Skouras, head of the United Artists Theater Circuit, Inc., was named president, and Arthur Hornblow, Jr., vice-president. Mike completed the board with Lee Shubert, his oldest friend on Broadway; Professor Charles Seligson, his lawyer; Richard Rodgers and Oscar Hammerstein II, who had given him their promise not to sell *Oklahoma!* until they had seen his process; James M. Landis, former dean of Harvard Law School; Edward Small and himself.

A contract between Magna and American Optical Company was signed. It contained a clause that, when the process reached the exploitation stage, a third company would be set up to do the exploiting, with Magna and American Optical Company as partners. Mike had not missed a page in his Cinerama primer.

The lens was nine inches in diameter; it was called the Bug Eye and it was completed in May, six months to the day since Mike had given Dr. O'Brien his deadline.

"The process has to have a name," one of the directors said at a meeting of the board.

"Let's call it Magnascope or Magnorama," another director suggested.

"No good," Mike vetoed. "The public is already confused with the glut of 'scopes, 'ramas and 'visions on the market."

His associates concurred. What, they asked, *was* a unique name?

"The name must be not only catching but one that will stick in the public's mind," Mike said. "Call it the Todd Process."

There was a stunned silence, broken by an executive from the American Optical Company.

"Whatever name is decided upon," he said, "it seems only fair that it should contain some reference to our firm."

"Agreed," Mike said. "We can call it Todd-AO."

It was.

Some were of the opinion that it should have been called the O'Brien Process. No one was less interested in this contention than Dr. O'Brien.

"Todd was the first to recognize the need to give the effects of Cinerama with a single camera and film," he said. "It is due to his vision and imagination, plus his drive and determination to stay with it during the difficult period of development, that it came into being. I am glad that the process has his name on it."

It was a hectic month.

On May 8, Junior, recently commissioned in the Navy, married Sarah Jane Weaver, the girl who lived next door when they had the big house in Irvington. His father and Sarah's parents were the only ones present at the ceremony performed by a Superior Court judge at Newport, Rhode Island.

"You two ought to get along," Michael told his father-in-law, president of a construction company. "Dad used to be president of a construction company too."

Before Junior was born, Mike realized. *I'm getting on. Next month I'll be forty-four, even by my reckoning.*

He did not dwell on it. He had a date that night with Marlene Dietrich. And Evelyn Keyes, one of the most beautiful girls in the world, was flying in from Paris to spend a few days with him.

A small, selective group of millionaires was invited to the Regent Theater in Buffalo on August 14 to witness the first screening of Todd-AO on a makeshift beaverboard screen, a test sequence in color involving two young couples at a picnic.

"I found myself wanting to reach for a doughnut," Richard Rodgers exclaimed, "and then for both girls!"

"This is for us," Oscar Hammerstein II said.

"Gentlemen, *it's an extension of life,*" Mike said, chomping on his cigar. *"You're in the show with Todd-AO!"* He grinned for the first time in more than a year. He had the greatest process in the history of motion pictures, his name was on it, he had just minted a slogan for it, and he had *Oklahoma!*, the most successful musical show of all time, to present on it.

In his moment of elation there was a single note of misgiving. If he had not changed his name, it would now be Gold-bogen-AO, a proud banner for his people all over the world.

Rodgers and Hammerstein drove a hard bargain. They held out for $1,020,000 cash and forty percent of the net profits, Magna to pay all distribution and advertising expenses. Also, they insisted on the right to purchase a substantial block of stock at the original price Schenck and Skouras had paid. Magna would have distribution rights for ten years with an option on three additional years, after which all rights would revert to Rodgers and Hammerstein.

Mike secured $1,050,000 from Skouras' United Artists Theater Corporation to close the deal, for half of the common stock in the new company to be formed, and persuaded Skouras as well as Schenck to sell Rodgers and Hammerstein some of their Magna stock at the original price.

Rodgers and Hammerstein had closed the most incredible deal ever made for a property, and the most important condition, one that would force Todd out of Todd-AO, was still to come.

"Evelyn Keyes flies out tonight to join Mike Todd in Paris," Harrison Carroll reported in the Los Angeles *Herald-Express* September 10, 1953. "The town is full of rumors that the two will wed, but Evelyn says no. 'Mike and I have talked about it,' she admitted, 'but I have had several marriages and I want to be real sure the next time. It has been a lot of fun the last two years; I have enjoyed my freedom and I don't know as I would want to give it up. I'll see Mike in Europe, but no wedding.'"

He had played the field as long as he could, but he wasn't gaited for it. He was, as the saying goes, a one-woman man. He had gone with Eva nine years, and almost eight years with Joan. He had to have someone he could trust, someone he could talk to.

Evelyn Keyes was a brown-eyed ash blonde, fey, irrepressible, honest with herself and warmly sincere. She was born in Texas, raised in Georgia and educated by men.

She was married to Barton L. Bainbridge, owner of a swimming-pool corporation, for two years. He could not live without her, and in the summer of 1940, one month after their separation, he sat in his car, held a rifle between his knees with the muzzle against his heart and squeezed the trigger.

Four years later she married Charles Vidor, a director at Columbia Pictures, where she was under contract. It lasted fourteenth months.

One evening in July, 1946, John Huston made an impulsive proposal at Romanoff's Restaurant, and she took him up. Their host, Prince Mike, went home for a wedding ring lost by a guest in his pool. They flew to Las Vegas and, with the pilot and taxi driver as witnesses, were married at 3:30 A.M. It lasted three and a half years.

"Next time I better hook up with a good husband rather than a good director," she said. "It wasn't a total loss, however. I read seventy-eight of Robert Hutchins' list of one hundred classics."

She played in scores of films, from the role of Suellen, the demure sister of Scarlett O'Hara, to *The Jolson Story*, and including such forgettable sagas as *Sons of the Legion* and *Smugglers Island*, but she was always more entertaining off the screen.

For a time she carried a thermometer in her purse. Asked why, she replied, "Oh, somebody might ask for the temperature."

Mike had never known a woman like her. She thought like

a man and was brutally frank. "What's this nonsense about women and children first?" she remarked with honest scorn when she read the script on *Titanic*. In her world there was no moral distinction between men and women; they were people.

She was a true liberal, and through her, Mike's political consciousness, evolved during his associations with Lloyd Lewis, Jake Arvey and the Democratic Party, became more acute.

With the possible exception of Gypsy Rose Lee, she was the only woman who never pulled a punch against Mike. And she hit harder than Gypsy. Her plain talk bothered him for a long time, but he listened. He felt a need for it and there was some worth to it.

She went to a psychiatrist, mostly to analyze Mike.

"He has a strong persecution complex working against him," she said at one session. "It's unworthy of him and infuriates me."

She was annoyed with Mike when he told of a criminal or someone who had done something he did not like, and added resentfully, "And he's a Jew."

"Why, in all your other stories about no-goodniks," she asked, "don't you mention that the people involved are Gentiles? It must be a basic insecurity . . ."

"That's your head-shrinker talking," he said. "I'll give you the whole drill. I'm insecure. If I admit I'm insecure, then it's proof I'm insecure. If I insist I *am* secure, that's a pose, I'm fighting it, the proof of my insecurity. Prenatal or postnatal, take your pick . . ." His amusement was greater than his scorn.

She wanted him to be a bigger man because he was a big man, greater than any of the many she had known. And she loved him, unconditionally and unselfishly.

He illustrated his feelings about marriage with a story.

"This porter made only twenty bucks a week in the bar but he managed to buy a sweepstakes ticket every drawing, for ten years. Then he hit. He quit his job, bought a carload of clothes and started buying $100 tickets at the race track. A broad saw the fresh dough and they got cozy.

"After a few months she spotted him at the $50 window. A warning signal. She dusted him at the $10 window; she didn't want to wait until he was broke. She was off and running.

"He tapped out, begged for his old job back, and got it under sufferance, still at twenty bucks a week. He kept buying sweepstakes tickets out of habit. Four years later his number came in again.

"When the man came with the good news, the porter exclaimed, '*Good God, do I have to go through that again?*' "

It was one of his favorite fables, if not Evelyn's.

"I'll never marry an actress," he told her one day. Then, noting her hurt look, he quickly added, "You're not an actress, Evelyn." She would be *Mrs. Mike* but only in a movie.

"To live with an actress," he would say, "you got to be able to worry about her hair. And when their bosoms start to drop they get panicky and run to head-shrinkers."

Bill Doll had to become a producer, and in October of that year he presented *Sherlock Holmes,* a play in three acts, written by Ouida Rathbone and starring her husband, Basil, with Thomas Gomez as the perfidious Moriarty.

It was fairly well received in Boston and drew $29,000 in three weeks, but Doll was worried. He needed money. Mike, who had come up for the opening, appraised the situation.

"I could give you dough, Bill," he said, "but psychologically it's better if you went into town in trouble."

Doll went into New York in trouble. *Sherlock Holmes* died after three desultory performances at the Century Theater and lost $120,000. Doll, personally responsible for $60,000, would be mimeographing press releases for years to get even.

Like Harry Bloomfield and Sammy Lambert before him, Doll had to learn the hard way. Todd's disciples knew every detail of all his tricks except how to perform them. There was a tendency, shared by friends and foes, to underestimate him. They confused intimacy—his informality with employees, "Call me Mike," and his lack of *outward* dignity—as proof of inability. His successes were charged off to uncommon luck, senseless gambles that happened to pay off.

Luck, his record proved, was the *least* significant ingredient of Mike's success.

Todd-AO Corporation was created in June, 1954, with full control of licensing the process. Magna Theater Corporation was allotted half of the A stock, AO the other half. B stock was split up sixty-two and a half percent Magna, the remainder AO. Kuhn, Loeb and Company, investment bankers, came into the deal. On the sixteenth of the month Magna sold $6,000,000 of debentures and later borrowed $2,000,000 from Bankers Trust Company.

Lorraine Manville had 75,000 shares in Todd-AO, representing $150,000 cash investment and the remainder which Mike had given her in repayment for the $400,000 she had staked him to stage *Night in Venice* at Jones Beach.

There were many skeptics. Nicholas Schenck, president of Loew's, Inc., Metro-Goldwyn-Mayer's parent company, for more than a quarter of a century, examined the 65-mm. film and shook his head. "It isn't practical," he said seriously. "This wide film won't fit in our cans."

Mike gave his first public demonstration of the process on June 22 and the stock skyrocketed to $20 a share. The following morning he received an offer from a Wall Street syndicate of $15 for every share he could deliver.

His 500,000 shares would bring $7,500,000. He had never had his hands on that kind of loot. It was tempting. But not enough. It was 1939 again, outside the Broadhurst Theater, the opening night of *The Hot Mikado*. Lee Shubert was offering to pay all the expenses for half of the profits. "It's a free ride, Mike. You can't lose, it's a sure thing." He had decided by flipping a coin, his last one. This time he did not have to toss a coin. He didn't want any free rides, let alone sure things. He was shooting for higher stakes. After he produced and directed *Oklahoma!* in Todd-AO he would be the biggest man in show business.

He had failed to include Messrs. Rodgers and Hammerstein in his planning. They were astonished that anyone could be under the misapprehension that absolute artistic control would be invested in anyone except Rodgers and Hammerstein.

Mike announced his vehement objection to any such assignment of power. Rodgers and Hammerstein did not waver.

Todd was confident. The board of directors, his board, had the last word. "It's suicide!" he roared at the climactic meeting. "We're buying *Oklahoma!* not to make a picture but to launch a *process!* The process *must* be the star. Oscar and Dick are friends of mine. I like them personally and I respect their work in the theater. But they know nothing about our process and, more important, they don't care. Why should they? *Oklahoma!* is their baby. In any question between the process and the play you know which will be sacrificed. They'll remain faithful to their play, *as it appeared on the stage,* and our process will go out the window. *Its* potential will never be realized. That's why I want to produce and direct it. To make sure the process is the star." He looked at his associates, one by one, the men he had chosen to be on his board. "I beg of you," he pleaded, "not to yield artistic control. You'll regret it the rest of your lives."

They did not listen and they did not hear. They knew what they wanted. They knew how they were going to vote. Everything was cut and dried. They looked down on Todd with the same contempt the lords of Cinerama had looked down on him. They *were* the same men, only the aliases were different. Their names were Money. They had the process, they had *Oklahoma!,* they had Rodgers and Hammerstein to produce it and Fred Zinneman, the hottest director in Hollywood, to put it on film. Todd should be grateful they let him put his name on the process, that was more than Dr. O'Brien got. Let him scare up a new racket to promote. They didn't need him any more. With him out of the company, the stock would go up.

Mike did not have to wait for the call of hands. He had read the votes in their faces. He had overmatched himself again. He was only half-smart when it came to finances. He became bored halfway through a transaction. They did not. They studied finances by the book. He wouldn't even read the book, he tried to write a new one. He was, he had to admit, a lousy business-man.

"I vote to give Rodgers and Hammerstein full artistic control," Skouras said perfunctorily and it was settled.

"I'm going to sell out," Mike confided to Schenck. "The stock is up to twenty-two dollars a share. In big lots I can get seventeen dollars, certainly fifteen."

"Please don't sell," Schenck begged.

"But there's nothing for me to do around here!" Mike said. "I'm not the producer, I'm not permitted to open my mouth on the production. Nobody wants me, why shouldn't I get out?"

"It would ruin the stock," Schenck said and added, meaningfully, "For all of us."

Schenck had appealed to him emotionally, and he could not turn him down. Uncle Joe had been too good to him.

He would not be forced to resign his directorship for another year. *Because of his friendship with Schenck, he would not sell his stock until it had dropped to five dollars a share, getting five million dollars less than he would have received when he wanted to sell it.* He did not mind that. What hurt was that, after all these years, he had learned so little. He was still naïve. He had left himself vulnerable and had been frozen out of the company he created. He had been, in his own word, *tooken.*

There was, he recognized, a fine line between him and those who had taken him. When he pulled a sharp deal he was called a con man. When they pulled one they were called astute traders. This time he'd thought he had had a sure thing, but he was beginning to realize that the world consisted entirely of exceptions.

It figured. He was one.

* 36 *

"I'll Tell You About Mike Todd . . ."

THE ANALYST

The lithe, sleek blonde in a Bikini lazed like a beautiful animal alongside the pool of Mike's hilltop home overlooking Los Angeles. She spoke with affectionate candor.

"Mike is a moral man. In fact, he's a prude. To him a wife's quote infidelity unquote is the worst sin on earth. The second worst is a husband being quote unfaithful unquote. It's a part of his Jewish morality. I used to enrage him, when he started ranting about some woman who was unfaithful, when I said that maybe there was a reason why she was, perhaps a cause that compelled her. 'Everything isn't black and white, Mike,' I used to say, 'there are shades of gray.' He's slowly coming around to believing it.

"He lives in a man's world. He's not at home with women. I have men friends. He doesn't dig it. He can't have a similar relationship with women. I regard men friends only as human beings. They are friends, sex is removed. It's different with Mike. He is innocent about women. He thinks he knows women. I don't think he ever did. To him women are women and men are men, and each is supposed to function in *one* way. Maybe—but I don't think so.

"He absolutely refuses to analyze. Anything. Mike doesn't know anybody else, really. And nobody knows Mike less than he knows himself. I honestly don't think he started to mature until he met me. He still has a long way to go. For example, when I met him, he was not politically aware. Oh, he said he was a Democrat but he really didn't know why. He ragged me because I ran with the liberal crowd. He called me a Communist. He used to say he didn't agree with McCarthy's methods but he liked his script. Mike is a great quote American unquote.

"Does he believe in God? He believes in a Force. He talks a lot about Jewishness and feels Jewishness strongly. He really *believes*. He has tremendous faith, like Christ and Napoleon. Yet there must be a lack of assurance somewhere. All this frantic running around must be a compensation. He has to prove something. I don't know for sure what it is. As a boy he was quite small. He was a little guy in a big family. Survival alone was sufficient reason for hustling. You can't get reasons out of Mike. He just tells quote stories unquote—all flavored, all amusing, many with a switch at the end—but no *whys*.

"He instills excitement in people. They're carried away by him. He's sincere, believe me. For a long time I thought he was lying. But he's telling the truth. When he gives you the mysterioso bit with the cloak-and-dagger overtones, when he talks of fanciful dreams, it's for himself more than for you. He is his audience as well as you. He's selling himself his dreams.

"Things have to be his way. He doesn't permit anyone else to function. He keeps complaining that people fail him, but the truth is he never gives them a chance. As a result, no one around him can show any initiative; practically all scare and freeze up. He insists on making all decisions. He won't hire anyone he can't dominate. The truth is, of course, he does things better than anyone else. But he doesn't give them a fair shake.

"Mike is all surface. He says he doesn't need a head-shrinker. Come to think of it, he doesn't. His compulsive talking and smoking, all his frenetic habits, certainly are neuroses, but he makes them work for him. They're a part of his success. He has absolutely no self-consciousness. He thinks nothing of picking up the phone and calling an Ambassador or the Secretary of State, and saying, 'I'm Mike Todd, I'd like to talk to you about something very important.'

"He has many defense mechanisms. Underneath he's a real softie. He puts on a tough front talking out of the corner of his mouth, chewing his cigar, accenting bad grammar. He becomes more ungrammatical when he's with so-called intellectuals. I guess it's his way of showing his contempt. Actually, he's terribly smart and knows an awful lot. Nothing can get him down. I should say nothing can *keep* him down. And he doesn't want any help from anyone.

"He's always on, every minute. He gets along everywhere. Everyone, high or low, gets his message. He quote gives unquote. He doesn't drink. He can't. One drink and he's drunk. He gets his kicks out of gambling. You can't tell by his face or his voice whether he has won or lost a fortune. Except maybe the cigar is a little more frayed. I don't dig gambling. I don't get the message.

"Mike sleeps exceedingly well: standing up, in a plane, anywhere. Yet he never truly relaxes. Even when he goes on a so-called vacation he doesn't play. He thrives on work. His mind never rests. He has to be center stage. He requires constant approval, especially from me.

"Beneath the façade is a wonderful, sensitive guy—but don't be fooled, he's not shy. He's the only truly generous man I've ever known. He is an honorable man, a man of genuinely good intentions. That's why he's hurt very often. He keeps saying that this person and that one hates him. That's because he knows in his heart that *his* intentions were honorable. He's oblivious of the fact that he might have said or done something that hurt the other person. He knows he didn't *intend* to.

"Marriage? Not right now. He's scarred. He takes marriage very seriously. Which is as it should be, I guess. Joe Schoenfeld of *Variety*, who thinks he knows Mike because he's buzzed around him twenty years or so, told a mutual friend, 'I know Mike. He never stuck to anything, including women. If Evelyn wants to hold on to him she'd better stay away from him.' I thanked the mutual friend for the advice. I think Joe is one hundred percent wrong. Mike does stick. For a guy of his years and his opportunities and the life he's led, he's had very few women."

Evelyn Keyes paused. "One more thing," she said. "Even Mike's worst enemy can't say he's petty."

THE MAN WHO WANTED A SON

The old man, meticulously attired in a gray tweed suit and matching haberdashery, sat on the balcony of his penthouse in Beverly Hills, gazing out at the city and the industry he had helped to build. His right eye was barely open, his speech was halting, every sybaritic moment of Joe Schenck's seventy-seven years was etched on his seamed face.

"Mike will undertake anything," he said. "Nothing will stop him. He'll move mountains if necessary. If it's not necessary he'll build a mountain so he can move it.

"To be able to go through bankruptcy for more than a million dollars you have to have the million and go broke all at once—or be a brilliant, likable personality capable of convincing a man who has a million to invest it in you. The million that Mike borrowed he got from sane, sound businessmen, like Henry Crown. He didn't get it from anyone who was also a promoter. How could Mike, with his inclinations, his manner of doing business, how did he sell sane, sound businessmen?

"The obvious answer is, he has qualities those businessmen don't have. He can paint pictures from his imagination. Is he a kind of genius? If a man is a genius who creates a masterpiece on canvas or in words, I suppose Mike is a genius for the pictures he created out of his imagination. He painted such wonderful pictures of nonsensical things, he made them real and logical to sane people.

"He always knew what he wanted and knew how to get it even if he himself could not create it. He *saw* Cinerama before the rest of us did. He visualized the necessary improvement on Cinerama before anyone else did. He convinced me, and I am not easily convinced. He always understood his subject thoroughly and he had the ability to transmit it. *A smart man cannot be deceived by something he fully understands.*

"Mike has a habit of being right. He fought bitterly against giving Rodgers and Hammerstein a free rein on *Oklahoma!*. He was outvoted. I would not have given them the control they received. It was a bad mistake. They did not use the process properly. Mike was right from beginning to end.

"You can't have a smooth relationship with Mike. If things run smooth he is not happy. He is a very difficult person to get along with. Often he doesn't know right from wrong. He can lead a person in the wrong direction knowingly. His intentions? Mike believes he is so great he can right anything, even knowing it is wrong.

"I don't dislike Mike and I don't approve of him. I wouldn't hurt him for the world. I don't say he should be forgiven. Nature created him as it did. We are products of heredity and environment. It could be that he was afflicted with bad heredity and environment and came to bat with two strikes against him.

"Liking a person is a personal thing. It's like liking a woman. You can't really explain it. Now Lee Shubert was a smart man. Nobody fooled him. He liked Mike and gave him anything he wanted.

"Or take what happened last night at Chasen's. For a long time Charlie Feldman has been going around town shouting his hate for Mike. Believe me, the hate of a good Jew for Hitler was nothing compared to Feldman's hate for Todd. How many times have I heard him say, 'May my right arm drop off before I touch him.' In a town of fluctuating hatreds this was the one you could depend on. Others came and went, but Feldman's extraordinary animosity for Mike, this was like the Rock of Gibraltar.

"So who comes over to our table last night and shakes hands with Mike? Charles Feldman." Schenck sighed heavily. "I've lost my faith in haters," he said. "I'm sure everyone in town will feel a little sad to see this one go. In a capital of atheism like Hollywood, what can a man believe in?"

The old man was tiring.

"Who can figure Mike?" he mused. "You could figure out a sane man. But a sane man cannot figure out a man at the point of insanity. I would say that if a man came to Mike this afternoon with a proposal to construct the largest skyscraper in New York City—with the proviso that all the construction would be done in Hoboken—Mike might take the proposition. He would think about it and find some virtue in the plan.

"Sometimes I have felt that he would rather lose my money and get something for himself—not money but some kind of praise—than to have a financial success. Has he cost me money? A man who makes money loses money. I have made and lost fortunes. *I have not lost any money with Mike.* And even if I had I would not admit it.

"I like Mike despite himself instead of for himself. He can only annoy you with his noise. If Mike's chatter could be set to music by Dick Rodgers, with lyrics by Hammerstein or even Berlin, he would be delightful. He lived at my house off and on for years. I put him out many times. He always came back . . . and I was always glad to see him."

He spoke of him as a gifted, errant son he dearly loved, the reminder of his own lost youth.

His man came out. It was time for Mr. Schenck's nap.

THE EX-WIFE

The taut, worn, lonely middle-aged woman sat outside her little trailer on the lot of a studio sound stage between takes. She had come the familiar route from ingénue to leading lady to character parts. Joan Blondell was playing her third act.

A grip stopped and patted the toy bulldog at her feet.

"He gets more than enough at home," she said. "He won't be unfaithful."

Few came to interview her any more. Her name was in lower case.

"I had my doubts about each marriage," she had told Armand Archerd, a newspaperman, shortly after the divorce when she was living in a rented trailer on a desolate stretch of beach north of Malibu. "I now have one rule about everything: whenever you're in doubt about something don't do it, because it's always wrong. I guess I expected too much out of life. I wanted a husband for always. After Dick and I were divorced I was ordered to a hospital for a complete rest. But I wasn't licked. I guess that was proved when I married Todd.

"I am very sorry," she said as she now sat on the studio set, "but there is nothing I can tell you. Nothing. I would like to help you but it is *impossible*." She paused. "I have blotted Mike Todd out of my mind. It was not easy. It took a long time. I had a breakdown. But I triumphed!" Her voice rose to a shrill emotional pitch. "*I remember nothing about Mike Todd.* As God is my judge, if I were under oath and he was on trial for murder, I could not describe him. I remember nothing about him. Nothing."

She had chatted with Mike for half an hour the day before.

"Yes, he came on the set yesterday," she admitted. "It upset me very much. He'll never do that again."

She changed the subject. "I hate Hollywood. I've never felt at home here, after all these years. I'll never send my laundry out again here. As soon as the picture is in the can I'm rushing to my little place in New England . . ."

Her thoughts returned to Mike. "The hardest thing in my life," she said heavily, "was to stop loving *little* Michael . . . Junior."

"We're ready, Miss Blondell!" an assistant director called out. Joan patted her little dog, stood up and went back to work.

THE FRIEND IN NEED

Jack Dietz, a balding, compact little man with tolerant, twinkling eyes, put down the script he was reading in his office on the Sunset Strip.

"Those old-time snake charmers, they don't know nothing," he said. "When Mike wants to charm anybody, they're charmed. Look at me. I've backed him from *Hot Mikado* to Todd-AO. You get to know a person in fifteen years. He's a tough man to do business with. But *he's honest*. He's a man of his word. The proof of it is old Lee Shubert. Lee was the toughest sonovabitch in the history of Broadway. Nobody fooled Lee Shubert. Mike was the only guy who ever got to him. Lee gave him everything to the last day of his life. I'm not even mentioning the ticket brokers. How he charmed *them*. Their sorriest day, was the day he quit the theater.

"Mike's had a lot of girls but his only true love is Junior. *If it hadn't been for Junior, Mike might have been a bum.*"

He opened his wallet and took out a yellowed card. On it was the legend: "Feb. 2, 1940. If I don't make *net* $50,000 by fall, 1940, I quit show biz. M. Todd."

"He didn't net the fifty and he didn't quit show biz. When I think back how our kids were going to have royalties the rest of their lives from so many shows. One by one every bubble burst. No wonder Junior is scared. He's a logical boy, he doesn't savvy this illogical business.

"How did I make out financially with Mike? I'm glad I can afford it. You don't go into business with Mike to make money. That went for Ziegfeld and all of them. Investing in a show is conversation. A game.

"You ought to have a best seller if half the guys who hate Mike buy books. Don't look at me. I love him."

Jack Dietz picked up the script for his next film production, *The Black Scorpion.*

RHAPSODY ON A G-STRING

"I was very much in love with Mike. He was wonderful fun to be with but he wouldn't make a good husband. We didn't have fights like he did with Joan. Maybe because we weren't married. . . ."

Gypsy Rose Lee, smartly dressed, led the way through her twenty-six-room home on East Sixty-third Street in New York. The walls of almost every room of the three floors were covered with paintings. Miros, Paul Klees, Picassos, abstracts by Julio de Diego, her third husband. Mike's Bouguereau had the place of honor in the living room.

"I don't know how many paintings I own," she chattered. "Some are still in storage. Mike was right about this house, you know. I bought it for $23,000. I've already turned down $175,000. We call it the House That Star and Garter Built.

"Mike's thinner now. The crew-cut I don't like. He's more fidgety now, but he was fidgety then too. *He is today what he wanted to be.* There's a lot of clown in him. He loves to amuse people. He has no hobbies. He doesn't talk seriously as he used to. He just can't sit down and talk seriously any more. He's wonderful to work for. He's never petty. He charms the girls, makes them feel good. He knows how to give a gift and a compliment."

She picked up one of her five Siamese cats and caressed it. "This is Gaudi. I got him in Barcelona and he speaks only Catalan. That one over there is Mee Chow Phumiphon, after the King of Siam. I'm vice-president of the Greenwich Village Humane League, you know. An orphanage for kittens. There are twenty-two million cats in the United States, and half are unowned. Everyone loves kittens, but when they grow up people let them run wild. We place twenty-two thousand cats a year. Before adoption we investigate the details of the home and the people, like the Cradle in Evanston.

"Mike's experiences with women are all stormy. No woman has really loved him except for what he is, I mean his public character. Bertha was strictly middle class. But then, so was he. If she was alive they'd still be married. Mee Chow Phumiphon, darling, come here."

THE ENEMY

Arnold Grant, a lank, bronzed man whose superb condition belied his fifty years, casually and expensively dressed in a knitted white sports shirt, gray slacks and white loafers, settled comfortably in a big chair in his suite at the Hampshire House overlooking Central Park.

It was Sunday, March 24, 1957, 6:15 P.M.

He began talking. He spoke in a modulated voice, not once groping for a date, name or reference. His gray eyes—now accusing, now disdainful, now condemnatory, always piercing and at least outwardly candid—crinkled with amusement every few minutes as he recalled what was to him a particularly pleasing incident, and his open face broke into an apparently guileless smile. He was obviously enjoying himself.

There was no bluster, no hysteria, only rarely a sign of emotion. Like a skillful lawyer who had prepared his case with infinite care, he meticulously welded his case of evidence against Michael Todd. It was not an interview but a soliloquy, not a reminiscence but a dissection, not an indictment but an autopsy.

"I have predicted that Mike will die in jail or by his own hand," he said. "He is not in prison only because he is one of the best psychologists I know. He is master of the Big Lie. He starts with a lie that is completely inane. He employs facts, accurate dates and names, as a foundation for a lie and then distorts them. He's a psychopathic liar.

"Most men worry that they are their own worst enemies. With Todd around I don't have that worry. Some say my bitterness toward him is a career. I've only tried to keep him honest. He is a dangerous, hurtful man. I have an *obligation* to my friends and clients to fight this man on his level. I don't want to see these people taken. As long as he's around I'll be after him."

He paused. It was 10:45 P.M. Arnold Grant had talked about Todd for four hours and thirty minutes.

SISTER-IN-LAW

"Toddy is a very simple boy, the same plain, sweet guy I met when he was twelve years old," Esther Goldbogen, Carl's wife, said as she prepared Friday-night dinner in the little bungalow on North Dillon Street, Los Angeles. "I don't agree with any of you who say he can't be a good husband. He needs a woman with a mind as sharp as his, like Marlene Dietrich."

Carl, half reading the evening paper, sighed heavily. "*Nu,* where are you going to find it?" he asked.

"I knew a widow with a million dollars in Long Beach," Esther went on. "She was a nice woman too. Culture, intelligence and with a heart yet. I was very much impressed. It would have been such a fine match for Toddy any way you looked at it. You know, he doesn't even know about it. By the time I got to tell him he was already going with somebody else."

"He sure can pick 'em," Carl remarked. "That Evelyn Keyes is a looker."

"And then my dear friend, Mrs. Jacobs," Esther continued, ignoring her husband. "You know, her daughter is Piper Laurie, the actress. A lovely girl. At least I told Toddy about her. He just laughed. 'Don't be silly, Esther,' he said. 'She's too young for me.'

"That man has a heart. In 1928 I wanted a collapsible buggy for my baby. When Toddy heard about it he got me one. How, I don't know. He didn't have money to eat. He would never let you know when he was hard up. That's the Toddy I remember most."

Carl nodded. "That's why I never gave it up. Come down in the cellar, I'll show you that buggy. But don't tell Toddy. He says I keep everything."

The front door opened and the daughter they had pushed in the buggy walked in pushing a buggy with her own daughter.

THE FOX

Matty Fox was offered $12,000,000 for a backlog of films by a television network. He turned it down and demanded $15,000,-000. "Matty, how can you turn down twelve million bucks?" he was asked.

"I want to be worth twenty-three millions," he said.

"How did you arrive at such a figure?"

Matty shrugged. "I just want to be worth twenty-three millions," he said with finality.

A big man, physically and temperamentally, he sat under a Corot in his swank twenty-second-floor penthouse on Park Avenue and assessed Todd fondly, frankly.

"Mike defies the law of gravity. Every day is a crisis, climax on climax. He will not compromise. I've seen him overdrawn

in the bank, negotiating for a million-dollar loan for ninety
days *and* arguing over the conditions as if he didn't care
whether he got it or not. He won't let money talk. 'Put up your
dough and shut up,' he tells his backers. It takes gall to live by
your wits in a highly competitive and jealous world. Mike always figures to brazen it out.

"He is a master showman but a poor businessman. During
the Todd-AO fight, George Skouras came to me and said,
'Matty, this guy is a genius. Nothing he would ever do would
surprise me. But he's undisciplined, a nonconformist. I oper-
ate a company with stockholders. I must conform to the rules
of organized business. Mike wants to make *Oklahoma!* on his
terms. There are limitations to our working capital. I can't think
as an artist but as a businessman. Mike is not a sound risk. His
record is the proof. You can't invest in unpredictability, Matty.
I'll have to vote against him.'

"It's awfully lonely fighting the world, but what's in a man
will out. Mike is never kidded by anybody. Being a 'character' is his calling card. He went to school for broken English.
He is tough. He has taken enough punishment to kill four men.
Now that Junior's growing up he's trying to save him from
getting lumps. Mike knows better. Junior would have to live a
few hundred years to have what is seared in his old man."

THE PRINCESS

A delicately featured Oriental, Midori Tsuji, sat on the terrace
of the Vialle Fiorentina, a fabulous villa on the French Riviera
at Saint Jean Cap Ferrat, placing calls to New York, Hollywood, Brussels and Caracas.

"Mr. Todd had gone through three secretaries in three weeks
when I hit him for a job," she recalled. "It was just before the
opening of *A Night in Venice* at Jones Beach. My last job was
with an animal feed mill in New Orleans, before that with a
horticulture magazine. I came out of Fresno and went to the

University of California two years, majored in history; I was going to be a teacher. The war came and I was interned in a Japanese alien camp at Topaz, Utah, for nine months. My father died in that camp.

"Mr. Todd wasn't interested in my shorthand speed. 'Our slowest form of communication,' he said, 'is cabling. All I want to know is if you have any personal problems, and can *keep calm.*'

"Everybody told me Todd was a crook, I wouldn't last a week, and if I did I wouldn't get paid. That was over five years ago. Mike Todd is a tender person, the softest man I ever met. Carries no grudges. Tosses them off as if they hadn't happened. He's intuitive, can tell what you're thinking by an inflection. He's upset often but not because of your error. Something's bugging him. He'll cool off when his problem cools. Then it's gone.

"He gave me a trip to Europe. When I came back I didn't know how to express my gratitude. Knowing him, all I said was, 'One big thanks.' He was embarrassed and didn't look at me. 'Yeah,' he said. 'Any calls?'

"We went to a chi-chi restaurant on the Riviera one night with Gary Cooper, Van Johnson, Eddie Fisher and some others. In a few minutes the manager came over to Mr. Todd and whispered in his ear. I guess Japanese, even American-born, were not welcome.

"Mr. Todd looked at the manager incredulously. 'You didn't recognize the *Princess?*' he asked. 'Princess Midori, of one of the oldest Chinese dynasties in . . .'

" 'Of course, of course, I *thought* it was her!' The manager bowed almost to the floor and apologized, 'Forgive me, your Royal Highness.' They give medals to celebrities at this joint. Gary Cooper and the others didn't get any but I did, with my name on it. I've been Princess Midori ever since. And when something is bugging the boss and he lets out a *geshrei*, I remind him, 'Watch your manners, boy, that's no way to talk to a Princess.'"

The phone rang. Caracas was on.

THE CRITIC

In a crowded two-room flat at 156 West 48th Street, an apartment house where Runyon, Winchell and Ed Sullivan once lived, Irving Hoffman, columnist, publicist and wit, played with two cats and answered a stream of calls on a phone hooked up with a loud speaker that enabled him to walk around the room, without a receiver, and do other things as he conversed. Parties on the line were disconcerted now and then, complaining of a broken connection as his voice faded in and out.

Even with special-lens glasses Hoffman cannot see two feet ahead. Once when he was escorting a beautiful girl to a first night, he whispered to a crony, "What does the broad I'm with look like?"

"I once told Mike, 'I have bad eyes but around you I'm hard of hearing.'" Hoffman smiled gently. "Mike covers his ignorance with fifteen stock phrases. But then, William Faulkner says all the wisdom of the world can be summed up in half a dozen clichés.

"Mike is a good showman and exploiter. Brass he's got. Give him almost any script and he can convince a lot of people it will be great. But he has a second-class-story mind. He's not in Ziegfeld's class or Earl Carroll's. Billy Rose? A little sharper but no creative talent. Photo finish between them. Mike has hustle and charm, he would probably make a good ambassador.

"Joe Schenck says Mike has to wind up *borvis* [barefoot]. Joe is usually right."

THE TEMPTRESS

Mae West wore a diaphanous white and turquoise negligee with a train; her face was heavily made up and her straw-colored hair was in a high pompadour. The biographer, attired in a sports pullover, blue denims and sneakers for his four o'clock appointment at Miss West's beach house in Santa Monica, California, wondered if one of them had confused the meridian.

"I didn't investigate *all* of Mike Todd's qualities," she said with a Westian smirk. "I may have passed up something very good. But I didn't investigate him as a man. Of course, it doesn't take me very long when I do.

"I couldn't make a burlesque of *Catherine Was Great* like Mike wanted. My type of writing was ahead of its time. *I* was ahead of my time. I attempted a new kind of play construction, my own original way. I would love to find someone to do plays for me but I can't. My work must be inspirational, it cannot be manufactured. Like Chaplin. He had to write his own plays too. We are very much alike. The same kind of personalities.

"Sex must be in the face, not the body. Marilyn Monroe and the others who portray sex today are very slight imitations. They don't create. That's why they don't and never will reach the heights I did. If you have to show your body, then you haven't got it, dear. . . ."

THE FRIEND IN DEED

Colonel John Gottlieb, a chunky man in his fifties, with a fearless, leonine face, attacked his filet mignon at Fritzl's in Chicago and talked in a staccato, episodic manner.

"My friendship with Mike Todd cost me three or four million dollars," he said.

"Mike is a victim of his own folly. He means well. He's an impresario. It takes a ton of money to live the way he does. When he's courting you he throws Cadillacs and diamonds at you even though he has to borrow three bucks from someone for breakfast. That's the nature of the beast. I know it costs me two or three hundred dollars a day to live, just walking-around money. To Mike that's spit.

"I tell you the truth, Mike Todd is more sinned against than sinning.

"Mike is my friend and I'm his friend. When he was in trouble he came to me for help. That's what a friend is for. Friends know our faults and help us to mend them."

THE HISTORIAN

The affable, bespectacled man in a bow tie was in his ringside seat behind a large desk of W. C. Fieldsian confusion next to a floor-to-ceiling window that overlooked his beloved Forty-sixth Street, a block off Broadway.

"Mike is a lovable renegade, a rogue, too courageous for his own economic good," Abel Green, editor of *Variety* said. "He's a resourceful entrepreneur rather than an impresario, more Shubert than Belasco, sort of an underwriter like Lever Brothers.

"He does everything in the grand manner. He'll call Bill Goetz in Hollywood to find out what time it is in California. Figuring out on his own watch would be too much trouble. Gauche? He doesn't mean it. He'll slip dough quietly. He's a good citizen.

"He wanted to throw a welcome party for Art Buchwald of Paris. French motif. Did he pick a French place? No. He took over the second floor of Lüchow's and converted the most German joint in town *into* a French restaurant.

"The two top stars in *Variety's* N.Y.-to-L.A., L.A.-to-N.Y., N.Y.-to-Europe and Europe-to-N.Y. listings week after week are Todd and Jessel. Counting transatlantic hops, Todd holds the championship. Frequently my copy boy, who keeps tabs on these peregrinations, is puzzled how come they can be from the Coast and back from Europe within the same week, flitting from Romanoff's to Maxim's, while I take a brisk walk to the donnicker.

"Mike is Morris Plan on Fort Knox. In his language he tries to out-*Variety Variety*. He's a glorified grifter, an exciting individual but not a guy Chase National Bank would float a bond issue on. He will K.O. himself in the grand manner. He can't afford his extravagances. Mike can parlay himself into the poorhouse. He'd screw up the menu in the poorhouse, you can be sure: there would be caviar and champagne for lunch."

HOLLYWOOD ADMIRER

Bill Goetz, motion picture producer, art patron and turfman, looked up from his desk at Columbia Pictures.

"I don't agree with Joe Schenck that Mike is a conflicting personality," he said. "Show me *another* side of Mike.

"I was having lunch at '21' with Dick Shepherd, who was to become my son-in-law the following week. Mike dropped by and said to Shepherd, 'I hear you're gonna get married and I wanna give you a present. Whatya want?' Dick was reluctant but Mike pressed him. If Mike insisted, he said at last, he would appreciate a TV set.

"'How much?' Mike asked. Dick didn't know what to say. 'How much?' Mike repeated. 'I haven't time to go shopping. Be practical. How much?' Dick finally said he had been looking at a set that cost $121.

"Mike took out a roll, and as he counted out the $121 he turned to me and said, 'Your daughter is marrying a booby. He could have grabbed me for five hundred.'

"His generosity is bona fide and boundless. He heard about a new-type radio. Before it was put on the market he bought a hundred and presented them to friends, with their names embossed in gold.

"He never keeps an enemy permanently: he cares about everybody and what everybody thinks of him.

"Mike takes success better than anyone else I know because he knows it won't last long. He knows he'll foul it up. Mike doesn't think there will be a tomorrow, but if there is he'll handle it. He's not as classy as Ziegfeld or as crude as Barnum, but he certainly is the greatest showman in many ages."

DEVOTEE

Eddie Fisher, singer of songs, was shooting craps at Monte Carlo. "I don't envy you," he said between rolls. "Trying to put Todd into the twenty-six limiting letters of the alphabet must be like trying to catch a breeze in your hands or like phrasing a child's smile. It's impossible. And he's impossible. In the best possible ways. Mike is indefatigable, irresistible, irrepressible and incorrigible. That sounds like a lyric but I didn't mean it to.

"If there is one basic quality I could underscore, it would be his absolute honesty. Telling the truth, he says, saves an awful lot of trouble. He puts the word right on the line without hedging. This doesn't always endear him to everyone, but, and here's his second rare quality, he does not want to endear himself to everyone. Third, and maybe I should have mentioned it first, Mike is a guy who knows no fear.

"The word *can't* does not exist for him. If something cannot be done one way he will do it another way, a *better* way. If I sound like a press agent it's only because we have a secret friendship pact and I aim to keep my end of the bargain as I know he will his.

"I auditioned for him in 1947. He made me come back six times before he decided I wouldn't do for his show. Recently, when I asked him why he had made me come back so many times, he said, 'Well, there was something about you and there was something not about you, and I couldn't figger it out myself what it was about you that I liked and what it was about you I didn't like. I was pretty busy seeing people, but the sixth time you came in, it was easy. I knew you had the right chemistry, magnetism and talent—but you were too green.'

"Sometimes his reasoning is lost in emotion or pique or plain mulishness. But no one will ever sway him from a decision once given, and Mike is one of the split-secondest decision makers of all time. It might be an intangible but with Mike it's never a maybe: it's yes or no, period, end of discussion.

"For all his brashness he is a gentleman, without courtly manner or, heaven forbid, polished speech but with integrity and respect for every human being, friend or foe. He doesn't believe in vengeance, considers it a waste of precious breath. He works constantly: life is nothing without work, he says.

"He's always on the offense, but, more often than not, he consumes himself and not others. The worst thing you can say about Mike is that he delights in shocking people. Long ago he learned that he could call *any* man's bluff if he called it loud enough. Talking loud has won him more battles than anything else. In fact, there's a Todd-ism that neatly, if ungrammatically, sums up his approach:

"*'Do you hear me good?'*

"He delivers it in decibels that echo from room to room, from block to block and even, some say, from continent to continent.

"Mike never looks *down,* at anyone or anything. When he is on top of the world he looks *up*—and he always brings a lot of people up with him. I love him. Do you hear me good?"

Eddie Fisher rattled the dice and shot a natural.

VOX POPULI

All around the town . . .

A former creditor, Herb Fields, playwright: "He was blowing everyone's royalties in those days. We got a settlement. Mike remains a dear friend. He has superb taste and sensitivity, a wonderful, expansive, generous man who gets the best out of everything."

His houseman, Frank Campos: "People ask me if Mr. Todd hollers at me as he does in business. Mr. Todd has never lifted his voice to me except when he's in the bedroom and I'm in the kitchen on the other side of the house. I wish I could do more for him but it's impossible to anticipate anything with him. Here it is seven P.M. and I don't know if he's dining out or eating at home. I guess he doesn't either."

Walter Winchell: "Mr. Todd is Very Odd. To paraphrase an old line, God spells His name with one d, Todd spells his with two."

An author, Thyra Samter Winslow: "He simply oozes sex appeal. He has Frankie Boy Sinatra and Van Johnson pushed completely out of the picture."

Harry Bloomfield, former associate and ticket broker: "Mike is the greatest judge of character the Street ever had. He knows every phony. He looked like a boy when he came to Broadway. Never talked out of turn. Great listener. He was laying back. When he came on, no one *pre*-sold a show the way he did. He can outwork any man in the world. When others are sleeping he's working. He could have made a fortune owning theaters, he *knows* real estate, but he didn't want to make money in an unromantic way. He never knows what he's worth and doesn't want to know. When he was bankrupt he gave seven-and-a half or a G to a newspaper guy who needed it. He'll give money to the needy when he has not paid his own bills. Everybody clips him a little, but he figures take a little and leave a little. Mike was never a hungry producer, never cut in on a broker. Do you know what it means when brokers back a producer the way they did Todd? They're strictly short-thing guys, one-man operations, and they have insight that's frightening. They're wrong once in fifty, no more. They went for Mike. If he had kept his skirts clean he could have been President."

Maurice Zolotow, writing in the *Saturday Evening Post*: "True to the gambler's code, Todd refused to welsh on his creditors. 'Why shouldn't I pay off?' he reasoned. 'I couldn't

have bought anything for a million bucks that would have
given me as much pleasure as paying off the debts. I was selfish
about it.' Although he has lived high, wide and handsome and
has been a spectacular gambler, he's a straight-shooter and his
credit is practically unlimited."

His West Coast secretary, Dick Hanley: "Mr. Todd cannot
buy one of anything, he must take two. Never a dozen eggs but
a crate. We were driving to the office from his home one day.
'How are things in the office?' he asked. 'Quiet,' I said. 'Everything settled?' he asked. 'Yes, Mr. Todd,' I said. 'Let's *unsettle*
it,' he said, and he wasn't kidding. That's the Michael Todd I
know."

George Seaton, President of the Academy of Motion Picture
Arts and Sciences: "Todd talks shorthand but he makes sense.
What drive! I'd like to get up in the morning with the energy
Mike goes to bed with."

Orson Welles (a letter): "Your desire to check what you
refer to as my 'version' of the Broadway production of *Around
the World* is rather surprising, since you say that this is 'for the
sake of accuracy.' In your last book, *The Joker Is Wild,* you
took the trouble to invent a scene between Joe E. Lewis and
myself. Now it so happens that I have never in my life heckled
even a bad comedian, and my feelings for Joe have been such
that I used to make special trips to Philadelphia to see him before he ever played in New York. Quite apart from our warm,
personal friendship, I admire him as a performer just this side
of idolatry. Although he has been nice enough to apologize
for the little fable you chose to concoct, I will always regret it,
and perhaps you will acknowledge that I have some reason to
be skeptical of your interest in accuracy. Being what he is, Mr.
Todd is lucky, I suppose, to have found you for his biographer."

(Nine days later, after learning all the facts, Welles graciously
wrote a detailed letter, answering fully all questions regarding
his relationship with Todd in *Around the World*. See Chapter
26.)

Bert Allenberg, one of Hollywood's three good talent agents: "Mike is *meshuggah,* but what big talent in our business isn't to some degree? He's the most generous man I've ever known. Once I made a deal with him for a client's services at his established salary. Three days later Mike called me and said, 'I like the way your man works, I'm going to give him $25,000 more than we agreed on.' And he did. He's generous with everything except his girls. One day I ran across him on the M.G.M. lot with a beautiful actress. We were all old friends and, not having seen the girl in several months, I embraced her. 'Cut!' Mike shouted. 'Oh, Mike . . .' I said, 'I'm an old man.' Todd grabbed the girl's arm. 'How do you think *I* got her?' he cracked as he led her away."

An erstwhile praise agent, Max Gendel: "If he had done it the American way, gone to high school, taken a correspondence course, read Dale Carnegie, minded his own business and behaved himself, today he would be third assistant manager of a Florsheim shoe store without authority to make change."

Max Youngstein, vice-president of United Artists, whose company would stake Mike for millions: "He was impossible when he was broke. Imagine what he'll be when he's a millionaire. He cannot be fooled, least of all by himself. 'There are no suckers left in the whole world. It's *almost* impossible to fool the public,' he says, the first man in our business to proclaim it. The realization of this proves how much greater he is than Barnum."

A former partner, Lowell Thomas: "I was not in on the business end of the deal and made no financial arrangements with Todd. It was, in the main, a pleasant relationship, but I must confess that I felt as if I had been swiped by the tail of a dizzy comet."

A guy in show biz, Emmett Callahan, husband of Ann Corio, the stripper: "I hate Mike but I love him."

His trumpeter, Bill Doll: "He's the last of the Big Time hustlers, and there never were any before him. He's on the lonesome side. He's ninety-five percent instinct. He doesn't know why he does anything. He's a realist. When he went into hock for a million he told everybody to get off his neck long enough so he could promote another show. 'You can't win on a dead horse,' he told 'em. He can be naïve. I took him to a revue and he watched T. C. Jones, a female impersonator, the whole show without realizing he was a guy. Nobody's put him down on paper yet. *Life* magazine worked on him six months, at one time had twenty or thirty people researching him. 'The only thing right about the article,' Mike said when the piece came out, 'was the amount of the bankruptcy, right to the penny.'"

On the wall of Doll's office was a photograph of Mike, enlarged to triple life-size, with the inscription: "Bill, you made me what I am today but I still like you."

CIRCE IN SLACKS

All the descriptions of her, including Hemingway's "timeless loveliness of her face," seemed inadequate when she entered the cluttered luxury of the living room in her apartment on Park Avenue.

Marlene Dietrich, impeccable in black silk slacks, white blouse with open collar, and black vest, greeted her visitor with a genuine warmth, as if she had not postponed and canceled this appointment at least twenty times.

She conversed uninhibitedly, now whimsical, now cynical, always entertaining, proving each minute she was, as Noel Coward said, "a realist and something of a clown."

"I used to be an impudent *shnook*," she said, "but I've calmed down and no longer say the things I used to." A moment later she was making the most audacious declaration.

"Mike said we had to stop going together. *Why, I asked, did I say or do something wrong?* 'I'm afraid I'll fall in love with you,' he said.

"*No man falls in love with me I don't want to have fall in love with me,* I told him.

"Mike has had incredibly bad luck with women. Is it because he is naïve? *All* men are naïve. Wonderfully, pathetically naïve. So innocent. The women are crooked. Devious. If men weren't naïve the System could not exist. They would not continue to go into the same experience over and over again.

"The American man must *prove* he's a he-man twenty-four hours every day. A little boy comes home and says, 'Jimmy hit me.' The first thing his mother asks is, 'Did you hit him back?' God forbid he should become a sissy. The European mother asks, 'Were you hurt?' "

The conversation was steered back to Mike.

"Wouldn't it be wonderful," she said, "if everyone spent money like Mike? If people were so secure they wouldn't have to hoard money. And think of the money in circulation.

"You should mention his Jewishness . . . Josef von Sternberg once said he would always be grateful that not once in our furious arguments did I call him 'a dirty Jew.' *What's that got to do with it?* I asked. Mike must have heard the same thing many times and was hurt. And self-conscious. That he is able to remain Avrom Goldbogen watching Mike Todd, according to your theory, is to his credit. Most celebrities *become* the image and are unaware of their true self."

HIS FATHER'S SON

The handsome, dark-haired, intense young man was barbecuing a roast in the back yard of his modest little farmhouse in Croton, New York. Sarah was busy with the baby, Cyrus.

"Unlike most men, Dad's objective is not to build an equity outside his living standard, which is considerable," Michael Todd, Jr., said in thoughtful, measured words. "He does not want to accumulate. To him activity is the god. He is always thinking five jumps ahead and has no time to lay a foundation.

"Dad conquered the world. He had to get over the show-off stage. There is a difference between show-off and pride, between ego and accomplishment.

"He is a man of real principle. His way of reckoning in regard to obligations sometimes is loose. That's the way he operates. But he is firm in principle. He will act and sacrifice on principle. Money means absolutely nothing to him when it is at odds with integrity. *When it comes to honesty, Dad is the most scrupulous man I've ever met.*

"They made him look bad during the bankruptcy proceedings, and I helped them, with my testimony in the furniture transaction. I *wasn't* briefed. On the way to court, Dad said to me, 'Tell it exactly as you remember it.' Nothing else. I told the story exactly as I remembered it. Dad remembered it differently. He remembers most things differently, as often to his disadvantage as to his advantage. I felt badly because I was so stupid. I don't know why I asked Dad to transfer that furniture to me . . . but it was the truth.

"We've always been close. I'll stay in show business about five or ten years, if all goes well, as his partner. Then I want to go in a real small company, real estate or something. The only important thing is time. Time is everything. Time with your family. Sarah and I are going to have six kids. Dad's work is his life, the end. I want my cake and I want to eat it. I have a fair chance of doing it."

The roast was almost done.

"Everyone tries to analyze Dad. His greatest asset, I think, the characteristic that sets him apart as a unique man, is this: *After he has lived an experience, good or bad, he can walk away from it without looking over his shoulder.*"

* 37 *

Hunch Bet

After many months of negotiations, he had persuaded Sir
Alexander Korda of London Films to sell his motion-picture
rights to *Richard the Third* and had secured commitments
from Sir Laurence Olivier and Vivien Leigh to co-star in the
production. They shook hands and the contracts were drawn.

Mike went to Korda's office to sign the papers. There were
no papers. There was no deal. Mike was acceptable to British
peerage but not to American financiers.

"I guess you overplayed the mug role," Korda told him. "And
you are not a member of the Union League Club or the Motion
Picture Producers Association." He became serious. "I'm truly
sorry, my friend."

Mike walked around Korda's office, dazed. He had spent a
great deal of time, money and hope commuting to London. He
had thought the end of his losing streak was in sight. He had
not had a big winner since 1945, *Up in Central Park*. Nothing
had gone right since he came home from the war. He had
flopped on Broadway. Then Bertha had died. He had lost
Del Mar Race Track and blown his job at Universal-International. He had gone into bankruptcy and Joan had left him. And
he had ace-deuced his way out of Cinerama and Todd-AO. He
was what he had been tabbed in Chicago in the early thirties, a
hard-luck punk. He did not know what to do or where to start.
Everything he touched crumbled.

He sauntered to a shelf and picked up a script at random. The title brought back memories, painful ones.

"How much do you want for this?" he asked.

"Back away from it, Mike," Korda said. "I've been trying to lick it for years. Orson Welles even shot some test scenes in Italy and Africa." He shook his head. "Total loss."

"How much?" Mike repeated.

"It's too tough to make and too expensive."

Mike's jaw hardened. "I dropped forty G's on this project a few years ago and I'm gonna get my dough back," he said as he pounded Sir Alex's desk with the script of *Around the World in Eighty Days.*

To represent him in negotiations with Sir Alexander, Mike enlisted the services of David B. Stillman, a shrewd, personable attorney who was extremely well versed in show business.

"In 1948 one of my clients claimed Mike Todd owed him $20,000," Stillman relates. "My client and Todd had been negotiating a co-production movie deal. I sued Todd. He was in bankruptcy. He was co-operative. I have always believed in giving a man a break; nothing is to be gained by crushing him. It took Mike four years to pay but he paid every cent of the twenty thousand.

"We had no further contact until July, 1954, when Mike telephoned and asked to see me. It was a Sunday. He said it was urgent and came to my home in Westport, Connecticut. He said he needed someone to represent him in a deal with Sir Alexander Korda. 'Why me?' I asked. 'If you can collect money from me you have to represent me.' Perhaps there was some truth in this jest, but Todd does nothing without careful thought and consideration. He was aware I knew Korda and could handle him. He and Korda had one thing in common: I had collected money from Korda too. We left for London the next day."

Sir Alexander and Mike reached a satisfactory agreement.

Korda was to supervise the English facilities of *Eighty Days*, the entire film was to be made in England and Korda was to get ten percent of the picture.

That summer Mike and Stillman commuted between New York, London and Hollywood. The picture was scheduled to start in March, 1955.

Mike's concept of the picture never varied one degree. To adapt Verne's masterwork for the screen he hired writer after writer until he found one with the right chemistry. His name was S. J. Perelman, one of America's top-drawer humorists.

Perelman was strictly Mike's kind of guy, neither insecure nor neurotic. He didn't mind when Mike junked a full day's dialogue and rewrote it in one hundred percent Todd-AO.

Mike said of Perelman, "He writes great dialogue but it is strictly *New Yorker*. The circulation of the *New Yorker* is three hundred and fifty thousand. I want this picture to be seen by over a hundred million."

He next engaged John Farrow to direct, telling him, "This show must not be directed as a movie. You must not function as a movie director. You are to carry out my concept with your ability."

Farrow agreed, but after the second day of shooting differences arose and Mike decided a young, intelligent director of good taste with absolutely no Hollywood experience would be best. He chose Michael Anderson of England, who had been earning sixty pounds a week.

William Cameron Menzies became associate producer. He had been around a long time and he used a couple of Academy Awards for bookends, one of them for *Gone with the Wind*.

In the early days of shooting exteriors in London, Mike noticed a young man walking a little faster than the rest of the crew. "Who is he?" Mike asked.

"The thirty-third assistant director," he was informed.

Kevin O'Donovan McClory, an adventurous, pixilated Irishman, was immediately moved up to thirty-second assistant, and

Mike took him to Paris. "Don't pack a bag, you'll only be gone a day," he told McClory.

Kevin flew 44,535 miles before his assignment was completed, and directed sequences in Paris, the Middle East, Pakistan, Siam, Hong Kong and Japan. He also assisted in the editing of the film in Hollywood.

To portray Phileas Fogg, the gentleman "of tall figure with noble countenance, unwrinkled forehead, magnificent teeth" and a zealous interest in whist, Mike selected the impeccable, urbane and imperturbable Britisher, David Niven, because he epitomized the public conception of Verne's classic adventurer.

Great casting calls for intuition, imagination and a magical gift to fuse human chemicals. "Cantinflas is the greatest living performer," Mike said. "Not only is he a magnificent actor and comedian, he's a noted bullfighter, musician, acrobat and can ride anything from a camel to a comet. Most important, he is essentially a pantomimist and will give the part true pathos. Get him."

"He can't be got," Todd's emissaries reported. "Cantinflas is the wealthiest actor in the world, and the most independent. He has his own company, he has never made an American picture and, though he receives fabulous offers every week, he says he never will."

Mike flew to Mexico and, within a week, Cantinflas agreed to play the part, on a handshake.

How did he do it?

"Mr. Todd assured me the film would be done properly," explains Cantinflas, "and that I could portray Passepartout as a Latin. So, to my audience in Latin America, I'll still be Cantinflas."

One of the major problems was finding an actor to play the heavy, Inspector Fix, an obtuse man who believes he possesses shrewd cunning, a caricature of Hawkshaw and Javert.

Mike chose Robert Newton, the gifted English actor.

Newton was eager to play the role. "This is my best part,"

he told friends. And, ironically, it was also his last on this earth.

Mike was back in Hollywood, casting the production from Bungalow 12 in the Beverly Hills Hotel, half a dozen constantly ringing telephones beside him. He had not yet decided on a leading lady, the native Princess Aouda. He saw a photograph of Miss Ceylon in the Miss Universe Contest at Long Beach and said he wanted her. The wheels began turning.

Miss Ceylon, a frightened beauty, arrived with police motorcycle escort, sirens screaming, in a state of complete stupefaction. She was escorted by her duenna, a "mother" from the hot plains of Nebraska. Mike dismissed the cops and began telling her that she was going to be the star of the greatest picture of all time. Her eyes became round as a startled gazelle's. Mike paced back and forth telling her about the role of the native girl, and, hardly looking at her after the first glance, said, "Be at R.K.O. Monday at ten A.M. for a test."

"I have to have my hair done Monday at ten," she said.

"Never mind about that," Mike said testily.

The girl said, "But yes, at Madame Kay's salon."

Mike paid no attention, he was talking on two telephones. He had lost interest.

Miss Ceylon had had her brief moment of glory without realizing it. She missed her destiny—stardom handed her on a silver platter—because of a ten o'clock appointment with a hairdresser.

Mike settled for a red-headed Virginian, Shirley MacLaine. She, an obscure dancer, Carol Haney's understudy in *Pajama Game*, became the heroine, Princess Aouda. Mike wanted a new personality and liked her whimsical, pixieish quality. "She's believable," he said, "and fits into the chemistry of the other three characters traveling around the world."

Mike had the four principals; all he had to do was fill in the small parts and he was set. But for Mike Todd there were no small parts.

He proved it, the hard way, in his casting of fifty "bit" parts that would appear on the screen only a few minutes, some but a few seconds. He made his point. There are no small roles in *Eighty Days* because he chose for each one an internationally famous actor deserving of his fame.

Todd called them cameos. A cameo, to Mike, is a gem carved in celluloid by a star.

"There have been many pictures loaded with big names," he said, "but the story has always been built around the stars. My idea was to have each star fit the part of the story. Our story was about four people who go traveling. When you go traveling you meet a lot of people. It's that simple.

"Say you want a guy to pound a piano in a honky-tonk. Who do you pick? Sinatra, naturally. Not because he's Sinatra but because when he sits down at that piano, with a bowler on his head and garters on his sleeves, he's for *real*. That's how I picked my people—they had to be for real. This thing wasn't burlesque."

How did he persuade the stars to appear? An associate says, "Mike never stopped talking. He sweet-talked the women and fast-talked the men and conned them all into believing only a real top name could *afford* to take alphabetical billing."

Noel Coward said, "Todd bullied me over an inferior lunch and I gave in just for the devil of it."

Louis Dominguin, Spain's greatest living bullfighter, agreed to come out of retirement to do a sequence after ten minutes of conversation with Mike.

"We forgot to mention money," said Mike, after the agreement was reached.

"How much do you need?" was the millionaire Dominguin's dazed reply.

The budget was theoretical. Mike went by one rule: anything that would improve the picture must be had regardless of cost. If it was planned to have 200 extras but he thought 1,000 would improve the scene, he ordered 1,000. Originally he guessed the picture would cost $3,000,000. The actual cost was over $6,000,000. No one had taken into consideration the infinite care and patience with which Mike would cut the picture.

The first deal for financing was with Columbia Pictures. Three weeks were spent drawing up the contract. Finally everything was set and only the formality of signatures remained. Columbia was to put up seventy-five percent of the cost and lend Mike the remaining twenty-five percent, accepting 100,000 shares of Magna as collateral. At that time he still had 200,000 shares of the original 300,000.

This was on a Friday afternoon and the negotiations took place in New York. "Monday we sign," Mike told Stillman and the Columbia representatives.

Harry Cohn, in California, heard about the deal and wanted no part of it. Mike flew out to see Cohn. He put his feet on Harry Cohn's desk, and Cohn raged, "Take your shoes off my desk."

Mike removed his shoes and put his feet back on the desk. Cohn eyed him in disgust. "What the hell do you know about making pictures? You never made one in your life. We make the pictures. You stick to your girlie-girlie shows."

Even Sir Alexander lost faith and sold his ten percent interest to Mike for $100,000.

Mike dumped every nickel of his own in and everything he could beg, borrow or grab.

Halfway through the picture he was in trouble. The long Western sequence at Durango had cleaned him out. He didn't have a quarter. He was telephoning Stillman five times a day in New York and was flying back and forth between New York, Colorado and Hollywood, scrounging all over for money.

The Monday before Thanksgiving of 1955 was Black Monday. He was at R.K.O. Studio in Hollywood shooting interiors, and he couldn't meet a $329,000 payroll. Shooting would have to be stopped.

Stillman called Columbia again. The New York office agreed

to lend Mike the $329,000 on the lawyer's word that Todd would make a releasing deal with them. Again Cohn got wind of the negotiations and put an end to them. He wanted no part of Todd or his picture.

Stillman contacted Roy Little, the financier, and tried to negotiate a one-million-dollar loan. Little offered ten million for the whole company, lock, stock and barrel. Todd would not sell.

The situation became desperate. Everybody was demanding money.

Stillman finally persuaded Arthur Krim and Max Youngstein of United Artists to look at some of the footage. Herb Golden of the Bankers Trust, backers of United Artists, was at the showing. There was a lot of footage but not many reels. What they saw was sufficient. They had enough foresight and courage to come up with a check for $500,000 without a definite deal, only Stillman's promise to negotiate a deal.

That was the day after Thanksgiving, 1955. The holiday gave Mike an extra day to get the check to the Coast to meet the payroll. They agreed to finance up to two million dollars. Then in July or August of 1956 Paramount Theaters came up with $750,000 additional.

At that time Mike was offered an advance of nearly $3,000,-000 for all foreign rights by a syndicate of foreign exhibitors. Although he was flat broke he turned it down.

The production of *Around the World in Eighty Days* made motion-picture history, shattering records and precedents with Toddian profligacy.

Fifty stars appeared in the picture, each playing a role germane to the story and none appearing as himself; 68,894 persons were photographed in thirteen different countries; the entire population of Chinchon, Spain, was used in the bullfight sequence, 4,348 souls. There were 112 natural settings, 140 constructed sets, 2,000 setups. Eleven studios were used, with thirty-two foreign locations and eight domestic. Film was transported one million and a half air-freight miles, and four million air-passenger miles were traveled; 680,000 feet of color film were shot; 74,685 costumes were designed, made and/or rented.

Mike cut and dubbed his picture in Hollywood with loving care the summer of 1956. Victor Young, the man who had written such popular hits as "Sweet Sue," "Love Me Tonight" and "My Foolish Heart," who had composed many of the most distinguished scores in the history of motion pictures and been nominated for the Academy Award twenty times, scored it.

A nabob of filmdom's sacrosanct upper echelon was invited to view a rough cut of the most discussed project in the film industry. When the lights went on in the sixteen-seat projection room of Kling Studio he turned to his host. "Quite a movie, Mike," he said.

Mike shifted his cigar and barked, "Bite your tongue when you call it a movie. It's a *show.*"

Around the World in Eighty Days opened at the Rivoli Theater in New York City on October 17, 1956, to a select, invited audience, without floodlights, TV or radio in the lobby.

Mike sat at the sound-control box in one of the back rows. He looked pale and tense. This was the count down.

The screen widened into infinity as the guided missile soared eighty miles above the earth.

The critical, sophisticated audience held its breath for a shattering instant and then sighed in collective wonder.

Mike's taut shoulders eased against the back of the seat. His showman's instinct saw his star rise with the bullet-shaped projectile into the firmament. His hunch bet had paid off.

Critical acclaim was unanimous: Mike Todd had a bell ringer.

The wheel had made a full turn. The guy who didn't know how to make a picture, who had just enough schooling to be able to read box-office grosses, had produced a picture it is estimated will gross between fifty and a hundred million dollars. The mug who had made his reputation with girl shows came up with what the critics call a classic that is absolutely clean, a family picture.

Avrumele had waited a long time for this night. He would never have a bigger one. Or a better one.

Sitting beside him when the cheering and applause began was the girl he introduced as Miss Lizzie Schwartzkopf, generally known as Elizabeth Taylor.

* **38** *

Miss Lizzie Schwartzkopf

It began June 30, 1956, the summer of *My Fair Lady*.

Mike was dissatisfied with the miniature of a schooner in his Singapore sequence. When he saw newspaper pictures of the *Kaiwo Maru*, a magnificent 436-foot Japanese sailing master in Los Angeles Harbor, he asked and was granted permission to take shots of her under full sail.

A rendezvous was arranged at Point Conception, some thirty miles off the Santa Barbara coast, for Sunday, July 1, five A.M.

With Toddian aplomb Mike chartered *The Hyding*—a 117-foot twin-screw yacht, with sleeping accommodations for ten, a comfortable main deck saloon and spacious dining room—for the week end.

To keep him company he invited Ketti and Kurt Frings and

Art and Marta Cohn. Kevin McClory, who was to assist Mike supervise the shooting, requested permission to invite his friends, Elizabeth Taylor and her husband Michael Wilding. The other guest was Evelyn Keyes.

The guests were advised to gather at Santa Monica Pier by one P.M. and be ready to board at one-fifteen.

Kevin arrived first with the Wildings, followed by Frank Compos, Mike's houseman, driving the boss's white Eldorado convertible. Last to come were Ketti and Kurt. Mike and Evelyn had boarded earlier that morning at Los Angeles Harbor.

Elizabeth, even lovelier than memory served, Wilding and Kevin made a beeline for the closest bar and started on Tom Collinses. They looked very salty in properly faded sailing togs, and their banter was strictly closed circuit.

The Hyding hove into sight at two o'clock and the party went out to board her in three small boats, one of them carrying the luggage, the greater part of which belonged to Elizabeth.

The day was gentle; a trifling breeze ruffled the sea. The sky was cloudless, visibility unlimited. It promised to be a perfect week end.

Mike, impeccably attired in a blue yachting outfit, the jaunty cap pulled over his eyes, greeted us at the rail with Evelyn at his side. He had never met Wilding before, Elizabeth only once, passingly.

Immediately after boarding, Elizabeth realized she had left her purse on the rowboat and was concerned, as it contained a treasured gold Fabergère cigarette case and gold Cartier compact. Mike said, "Don't make a Dreyfus Case out of it. We'll get it back."

Frank broke out the first of several cases of Piper Heidsieck champagne, and Dick Hanley, Mike's secretary, kept a recording of *My Fair Lady* spinning ceaselessly on the hi-fi.

The afternoon lazed by, everyone but Mike and Kurt Frings

sun bathing. They played gin rummy. Much champagne was consumed, and the conversation was desultory.

Mike had arranged for a late dinner in Santa Barbara and made every attempt to be a good host, but he seemed strangely ill at ease and his usual lingo was tempered by intelligible civilian sentences. For the first time he complained about expenses, particularly the cost of frequent trips to Europe. Evelyn attempted to change the subject, and Mike retorted, too heatedly, "You don't see the bills, I do." The atmosphere was tense, and the only ones oblivious of it were Elizabeth, Kevin and Wilding, engrossed in a whispered conversation.

Before leaving the restaurant Mike pulled Kevin aside and, with clenched fists and furrowed brow, upbraided him for his excessive drinking.

Kevin laughed. "Did I ever tell you the joke about the man with the hollow wooden legs and how he fell overboard?"

Mike grimaced and muttered, "Jokes he gives me."

It was not a satisfactory evening.

When the motor launch with cameras and crew pulled alongside at five o'clock Sunday morning, the sea was rough, the sky overcast and Mike proclaimed a new deal. He ordered Frank to shut off the liquor until sundown.

The shooting of the *Kaiwo Maru* took little more than two hours. The wind was right to show the three-masted schooner at her best; the training crew, seamen and captain were co-operative, and Kevin quick and efficient. They were back on board for breakfast, soaked to the skin but pleased with the early morning's work.

Kurt and Mike played gin rummy most of the day; Evelyn lay on a mat in the flirting sun; Ketti stayed in her cabin. Elizabeth and Kevin huddled in deck chairs and chatted in café society shorthand. *My Fair Lady* kept spinning.

Mike was disturbingly taciturn, only looking up from his cards occasionally to scowl at Elizabeth and Kevin. In midafternoon he took Kevin aside. "What's with you and Taylor?" he asked.

Toward evening the champagne corks began popping again. Elizabeth made an offhand observation about something or other, and Mike said, "Honey, you're a latent intellectual."

Elizabeth's eyes narrowed but she made no retort. Instead she held out her champagne glass, and before anyone else could, Mike jumped up and filled it, saying, "Go as far as you like. It's your head." She had been complaining of a severe headache.

Before the guests disembarked in Santa Monica, where they were to have a late supper, Elizabeth changed to skin-tight flamingo-colored toreador pants and a violet-blue cashmere sweater that matched her eyes. Mike was standing at the rail as she came up the stairwell onto the deck. Their eyes held, and for a split second Mike's face reflected total fascination.

Elizabeth said later, "I know Mike was upset aboard the yacht. It all added up that he was extremely displeased. When we came home that Sunday night I mentioned to Michael W. that Todd had been upset, or I should say, that he seemed to dislike me, which I couldn't understand because he didn't know me at all. Why, he hadn't said ten words to me the entire week end."

Less than two weeks later Mike gave a lavish buffet supper party for Mr. and Mrs. Ed Murrow, the distinguished commentator and his wife. Mr. Murrow had come to Los Angeles to narrate the prologue of *Eighty Days*. Elizabeth and Michael Wilding were among the more than one hundred guests.

Mike's rented house overlooking Sunset Strip, with a panoramic view of the city, was a perfect setting for the occasion. It was a warm evening and the women were clad in flattering summer dinner dresses. All but Evelyn. She wore a black Mexican skirt embroidered with silver paillettes and a simple white shirtmaker blouse with a stand-up collar that set off her deeply suntanned face and boyishly cropped white-blond hair. Her informality of dress and manner was in direct contrast to Elizabeth, who floated in while supper was being served, wearing a stunning tight-waisted ivory taffeta creation, strikingly décolleté. Her beauty was startling.

Mike supervised the corps of waiters expertly, attended to the comfort of his guests with meticulous absorption and deferred to his knowledgeable guest of honor to set the high key of conversation.

Elizabeth dropped gracefully to the floor, her wide skirt spread about her, her supper plate on a low coffee table. As the evening and champagne wore on, she became introspective and talked candidly and intelligently about herself and the life she had lived as a motion-picture star since the age of twelve.

One bad marriage behind her, the second obviously ill-starred and about to be dissolved, she was fearful and lonely, looking for comfort and solace like a lost, frightened child. That she had reached the ultimate state of unhappiness and despair was apparent when her tears overflowed during this conversation and she ran to the bedroom to dry her eyes and powder her nose.

Mike was immediately aware of her absence. "What's with her?" he wanted to know.

Given a fast run-down of the conversation he said, "Poor kid. She needs someone to look after her."

Only a handful of the guests remained. Wilding had left hours before, pleading an early studio call, and Kevin had volunteered to drive Elizabeth home. Evelyn played records. Mike's eyes followed Elizabeth. It was after three when she left with Kevin.

Elizabeth relates: "We were invited twice to his house. You know, you were there. One night with the Murrows. The other was that little barbecue when Mike wound up playing gin in the back with Lopert. I went back a few times and kibitzed a little but that was all. I didn't think he even saw me.

"Nobody seems to want to believe that Michael W. and I decided on a divorce before Mike came into the picture. But it's true. Our marriage had failed completely. This wasn't a sudden, impetuous decision. We had been thinking about it for three years. It was something both of us agreed on. Life had no more meaning. I was dead, old at twenty-four. It was just smog and no sunshine. We would wake up in the morning without hope, with nothing to do or talk about, with no reason for living out the day. At last we decided to separate and we took the step.

"The day after we separated legally and it was announced in the papers, Mike called me. Oh, wait a minute. There was one other occasion I saw Mike. He invited us to Kling Studio to see *Eighty Days*. The next day he called and asked how I liked the picture. In fact, he called five times and asked how I liked it. But nothing serious, it was just a joke.

"Anyway, the day after my legal separation he called and said he wanted to talk to me about something serious. I had no idea what. I had a feeling it might be for a picture.

"I met him in Mr. Thau's outer office at Metro, and Mike asked me to come down to the old office he had in the Thalberg Building, the one he used when he was on the lot shooting *Eighty Days*. He sat at the desk and I sat on the couch. There was a little coffee table between us. He has since told me he was very nervous, but he didn't show it. He never rose from that chair once. His voice was gentle. He spoke very softly for about forty-five minutes. He told me that he loved me, that he had been thinking of me constantly, and he said he was going to marry me. We had never touched hands.

"I could not believe what I was hearing. I've since told him I felt like a mongoose mesmerized by a cobra. It seemed so unreal, and yet I knew it was like a prophecy and that every word would come true. We kissed but it was perfunctory.

"A week after our talk in his office at Metro," Elizabeth continues, "I went on location for *Raintree County*. That was when our courtship began—by telephone. Mike called me every day, five to ten times. We talked for hours, sometimes until five in the morning. That's how we got to know each other. For five weeks.

"Once he flew down to see me and then he asked me to come to New York, and I secured permission from M.G.M. to go for two weeks. When the plane landed at La Guardia I was the first out, and before I hit the last step Mike's arms were around me. People were pushing and scrambling to get by, and there we were in the middle of the crowd necking. Couple of days later we went to Atlantic City and he bought me a ring. I must show it to you. . . ."

She ran into her bedroom and brought out an old-fashioned gold band set with garnets. "It was our official engagement ring. I feel unfaithful, not wearing it."

David Stillman, his brother Louis and their wives planned to have dinner at the Metropolis Club. David asked Mike to join them. Mike said he would bring a girl but didn't mention her name. It was arranged that they'd meet at Louis' house.

Mike arrived before David Stillman and introduced his date as Miss Lizzie Schwartzkopf. They sat and had cocktails. After looking at Liz for several minutes, Mrs. Louis Stillman said, "You know something, you look very much like Elizabeth Taylor, but you're heavier."

Mike promptly slapped Elizabeth's bottom and said, "See, I told you you're getting fat."

The change in Mike was first apparent in New York after the Labor Day week end. From the Thursday preceding the holiday to the following Tuesday he disappeared from his usual haunts and ducked his friends. It later turned out he had chartered a plane and taken Elizabeth to Atlantic City.

He was like a kid. Research proved conclusively he was forty-nine, but now he claimed to be forty-seven and produced a new, official birth certificate to prove it.

The following Sunday he took Elizabeth to Croton to meet Michael Junior, his daughter-in-law, Sarah, and his grandchild. He was not himself, his real self, from the moment he entered his son's house. Here he was the older Todd, a grandfather. Elizabeth was younger than his son.

Mike took his four-month-old grandson, Cyrus, in his arms. "Butch," he said, "how would you like Liz here for a grandmother?" The baby gurgled, and Liz, very sober, said, "I could be, Mike. I just finished playing a grandmother in *Giant*."

Elizabeth was quiet, subdued, on the way back to New York in the limousine. She said pensively, "I hope they liked me."

Mike, fatigued by the strain, stretched out and fell asleep with his head cupped in Elizabeth's hands. The sun set behind the Palisades, the lights of New York challenged the stars, the lovely Hudson rolled by, and Liz hummed and sang the lyrics of current song hits as they came over the radio. As the car entered Manhattan she sighed. "It was a beautiful day, one of the most beautiful I've ever known."

The Mike Todd-Elizabeth Taylor romance hit the front pages and all the columns. Leonard Lyons quoted Mike: "It must be love. Liz isn't even in my movie." Louie Sobol reported that Liz had repeated she was "passionately in love with Mike" in front of him and Edward G. Robinson, and quoted Mike as saying, "If we marry I don't intend to send out any releases. It's not going to be for box office."

Mike was in love. It wasn't only Elizabeth's beauty and youth. She was more mature about a lot of things than he was, and beauty wasn't exactly a novelty to him. "What we've got is so great and so right it scares me; I'm afraid I'm dreaming and all of a sudden I'm going to wake up. We've got the right chemistry," he said. "She digs me."

"I'm the most fortunate woman in the world," Elizabeth said. "Mike is just the opposite to the character he professes to be. Underneath he is a softy. I have never known anyone as gentle, with such integrity and honesty, and sentiment. Isn't it wonderful to be proud of another human being?

"He's more a man than any man in the world, I think. Even his faults, they're almost strength. Sure, he's full of hot air, but it's the kind of hot air that doesn't hurt anybody. I'm so lucky.

"The night of the New York opening of *Eighty Days* I died a thousand deaths until it was over and I knew it was the hit we thought it would be. Never have I ever been so worried. I helped with the sound control. What can be as important as sharing the success of your man? I want to be a woman to Mike's man. That is why I want to, why I *must* retire. A home, a husband, a real family means so much more to me. I don't say I'll never act again, but if I do, it will be for Mike.

"I am well aware that both of us must adjust to a life together. I'm well aware how spoiled I am. But I'm changing. I'll improve. No, I couldn't possibly continue acting. And we've decided on one thing: Ruth's prayer, to which I have added one word: 'Whither thou goest, I will go, Buster.' "

Mike called himself the New Todd, and as their jet-propelled romance progressed he was like a bundle of dynamite with a lighted fuse, ready to go off any minute. He was tremendously alert, living it up every second, as if tomorrow might never come.

He gave Elizabeth an emerald-cut diamond he insisted was *not* thirty carats but only twenty-nine and one-half and boasted what a bargain he got at $92,000. He loaded her with expensive and beautiful gifts and phoned her every hour of the day and night he wasn't with her. He spent half his time doing delightful, totally unexpected things for her, and when she was in Harkness Pavilion for a spinal operation he sent Art Cohn the following telegram:

DEAR BOSWELL WORKING HARD FOR YOU AND POSTERITY MAKING
LEGENDS ALSO GOING TO HOSPITAL TO VISIT LIZ AND AS LONG AS I
AM THERE NOT TO WASTE A VISIT STAYING FOR CHECKUP THIS MY
BOY IS LOVE PLUS EFFICIENCY SUGGEST YOU REST UP I AM COMING
BACK THIS NEXT WEEK

AVROM

He filled her room with priceless paintings and spent hours
in consultation with the doctors. When she was released he
tended her with loving care, his eyes never off her lest she
attempt to reach for something or get up from a chair without
his help.

Mike and Elizabeth were severely criticized because their
romance was too public and too publicized. Close examination
of their situation proves it could not have been otherwise. Mike
was a world-famous showman. He made it his business to be
publicized. Without publicity there would be no Mike Todd.

Elizabeth is a motion-picture actress of first magnitude. She
has been, and is, consistently gracious to her fans. Even when
she endured excruciating back pains she smiled, signed auto-
graphs, was co-operative with the press. Had she been less so,
she would have been as harshly criticized as she has been for
proclaiming her love for Mike unashamedly.

Like many actresses, she is basically shy and covers up with
flip repartee. She has an agile mind, is intelligent and introspective. Little has ever been expected or asked of her other
than that she expose her great beauty to the telescopic eye of
the world press and fulfill the role of a glamorous star.

Whether in Rome, Paris, London, New York or Hollywood,
Elizabeth Taylor has comported herself with greater decorum
than many other major film personalities. It is, however, impossible to be a cynosure without eliciting some disapproval.

Certainly she is spoiled, extravagant, often demanding of attention. But these are the failings peculiar to great beauties since the beginning of time. She is given to occasional petulance and whims but she is learning to control herself.

Over the years Elizabeth has graciously granted hundreds of interviews. They are amazingly candid, honest, intelligent.

Mike was not a mug. It was a role he played for so long he couldn't stop even if he wanted to. He didn't want to because he derived as much fun out of it as little boys do making believe they are gangsters.

Beneath the publicity, the Hollywood chatter, the Broadway gossip, was the close and personal relationship between two lonely people searching for a haven. With Elizabeth, Mike was totally relaxed. He could be himself. Not Mike Todd but Avrom Goldbogen. He didn't have to prove anything.

His love for Elizabeth was not a passing emotion. Mike rarely did anything impulsively and without deliberate consideration. He only gave that impression.

Elizabeth had considered herself a total failure at twenty-four. With two bad marriages and a string of short-lived romances behind her, she saw little ahead but that loneliness peculiar to celebrities.

Being a star no longer held any fascination for her. Beauty, fame, great earning power were ashes in her mouth. She was not ungrateful, only tired and disillusioned. She wanted someone to say, "Come, Elizabeth, stop worrying. You never have to go to a studio again, you never have to face a camera. Trust me, put your faith in me. I love you. I won't let you down."

Their public love making was no different from that of any man and woman in love, who hold hands in movies, occasionally kiss in a restaurant. If they were continually quoted, it was hardly their fault. They were perpetually on display. Often they said things they should not have. But who doesn't? Their answers to questions were not rehearsed, they couldn't erase errors once they were quoted.

They were learning to live together, to know each other, and they made mistakes like any two people in love. They quarreled and made up like the rest of us. But that they were genuinely in love is beyond question.

Elizabeth was granted a divorce in Mexico, January 30, 1957. On February 2 she and Mike were married at the home of Enrique and Ferdinand Parra, four miles south of Acapulco.

The ceremony was performed at sunset, the hills softly etched against the sun's golden afterglow. A handful of relatives and close friends witnessed the simple civil ceremony performed by the Mayor of Acapulco, Mario Lopetequi.

Later, additional guests arrived to attend the spectacular party in the fabulous terraced gardens illuminated by kerosene torches. A grandstand was erected in the huge circular driveway and decorated with sixty bushels of gladioli and orchids. Cuban dancers from Mexico City entertained the guests. Villagers came down from the hills to watch the one-hour fireworks display and to dance.

A full moon grinned down as Mrs. Avrom Hirsch Goldbogen was carried by her husband to a honeymoon cottage.

They both insisted this was for keeps, until death did them part. Between Avrumele and Lizzie Schwartzkopf the chemistry was right.

Epilogue

From the day, two years ago, Mike Todd, a total stranger, telephoned my husband, Art Cohn, to compliment him on his book, *The Joker Is Wild*, their destinies were entwined.

They became associated actively in May, 1956. Art, after thoughtful consideration, undertook Todd's biography. The book completed, he accepted an assignment to do the screenplay of *Don Quixote*, Mike's next project.

A singular relationship developed between the two men. Art sensed the innate loneliness of the spectacular showman, and Mike grew to depend upon Art not only for his writing ability and well-organized mind but for his ability as a human being to give love and warmth and meaning to each moment of life.

In Mike, Art found the excitement he was constantly searching for, and the freewheeling attitude toward life he admired. Though their goals were entirely disparate, they both believed in getting there first class.

Mike said of Art: "He knows what I'm going to say before I do." And Art did. He anticipated Mike's thoughts, actions, emotions.

Art said of Mike: "He needs me. He knows I like him for himself, not for the razzle-dazzle."

Each was a dynamic personality driven by the desire to live fully. Each was reaching for a star.

Immediately they met, Art became obsessed by the same urgency that drove Mike. They both pressed too hard, did too much. They were in perpetual motion.

Mike was scheduled to leave Friday night, March 21, for New York on the *Lucky Liz*, his twin-engine twelve-passenger Lockheed, to attend the Friars Club dinner in his honor at the Waldorf-Astoria. Elizabeth was to go with him.

Art had a reservation for the same night on the nine P.M. United Airlines flight to San Francisco, where his daily column was appearing in the San Francisco *Examiner*.

Elizabeth became ill. She was running a temperature of 102.

Art canceled his trip to San Francisco. Mike needed him. They would have time to discuss the *Don Quixote* script during the flight.

Friday morning the sky was overcast, a high wind whipped the hilltops. By evening there was a torrential downpour. Neither Mike nor Art wanted to leave. It did not occur to either to postpone the trip.

The *Lucky Liz* took off from Burbank Airport at 10:41 P.M. The pilot said the weather was good up above, it would be a smooth flight.

At ten o'clock the following morning I learned the plane had crashed and exploded in a valley between cloud-enshrouded mountains, thirty-five miles southwest of Grants, New Mexico, shortly after two A.M. My life crashed with it.

Within me is a loneliness that is wrenching, agonizing, devastating. But I don't question Destiny.

Thinking back over these two years, going over the days step by step, there is no doubt in my mind they had a rendezvous with Death in New Mexico on the 22nd of March, 1958. Nothing, nothing on this earth, could have kept them from that Appointment.

MARTA COHN

Beverly Hills, California
April 15, 1958

ART COHN was born in New York City and spent his childhood in Schenectady, New York. He launched his writing career in Long Beach, California, as a sports writer for the Long Beach *Sun and Press-Telegram*, going on from there to the Oakland, California, *Tribune*, where he was Sports Editor for seven years.

World War II took Mr. Cohn from New Guinea to the Middle East, and finally to Ceylon, as a war correspondent for International News Service. In 1947 Mark Hellinger brought him into the motion-picture industry. The first film produced by Cohn, *The Set-Up*, was awarded the International Critics Grand Prix at the Cannes Festival in 1949, and was hailed by American and European critics as the greatest fight picture ever made. As the personal representative of Howard Hughes, then head of R. K. O. pictures, Mr. Cohn collaborated with Roberto Rossellini on the screenplay of *Stromboli*, starring Ingrid Bergman. Returning to Hollywood, Mr. Cohn wrote and produced nearly a dozen motion pictures before he, his wife and one of their sons left on what was to be a three-month holiday to visit the Rossellinis. They stayed in Italy two years; Mr. Cohn wrote four pictures for Italian motion-picture companies, and the Cohns traveled in many countries, climaxing their European stay with a trip to Israel in 1955.

When the Cohns returned to Hollywood, Mr. Cohn completed *The Joker Is Wild*, his biography of the famous comedian Joe E. Lewis; it was published by Random House in 1955. He also adapted the book for the motion picture of the same title. At the time of his tragic death in the plane crash with Mike Todd on March 22, 1958, Mr. Cohn had nearly completed Mr. Todd's biography, THE NINE LIVES OF MICHAEL TODD, with the exception of the two final chapters. However, Mr. Cohn's wife, Marta Cohn, was readily able to construct them from the copious notes Mr. Cohn had taken.